Essays

Scratching the Surface
Adrian Shaughnessy

1995–2013

This book is gratefully dedicated to all the people who commissioned me to write for them.

'You can only get beyond the surface
by working with the surface.'

Richard Avedon

Contents

Introduction

Introduction
2013

Why would anyone want to read about graphic design? Who wants to read about the legibility of typefaces, or the latest ideas surrounding web-enabled fonts, when you could be devouring the hot new celebrity sex scandal, or a prize-winning novel? For most people, graphic design is part of the vast, throbbing cultural ecosystem in which we live. It is ubiquitous, which means that, like the weather, we just accept it as an aspect of life over which we have no control and scant interest.

Despite the fact that graphic design is often deployed for serious matters (medical instructions, road signage, the dissemination of vital information, for example), it is rarely a subject of pressing interest, unless of course you are a graphic designer. And even then, designers are usually too busy to spend time reading about their craft. For professionals, driven by the twin demands of financial survival and the need to constantly produce high-quality work, there is not much time left for serious reading about the subject.

If it is hard to see why anyone would want to read about graphic design, it is even harder to comprehend why anyone would want to write about it. Writing about graphic design sometimes resembles being alone in an echo chamber. If you like the sound of your own voice, you might be fine with being both performer and audience; but most people who write want to be read and to have an impact.

The writer on design also comes up hard against the old canard that 'graphic designers don't read'. I know plenty of non-reading designers, and their 'non-reading' habit doesn't appear to stop them from being smart, thoughtful and sometimes brilliant designers. They have what Rudolf Arnheim in his book *Visual Thinking* (1969) calls the ability to 'think with the senses'. Clearly, the part of the brain that deals with visual matters (perception, form, comprehension of images, visual relationships, etc.) is capable of functioning independently from that part of the brain that processes language.

Yet, oddly, almost perversely, there are many designers who do read. And not only that, there are enough of them who like reading about design to make writing about design a worthwhile occupation. (Well, let's say, a worthwhile activity, since the word occupation suggests earning a living, and earning a living writing about graphic design is like making combs for bald men – not much money in it.)

My own journey from designer to writer started when I realised I wasn't the best designer in the world. This was a shock. I thought I was pretty good. But once I started my studio (in 1988), I realised that my talents were not those of the heroic solo designer. Instead, I discovered that my primary talent was for running a studio full of talented people. I found that I could coordinate and blend them in a way that gave our clients stimulating work, and satisfied me as a graphic designer.

As we grew as a studio (at one dizzy point we were forty people) I discovered that language, both spoken and written, played an increasingly important role in our development as a creative entity. It was how I created a fluid interface between clients and studio that resulted in high-quality work, even when the outcome was purely visual; and in addition, as the business of design became more serious throughout the 1990s, clients increasingly demanded written proposals, and I found that more and more of my time was spent writing proposals for clients. At first I found writing these documents a crashing bore, but I also realized that unless I did it well, we wouldn't succeed in acquiring new clients, or convincing existing ones of the value of our work. So I forced myself to become good at it. [1]

Over time our proposal documents became rich mixes of text and images. I often liked them more than the final projects. But this wasn't the type of writing I wanted to do. Back then I was being distracted by the mid-90s interest in design theory and the burgeoning discourse around graphic design. The existence of this activity came as a surprise to me; I was aware of radical theorising in other areas of the arts – music, cinema and literature. But graphic design was something I did for a living. I was far too wrapped up in doing it so see it with any objectivity.

Nowhere was the interrogation of design more apparent than in the pages of *Eye* magazine. When *Eye* appeared in 1990, under the editorship of Rick Poynor, I was captivated. I knew instantly that I wanted to be part of the debate. In 1995, Rick kindly commissioned my first piece of serious writing [see pp.193–197] and despite disagreements about various matters over the years, we have remained friends. For me, he is the benchmark for clear, insightful and critical writing about graphic design.

In 2003, I gave up studio life, and set about earning a living as an independent designer, a design consultant, and as a writer. I use the word writer rather than author: I do this because I have always felt that graphic design – even in its most quotidian forms – is authorship. Not always of the most elevated kind, but authorship nonetheless. Graphic design is widely regarded as a secondary art form: it needs clients, content providers, and numerous other midwives before it can exist. It is an applied art, dependent on others for its existence. And yet, in its higher forms, it is my belief that it can be as potent and beguiling as any form of primary art.

As the designer Michael Rock noted in a famous essay ('Fuck Content'): 'Stellar examples of graphic design, design that changes the way we look at the world, are often found in service of the most mundane content: an ad for ink, cigarettes, sparkplugs or machinery. Think of Piet Zwart's catalogues for electrical cable; or the travel posters of Cassandre or Matter; or the new wave work of Weingart, Greiman and Freidman; or the punk incitations of Jamie Reid, in which the manipulation of form has an essential, even transformative, meaning.'[2]

I believe this to be true. I also subscribe to the view expressed by the designer James Goggin that 'graphic design now occupies a position where it should be confident enough as a discipline to be both a vehicle for fulfilling social needs and for expressing independent thought. A discipline equal to art, not aspiring to art.'[3] And it is against the backdrop of this sort of thinking that I offer up this collection of essays and journalism.

You will have to read some of them to decide whether I have the right to call myself a writer. But people keep asking me to write for them and that only encourages me to think that it might be worth carrying on. I also know that graphic design is dismissed by many people as superficial: by scratching at design's apparent superficiality, I hope to show that this is not the case and that it is a subject worthy of serious attention.

1. There was another reason why I wanted to become good at writing proposals and treatments. This was the loathing of the 'creative pitch'. Where once clients had chosen studios on the basis of their portfolios and meeting them, they now insisted on competitive – and usually unpaid – pitches. Competitive tendering became a fundamental part of studio life in the 90s, yet we sometimes found that we could bypass the need for a full-blown competitive pitch (in other words, doing the job in order to win it) by submitting a written proposal. Didn't always work, but when it did, it saved days of studio time.

2. www.2x4.org/ideas/2/Fuck+Content (December 2012).

3. *Iaspis Forum on Design and Critical Practice: The Reader* by Magnus Ericson, Martin Frostner, Zak Kyes, Sara Teleman and Jonas Williamsson [Eds.]. Sternberg Press, 2009.

Graphic design

The politics of desire and looting
2011

The riots that ripped through English cities during four days in August were more ferocious and catastrophic than similar outbursts in the recent past. They have caused a prolonged and unprecedented bout of soul searching amongst all strands of British society. How could this happen? What caused it? Who is to blame?

Blame has been heaped mainly on the cuts-obsessed, expenses-fiddling politicians; on the Metropolitan Police who inadvertently triggered the rioting by shooting a man in the street; on the nation's underfunded education system; and on city councils who rushed to close youth centres in the wake of the cuts in social funding imposed as a result of the global economic crises.

Opprobrium has also been directed at the parents of rioters (special venom is reserved for single mothers – the great bogey figures of the British right-wing press); at role models in entertainment and sport; at the despised and greedy bankers; even British rappers have had accusatory fingers pointed at them.

One group has so far escaped blame: designers. Hardly surprising – who could possibly think that we mild-mannered individuals are somehow responsible for murder, theft, arson and civil disobedience on an apocalyptic scale? And yet, a salient feature of these riots has been the fact that the main target of the attacks has been the shops of the major retail brands of British commercial life.

In previous modern-day riots, the aim has been to expose grievances relating to social injustice. And although the young of multicultural urban Britain have many genuine social grievances, on this occasion they made their objective the acquisition of free stuff.

The principal target was a highly successful chain of shops called JD Sports. It sells fashionable street wear. Other popular targets included mobile phone shops, electrical goods stores, and outlets of leading UK fashion brands. All these shops spend huge amounts of money on branding, on store layout, on window displays, and on slick advertising. Their ads leap at us from newspapers, magazines, TV, radio, and the Internet. Celebrities endorse their products. They are little shrines of desire. Despite one or two gleefully publicised cases, the majority of the rioters came from poor homes in the least desirable, least well-resourced areas of England's major cities. They come from places with low achievement rates in education, and where employment prospects are low.

These young people are not poor in the sense in which we understand poverty in the undeveloped world. They have Blackberrys (the encrypted Blackberry messaging system was used extensively to coordinate attacks), fashionable jeans, and cool footwear: but they are poor enough to have a sense of being excluded from the great orgy of consumer acquisitiveness that is flaunted in front of them daily.

Specifically, they are excluded from the world of unfettered acquisitiveness created by the brand owners, advertising agencies, art directors, graphic designers, photographers, product designers, retail designers, architects, stylists, retouchers, and copywriters at work in modern Britain.

I'm not advocating a puritan revolution. I don't want to ban advertising, or return to the bad design that characterised British shops in the 1970s – they were brown, musty, and unwelcoming. Nor do I think a single designer has ever gone to work thinking, 'Today I must create something that drives the underprivileged youth of modern Britain mad with desire and envy.'

But for the past three or four decades the major role of graphic design has been to create the branding and collateral of desire. For those who can afford entry into this world – no harm is done. For those who can resist the blandishments of this world – no harm is done. But for those who have neither the education nor emotional maturity to deal with this, immense harm is done.

Some designers have been warning about the unwanted side effects of the design revolution, most notably Ken Garland. As far back as 1964, he launched his 'First Things First' manifesto; and more recently, designers such as Jonathan Barnbrook and the supporters of *Adbusters* have issued similar caveats.

These warnings are often mocked as 'idealistic' and 'naive'. But from now on, it's going to be hard for critics to dismiss them. There really is a price to pay for creating the seductive tropes of modern commerce. We've seen what happens when you create a beautifully manicured world of desire, and then say to a big chunk of the population, no entry. Seductive design is emphatically not the main cause of the riots, but it is a contributing factor, and we'd be dishonest to deny our part in it.

What is to be done?

Interestingly, for some time now, I've watched the emergence of a generation of design students and young designers who don't want to become the agents of commercial seduction. They are looking for a new role – one where social value is the new capital, not the sales charts of brand owners. Suddenly, they seem like the only acceptable future for design.

Social design
2009

It's never been clear to me what the term 'social design' means. It's a topic that many people pontificate on, but what does it mean to working designers trying to earn a living in the commercial arena? The answer might just have been thrown up by the recent shifting of cultural tectonic plates caused by the global financial crises: social design is design for the common good. And it might even be the next big thing.

The notion of 'social' design has been around at least since the early modernists pioneered the concept of good design for everyone, and not just moneyed elites. In recent decades, however, this view has been eclipsed – crushed even – by the dominant notion of design as the lubricant of consumer desire. But now the cultural climate has changed, and the 'common good' has become a concept that nearly everyone gets – even big business.

And yet what evidence is there that the common good can become a compelling force to rival the desire for wealth and endless consumption? Well, it's clear that the free market orthodoxy that has prevailed since the 1980s has been dealt a near-fatal body blow by the profligacy of the banks, the sight of our MPs with their snouts in the trough,[1] and the toxic impact of rising unemployment. These and other well-publicised instances of greed have led to a palpable disillusionment with a culture where money is the only yardstick of value.

There's yet more evidence of a shift in priorities. It can be seen in the growth of the environmental movement, which has long since passed from the ideological to a real concern amongst real people, and even big business senses a benefit in ethical conduct. Cadbury has just launched its new Fairtrade certified chocolate bar. Why? Because they can see that the notion of the common good has entered the national blood stream.

Yet despite these many shifts in cultural politics, what are the chances of social design becoming a credible and sustainable activity for designers? I recently saw one small example of what might be meant by social design when I visited Applied Information Group (AIG)[2] in London. Tim Fendley's buzzing studio is mainly engaged in designing wayfinding systems for cities – in other words, it does social design. And AIG is booming.

Wayfinding is an unequivocal example of social design. It has a social benefit that designing, say, a shampoo label doesn't. This doesn't mean we have to stop designing shampoo labels – or that they shouldn't be well designed – but it does mean that we have to start designing labels (not to mention the bottles and the shampoo itself) that are ethically sound and truthful.

Of course, there will always be work for designers who refuse to bother with the new ethical dimension in business, and I'm also aware that there is a great deal of holier-than-thou hypocrisy surrounding the question of the 'common good', but I'm going to stick my neck out here and say that as more and more clients move towards an ethical position, and as more and more designers see a moral and – let's not be shy about this – a financial advantage in being ethical, there is a real opportunity for designers to set the pace and become exemplars of socially focused activity.

To many ears, that will sound like smarmy do-goodism; but I think it's a far more realistic proposition than the delusional mantra 'everything will be back to normal in a couple of years', which I hear uttered by people who have failed to grasp that the world has changed. Not only has the world changed, but it will never be the way it was. And I think we can say the same about design, too.

1. The MPs expenses scandal erupted in the UK when elected members of parliament of all parties were found to be inflating their salaries with often-outrageous expenditure claims. One Conservative MP famously charged the UK taxpayer for 'cleaning the moat round his castle'.

2. Since renamed Applied, after joining the Edenspiekermann partnership.

Chaumont Poster Festival 2010

Try and picture it. A small provincial town in Britain the size of say, Sevenoaks or Melton Mowbray; now imagine every pub and café full of graphic designers talking about Russian constructivist posters and the state of modern typography; next, try and envisage the local churches, libraries and disused industrial buildings full of exhibitions by leading graphic designers from around the world. Unthinkable, isn't it?

We don't do stuff like this in coalition Britain. We do *Antiques Road Show* and National Trust gift shops. But give over a whole town to the glorification of posters and the graphic arts? Not likely. Yet this is exactly what happens annually in the French town of Chaumont, two hours by train east of Paris.

For the past 21 years this unassuming municipality has held a three-week graphic design festival. At its heart are an international poster competition (although international in this context means only one British entry) and a major blockbuster show (this year, an exhibition of Russian constructivist posters). As graphic design events go, the International Poster and Graphic Design Festival of Chaumont is about as good as it gets.

This year's event was the first under new director, Etienne Hervy, the former editor of *Etapes*, France's leading graphic design magazine. Hervy has only been in the job for a few months, yet he managed to pull together a show that offered a sophisticated portrait of current graphic communication. He has also been hired to run a permanent collection of graphic design in Chaumont.

I first went to the festival five years ago and fell in love with its fizzy cocktail of intellectual enquiry and graphic radicalism. This year I was invited to curate one of the exhibitions. Hervy gave me thirty giant sewer pipes dotted around the town and asked me to commission thirty image makers to each produce an A0 poster to be mounted on each pipe. We titled the show 'En Tube – Concrete Image'[1] (or as the illustrator Andy Martin, one of the contributors, re-titled it – 'The Sewer Pipe Show').

On my short visit to this year's festival over the opening weekend I was unable to find all thirty posters. When I asked why some of the exhibits were missing, I was told that many of them had been peeled off their concrete plinths within hours of going up; it wasn't clear whether this had been done by disapproving locals or hardcore graphic design fans.

The first thing to hit the visitor emerging from the Chaumont train station was the festival's brilliant identity and signage system by French designers Helmo. Their graphic system of crisscrossing red, yellow and blue stripes was applied to shop windows, paper table mats in the local restaurants, and specially constructed freestanding units. It was deployed in publications and leaflets, and even used to decorate Etienne Hervy's car.

Also notable was the event's electrifying poster by Dutch wizard Karel Martens [see p.354]. A bravura display of highly-engineered graphic expression, Hervy describes Martens' poster as 'a masterwork of printing ... a good example of the use of colours and the command of letters distinctive of Dutch graphic culture ...'

This year's catalogue, traditionally a major component of the Festival's visual collateral and usually designed by some heavyweight graphiste, was the work of French designer Frédéric Teschner [see p.355]. A gorgeous document, it provided a guide to the major exhibits and made a covetable souvenir. Teschner also had a small show within the Festival and the posters he entered in the main poster competition were amongst the best on display.

What else was there for the graphic design zealot? Take your pick from a dazzling exhibit by Norm; a show called 'Open Projects' devoted to design shaped by user participation; a screening of *Logorama* by H5 [see pp.202–204], partnered with their installation 'L.I.P.' (Logos in Peace) – a cemetery fittingly situated in a church with headstones commemorating the death of various corporate logos; a vast exhibition of student posters responding to the question 'What is graphic design?'; a show devoted to re-imagining the book; and a host of smaller exhibitions, workshops, lectures and music events.

The two main attractions, however, were the international poster competition and the Russian show. The competition posters – elegantly displayed in a disused barrack – struck me as less engaging than on my previous visit. This may have something to do with the ongoing colonization of public space by media owners that has allowed radical poster art to be swept aside by acres of anodyne billboards.

Most of the posters in the competition were advertising small cultural events; this meant that for the most part they were speaking to a knowing or semi-captive audience, and as a consequence tended to be self-referential and somewhat underpowered. Nevertheless, there were plenty of impressive exhibits and an abundance of evidence that if the poster is to survive as a medium for communication, it will be designers – not commissioners – who ensure its survival.

The Russian show induced a giddy sensation of being present at the birth of modern visual communication. There is hardly a graphic technique or visual trope in use today that wasn't first pioneered by the Russian masters. And yet as I drooled over the technical and artistic verve on display, I couldn't help noticing that here too were the beginnings of graphic design as a tool of coercion and persuasion. Here was graphic design being used to sell something: in this case the benefits of collectivism and industrialisation. But it's a path that has led us inexorably to L'Oréal TV commercials and billboards selling holidays. Propaganda is propaganda, no matter what the message.

Graphic design has few better advertisements than the town of Chaumont. To quote Luc Chatel, mayor of Chaumont, the Festival is an 'assertion of graphic design as a creative form of art, able to imagine many different purposes for itself ...' I can't help wondering if there's a mayor in the UK capable of uttering that sentence? I doubt it.

1. 'En Tube – Concrete Image' was an exhibition I curated for the 21st Festival International de l'Affiche et du Graphisme de Chaumont. I invited a group of artists to each design a poster which was mounted on a giant upturned concrete drainpipe situated around the French town of Chaumont.

AIGA conference: the next generation
2008

The recent AIGA Next conference in Denver, Colorado, USA, was well named: it really felt like the 'next step'. In fact, it wouldn't be overstating the case to say that it offered a compelling blueprint for the way designers might think and act in the future.

Up until now I've thought of design conferences as fulfilling a largely social function: the presentations are a sort of glue that holds everything together, but the real action takes place in the bars and cafés where designers meet and swap war stories from the front line. AIGA's Next conference was different – the lectures, talks and panel discussions were the high points and acted as catalysts for debate, argument and inspiration in the late night bars and hotel lobbies.

As a Brit attending the event, I occasionally felt like the poor relation turning up at a chic family wedding. The sheer scale of the conference was dazzling. Of course, everything in America is bigger; the helpings in restaurants, the vehicles that clog the freeways and the waistlines of the customers in the donut shops. But it took a while to adjust to the vast Denver conference centre that was home to 2500 designers and design educators for four days. It was like an aircraft hangar with carpets. Not that the designers had it all to themselves. The venue was shared with a beer festival, but it was easy to tell the designers from the beer fans. The beer fans were more serious.

What really took the breath away was the range of events: it was a mouthwatering line-up of subject matter presented by smart thinkers from all corners of design. Speakers included: Ed Fella, Tobias Frère-Jones, Jessica Helfand, Jonathan Hoefler, Maira Kalman, Daniel Libeskind, Ellen Lupton, Michael Bierut, Christoph Niemann, Alice Twemlow and Garth Walker. Subject matter included: 'The Designer's Guide to China'; 'How Does Design Research Impact Design Practice?'; 'Intellectual Property Basics – A Designer's Guide to Copyrights', 'Trademarks and Patents'; and a talk with the intriguing title, 'I'm Sleeping with my Client'.

This is only a tiny sample of what was on offer, and it was impossible to get around everything. I missed far more events than I was able to attend. Certain presentations caught the collective imagination. From a British point of view, Wolff Olins' executive creative director Patrick Cox's defence of the London 2012 logo seems to have converted a few doubters. The other event that got people talking was a presentation by a biologist on Biomimicry: it's a subject that is attracting designers of all kinds, and apparently companies are turning to nature's strategies to make the smart products of the future.

Two thoughts struck me after my four days in Denver. The first was the high number of women attending and presenting. It felt like roughly 50/50 with perhaps a small bias towards the female side. It's doubtful if the same balance would be achieved in Britain – or Europe for that matter – but it gave the conference a well-rounded wholeness that was refreshing.

The second thought was that here is a challenge for D&AD. If Simon Waterfall[1] wants to raise the bar at D&AD, he and his board would do well to study the way AIGA caters for its members. Denver may have provided a blueprint for designers, but it also provided a blueprint for the way design's professional bodies should conduct themselves.

1. Simon Waterfall had recently been appointed President of D&AD and held this position from 2007 to 2008.

2012 Olympic logo ate my hamster[1]
2007

Three days after the launch of the logo for the 2012 London Olympics, *The Sun* – Britain's biggest selling tabloid newspaper – still regards the furore surrounding the new symbol as front page news. Not only is it widely regarded as a badly designed logo, but nearly 30,000 people have signed an online petition demanding its withdrawal. And now, in its animated form, it is said to cause epileptic attacks.

Designers often bemoan the lack of coverage given to graphic design in mainstream media. Yet when design catches the attention of journalists and commentators it usually results in a vicious mugging rather than hearty praise. Since the organisers of the 2012 London Olympics unveiled their new logo (or 'brand' as they call it), we Brits have been treated to the sight of our national press in fixed-bayonets assault mode. This is normally an unappetising sight, but on this occasion – although it wounds me to say it – the self-righteous indignation of the British press is justified. The London 2012 logo is a solid gold stinker.

Earlier this week the inboxes of British designers filled up with links to the London 2012 website. I went to the site determined to maintain an open mind. I wanted to like it. I wanted to swim against the tide and defend it against instantaneous dismissal by friends and colleagues. Surely it must have some redeeming features?

I logged on expecting a typo-illustration with willowy gymnasts waving banners – the sort of coy emblems you see at the end of CNN commercials from countries with suspect human rights records. Instead I got a piece of clumsy, oafish design; a self-conscious gesture of forced trendiness that failed every test you can apply to a new logo – clarity, precision, memorability. The Wolff Olins 'brand' for the London 2012 Olympics looks as if it has been designed by a committee desperate to prove its street credentials.

The London 2012 chairman, Sebastian Coe (Lord Coe, a former athlete and a former Conservative MP) announced: 'We don't do bland. This is not a bland city. We weren't going to come to you with a dull or dry corporate logo that will appear on a polo shirt and we're all gardening in it, in a year's time. This is something that has got to live for the next five years.' The logo is an example of the sort of design you get when politicos and business people try to be hip. What we've ended up with is a logo commissioned by middle-class suburbanites who do 'gardening in polo shirts'. In other words, it's a laughable attempt at 'cutting edge' design.

For Brits there's nothing new in the spectacle of the press rounding on new logos. In today's *Independent* newspaper, an article appears entitled 'Design disasters: logos that proved a flop.' It lists British Airways' ethnic tail fins (famously despised by that well-known design critic Margaret Thatcher), and Wolff Olins' 1991 'prancing piper' logo for British Telecom. Wolff Olins must be getting used to appearing on the front of *The Sun*: at the time the tabloid ran the headline 'BT blows £5m on a trumpet'.

But in the era of the Internet, the reprisals for getting it wrong are even harsher. The organisers clearly attempted to use the viral power of the Internet to spread awareness of the new logo and to encourage 'participation': visitors to the site are encouraged to create their 'own designs' and post the results. But rather than leading to mass acceptance, the Internet has provided a forum for vast numbers of people to savage the organisers: it has become a platform for Olympic bashing – and rightly so. This is public money we are talking about.

Both the left- and right-wing press seem determined to damn the new logo.[2] The emotive language of the logo's detractors is widely and gleefully quoted: 'toilet monkey'; 'broken swastika'; 'some sort of sex act involving Lisa Simpson'. Supporters are hard to find amongst the vitriol and abuse. But there are some pro voices. The *Creative Review* blog has comments from both sides of the argument. Peter Saville has given it his languid approval ('incredibly noticable, brave and confrontational'), and the prominent British designer Michael Johnson wrote a lukewarm appraisal in *The Guardian* ('It's trying to be "vibrant" and "youthful". The website suggests you download bits for children to colour in. When animated it has an edginess not normally associated with the Olympics'). *The Independent* reports the existence of two petitions devoted to supporting the logo: 'But they attracted seventy signatures in total, many of which seemed false, including Ms Lisa Simpson, of Springfield, USA.'

The gist of the arguments from the logo's champions is that at least the marque has the virtue of stirring up debate and controversy. But this is a facile defence and plays into the hands of branding and marketing people who will see the London 2012 logo as a dazzlingly successful paradigm of hype and spin. Wolff Olins has been silent on the matter. It is rumoured to have been paid £400,000 for its work. Why should it worry? Its phone is probably white hot with calls from corporations desperate to gain a fraction of the PR that its 2012 logo has generated.[3] Meanwhile, yet again, graphic design skulks off into the corner wearing a cap with a D on it: D for dreadful.

1. This was my first response to the London 2012 logo. I hated it. But as the two following essays [see pp.31–41] show, my view changed over time. I still think it ugly, almost offensive, but I have come to admire its intention and ambition.

2. The nominally left-wing *Guardian* carried the epilepsy story on its front page.

3. It transpired that this was not the case, though it's doubtful if Wolff Olins' reputation suffered in any way from their London 2012 logo.

Wolff Olins: expectations confounded
2008

Since the 1960s, commercially-minded designers have complained about their lowly status in the business hierarchy. They have complained about not being listened to in the way other professionals are – accountants, lawyers, management consultants. But most of all, designers have complained that business doesn't take design seriously enough.

In the 1980s, smart design groups realized that the way to muscle into the boardrooms was to downplay intuition and creativity, and elevate strategy and research. The result of this shift in emphasis was that the business world started to take design – and designers – more seriously. But there was a snag; the creative work that resulted from this change of tack was often sterile and formulaic. Sameness became the norm and blandness ruled throughout corporate design.

But surely it's possible for designers to possess the knowledge-based skills that modern businesses require, and yet still produce work that is engaging and different? If there's anyone who can claim to have consistently done this, it's Wolff Olins. Since the 1960s (it was formed in 1965), the group has been at the centre of most of the key developments in visual identity and brand expression. Founders Michael Wolff and Wally Olins have earned guru-like status within modern corporate communications. Olins' books on corporate identity and branding have defined the terrain for a generation of business-minded designers. And as the creators of the Bovis hummingbird, the prancing BT piper, the Orange identity, and most recently the London 2012 logo, Wolff Olins has always operated on a big stage.

The group is currently enjoying a fertile period. A run of high-quality work over the past two or three years is causing design's chattering classes to reevaluate them. And in the case of the London 2012 logo, it has been catapulted into a media firestorm that probably hasn't burned itself out yet, and the intensity of which hasn't previously been seen in design. More on this later.

This *purple patch* is encouraging clients to beat a path to the group's London and New York offices. The client list is gold-plated: New York City, Sony Ericsson, (RED), Macmillan

Cancer Support, GE, Tate, Adidas, Unilever, Southbank Centre and the New Museum, New York's only museum devoted entirely to contemporary art. There's also a smart new Wolff Olins website which suggests a fresh, genuinely modern sensibility at work.

So it seemed like a good moment to see if Wolff Olins – part of the Omnicom media conglomerate – has found the secret of being taken seriously by top-flight clients and yet still managing to produce work that is successful, newsworthy and distinctive. On a cold day in January, I went to their spacious offices near King's Cross to find out.

Having written disparagingly about the London 2012 logo, I expected to be treated like a tramp on the tube with poor personal hygiene. Far from it. Chairman Brian Boylan and executive creative director Patrick Cox were friendly and discussed what I'd written with calm objectivity. They're both good talkers, articulate and perceptive, and when they describe the way they merge sharp business thinking with softer, more intuitive creativity, I found it easy to see why their blue-chip clients value them so highly.

I even found myself reassessing that logo. I still think it's a mistake, but my gripe with it has always been aesthetic: the drop shadows and the garish buzz of the nu-rave colours make it into a visual irritant rather than an inspirational graphic statement. And yet, the web 2.0 philosophy that underpins it – users are encouraged to make their own versions of it – is inspirational, and a blast of freshness into the airless world of stodgey brand thinking.

Both Boylan and Cox stand by the 2012 work. I expected them to be evasive – constrained by gagging orders from the London 2012 committee – but the opposite was true. They discussed it freely and with quiet enthusiasm, which made me realize that Lord Coe and his team committed an Olympic-sized error by not allowing Wolff Olins to defend its work when the media rumpus started. Its considered response would have deflected some of the criticism.

Both Boylan and Cox see the London Olympic work as an exemplar of their philosophy of branding. 'Our view of branding,' notes Boylan, 'is that the brand is no longer a single neat and tidy logo that you stick in the same place every time.

Our thinking on brand has moved on. The brand is the platform, the brand is flexible, the brand is a place of exchange, and it is not fixed, so there is not one logo. There is recognizable form and recognizable communication and behaviour, but it's not one type of constrained and fixed thing.'

This strikes me as enlightened and progressive, but it only works if the execution remains in the control of skilled people who fully understand the brand's visual codes. The dismally designed literature (not done by Wolff Olins) that is currently being pushed through letterboxes in East London shows what happens when communication is freed from its moorings; it slips into muddle and cliché.

Although Bolyan and Cox remain committed to the 2012 work ('I stand by it on the basis of conviction. Sometimes you just know, and in this case, I just know that it's right,' says Boylan), the media ramifications of the logo have left them bruised. Unknown to me, Boylan and Cox were subjected to a vicious campaign of harassment by the national press. Cox, who has young children, found the door-stepping and intimidating phone calls accusing the company of malpractice, particularly upsetting. 'We didn't mind the criticism from within the design community,' he says, 'but what we got from the media was pretty unpleasant.' Boylan agrees: 'The experience has actually made me sympathetic towards celebrities who are subjected to this sort of treatment. And it didn't come from the tabloids. It was the weekend broadsheets.'

The 2012 logo is only one of many high-profile branding projects that Wolff Olins has undertaken recently. In the room where we meet, we are surrounded by giant blow-ups of logos and bits of brand architecture, done for its top drawer clients. They make an impressive display: a series of smart graphic statements that look like the product of careful thought, but which retain the kick of freewheeling creativity. I was curious to know how Wolff Olins has avoided producing the bland monstrosities that big brand agencies are so adept at?

The group's philosophy has been forged over a long time. In 1992 the company moved from identity to branding. 'The move can be defined as a move away from corporate strategy made visible,' says Boylan. 'In other words, corporate identity was very much about the corporation and the corporate world –

a bit one-way, a bit inside-out, and a bit rational. Today we see it much more about the relationship between the corporation and the consumer, and the corporation being positioned in the real world. We see it as much more two-way, and a bit more emotional than rational.' As an afterthought, Boylan notes: 'Curiously, identity is a more meaningful term to describe what we do today, and branding less so.'

He continues: 'After the management buyout in 1997, we had a partnership model, with five strong partners with different views. Four of those people left after the acquisition by Omnicom in 2001, and Patrick [Cox] came on board. Not only are we now a smaller number of people, but also we are much more focused and aligned in our views. We have a singular appreciation of what it is we're trying to achieve – both for our clients and for ourselves. Patrick and I, as two of the leaders of the business, are much more aligned than I was with the previous people.' Cox adds the point that 'we're very lucky to have people in the organization who are aligned with that thinking too: Karl Heiselman, the CEO, and the creative directors in both offices and our senior strategists.'

The result of this new-found alignment, according to Boylan, is that Wolff Olins now speaks with one voice where it previously spoke with many, and it now offers the seamless integration of strategic business thinking with intuitive creativity: 'The fundamental thing, though,' says Boylan, 'is that it's not all done sequentially. It's not about arriving at a strategy, full stop, and then handing it over to other people and saying now illustrate this strategy.'

Yet as Cox and Boylan are quick to point out, to make this philosophy work, you need good people. Both are clearly proud of the intellectual heft of the Wolff Olins team, and as an example they mention Mohsin Hamid, MD of the London office, whose novel *The Reluctant Fundamentalist* (2007) was one of six books shortlisted for the Man Booker Prize in 2007. 'Although Moshin is ex-McKinsey,' says Boylan, 'he's primarily a creative person. And that's what is important about him.'

Boylan is fond of the word intuition, and uses it often. He is keen to emphasise that intellectual firepower is no good if it results in what he calls branding by numbers. 'Our process is about getting a deep understanding of our clients,' he says, 'which is why we have people who come from a more strategic and business background. But then we start exploring, and that's where the intuition comes in. All in all, from beginning to end, it's a creative process, as opposed to a step-by-step logical process. Because if you only followed a logical process you'd inevitably arrive at a dry answer. Some of the answers we arrive at are beyond logical processes.'

Looking at current Wolff Olins work, and talking to Boylan and Cox, there's a sense of a company stretching itself – and stretching its clients, too. It's a view that is reinforced by digging around in their new website. Some of the statements have an almost utopian flavour, and there's a sense of being in tune with new advanced business thinking and radical approaches to traditional business practices. Some of it is borderline new age: Boylan makes a wry comment about being a child of the 1960s.

But how good is the work? Does it measure up to the visionary rhetoric on their website? Is it, to use Patrick Cox's favourite word to describe their work, 'extraordinary'? Inevitably, their best work is in the cultural sector, but perhaps their most important achievement is in the way they've moved branding away from the tyranny of petty rules and suffocating diktats, into something more fluid and expressive.

Wolff Olins' work is as good as it gets when working for big public-facing businesses that need to measure and evaluate everything they do. But, small design groups who rely purely on intuition and their innate aesthetic abilities also do good work. In other words, brilliant pieces of visual communication are done without the intellectual pyrotechnics Wolff Olins can call upon. Yet what makes Wolff Olins' achievements so remarkable is that its work is done in the full glare of public and corporate scrutiny. It has to sell its ideas to hard-nosed business people and public bodies drowning in accountability and evaluation criteria. High-end creativity is not easy in this environment, and it's rare to find it.

'What we do can't be bottled,' says Boylan. 'This means that we will never have twenty offices around the world. Our approach is based on results and something that's appropriate for the circumstances of the client. Intuition is important because all rational will get you is rational. There has to be space for thinking and rethinking and imagination. I've been here 27 years, and I still get excited every day.'

Learning to love the unlovable
2012

Along with many others, I was quick to pour scorn on the Wolff Olins-designed London 2012 brand identity when it first appeared in 2007. But I find that my opinion has changed. I'm now convinced that there is genuine merit in what Wolff Olins did – even if the brand implementation sometimes makes it hard to see exactly what that merit is.

The reason for this conversion is the outcome of two sessions with Wolff Olins' chairman Brian Boylan and Patrick Cox, the company's former executive creative director. The first meeting took place when I visited the firm's London office to interview Boylan and Cox for a previous *Creative Review* article [pp.31–35], shortly after the logo was launched; the second occurred a few weeks ago, when I took part in an event at Wolff Olins' HQ, during which Boylan and Cox presented, for the first time, a candid and revealing account of their work for London 2012 to an invited audience of staff, friends, clients and media.

I still stand by my view that the 2012 logo and its accompanying brand collateral are ugly, or, to use Patrick Cox's more considered adjective, dissonant. But I now also see the work as an example of prescient thinking and iconoclastic intent: in other words, Wolff Olins sets out to create something that deliberately jarred; that was suited to the age of participatory media; that was never static; and which trounced genteel Olympic notions of fluttering ribbons and jingoistic flags.

Boylan and Cox talk eloquently about their work; they avoid brand guff and grandiose assumptions. They explain their intentions calmly, rationally and – it must be said – persuasively. All of which makes it inexplicable that the London Organising Committee of the Olympic and Paralympic Games (LOCOG) prevented them from speaking about their work when it first appeared in 2007. Even at a press junket at the Roundhouse to launch the brand identity to the media, Wolff Olins was barred from presenting its own work.

The man who took on the role of the work's explainer-in-chief was Sebastian Coe, leader of London's bid team to host the 2012 Summer Olympics, and now chairman of LOCOG. Boylan is fulsome in his praise of Coe's enthusiastic support for the radical proposals put forward by Wolff Olins; but Coe's public defence was weak and only gave fuel to the campaign's critics. Boylan and Cox would have made better advocates.

The gagging of Wolff Olins, and Coe's lacklustre defense, had two consequences: the first was that the 2012 logo haters carried the day; it's hard to find evidence that the branding is widely liked, and I still meet intelligent people who think it was just another example of a slick branding agency trousering a wad of cash for a few blocks of colour that might or might not look like Lisa Simpson giving someone a blow job.

The second consequence was that Boylan and Cox were forced to endure a sustained attack from both the tabloid and broadsheet press. Boylan had reporters shouting through his letterbox, and Cox and his family were forced to move house for a few days. The harassment even extended to Luke Gifford, at the time a key member of the 2012 design team (in fact, it was Gifford who first sketched the now famous jagged 2012 symbol). Post-Leveson[1] it would not be in the least surprising to learn that their phones were hacked.

By Wolff Olins' own admission, the 2012 work as we know it today, has not been fully realized. Not all elements of its brand master plan have been implemented. But it is the fate of all graphic and branding work that it is judged by what we see, and not by the back story that shaped the final outcome. And yet, now that Wolff Olins has shared its thinking it is at least possible to come to a fuller understanding of its intentions.

The story begins in 2005 when the International Olympic Committee (IOC) awarded London the right to host the Olympic Games in 2012. The bid was based on four ambitions: the London Games were to be aimed at the young; cultural activities were to be championed as well as sport; London was not to be the sole focus of Olympic activity; and finally there was to be a post-Games legacy to inspire future generations to take up sport.

It was against these stated aims that Wolff Olins presented LOCOG with its branding blueprint. Boylan makes the point that unlike previous Olympic organizing committees, LOCOG had the good sense to request a brand identity rather than the customary logo with ribbons, flags and ethereal gymnasts.

Accordingly, Wolff Olins unveiled a strategy that can be summarized as 'going beyond sport, going beyond London and going beyond the Games'. To achieve this it proposed turning the calendar year – 2012 – into the focal point of the communications architecture. It reasoned that this was a way of 'claiming the future', and of making the Olympics into a time that could be shared by everyone, and not just two weeks for the exclusive benefit of athletes, sports fans and IOC officials.

In the Wolff Olins' scheme the word 'London' and the Olympic rings were relegated to subsidiary roles. There was no need to overstress London, they argued, since unlike Sydney, Barcelona and Beijing, where the Olympics were used to establish the aspiring metropolitan credentials of these cities, London was already one of the world's megacities. And if the logo was intended to live beyond sport it was also unnecessary to overemphasize the rings.

The Wolff Olins proposal was based on three recommendations: firstly, the branding should encourage and promote participation; secondly, the communication strategy should take the Games 'off the podium and into the streets'; and finally, all aspects of the Games should be treated as 'never before'; in other words, here was an opportunity to stage a global event in the 21st century which didn't do things just because they had been the norm in previous Olympics.

To achieve these goals, Boylan and his team offered up some radical un-Olympic-like ideas. One of the more daring of these was the notion of a 'ninth lane'. Normally, stadium running tracks have eight lanes; Wolff Olins proposed painting a 'ninth lane' through every city, town and village to foster the idea of participation and promote a view of the Olympics as more than just an event for elite sportsmen and sportswomen. And although in 2007, social media was not as entrenched in our lives as it is today, Boylan and Cox foresaw an important application for their ninth lane in digital media, as an area that could be owned and populated by everyone.

But the ninth lane concept, along with other schemes designed to encourage participation and to break with convention, was not implemented. Other ideas, however, made it through the LOCOG and IOC approval process. For example, London 2012 is the first Olympics to have one marque to cover all aspects of the Games: normally there is a separate logo for the Paralympics, but Wolff Olins pressed for a single unifying marque, and after much resistance, convinced all parties that this was the correct path to take.

And yet, despite all these conceptual fireworks, it is the 2012 logo that has been the focal point of the brand activity. And ironically, it is in the logo that we see Wolff Olins' participatory strategy at its most lucid. There are, in fact, three categories of logo. There is an official version for use by the Games and by the sponsors; there is a 'Festival' version (without rings) for the cultural Olympiad and non-sporting events; and there is the 'Inspire' version where the public are encouraged to make their own versions by infilling the shapes with whatever imagery they choose.

The marque itself is famously oddball. Undoubtedly, and to its credit, it lives up to Wolff Olins' ambition to create a brand identity that avoids 'stars, leaping figures, nationalism and nostalgia'. Patrick Cox and the creative team set out to produce a symbol – and a graphic language – that would live in the world for six years: 'This meant it could never feel tired,' he notes, 'or just be another one of those Olympic things that you get used to.' The logo design grew out of research into the world of handmade marks: 'We knew we didn't want a piece of typography,' Cox says. 'We wanted a marque that looked like it was made by human beings. But above all, we were looking for dissonance. We wanted it to sit outside of what we are comfortable with. We didn't want a logo with something swishy and a bit of Swiss typography.'

Boylan is equally emphatic in his aims for the brand: 'We didn't want consistency. We didn't want compliance. We wanted to make some tools that could be handed over to others to do what whatever they liked with. You could say, we prescribed anarchy.'

'Prescribed anarchy' takes us to the nub of the matter. Personally, I find the aims and intentions that underpin the 2012 campaign to be wholly admirable. The ambitious, 'open source', unprotected rationale behind the campaign is genuinely inclusive, and although designed and planned in 2007, brilliantly anticipated the coming participatory spirit of the age brought about through social media. Wolff Olins also foresaw the era of fluid and iterative identities where the logo never looks the same twice.

The work also deserves credit for throwing down a challenge to two entrenched groups: copyright protection lawyers and, perhaps surprisingly, branding agencies. Let me explain: many of the best ideas that Wolff Olins proposed were quashed by lawyers protecting the interests of the Games' sponsors. By Boylan's own admission, the notion of the 'Inspire' logo, where everyone is given the chance to make his or her own versions, 'never gained traction'. Why would it, when we are surrounded by stories of LOCOG brand police clamping down on any attempt to use the logo for non-official purposes? A look at LOCOG's website 'Using the brand' would scare anyone off.

But in what way are branding agencies (of which Wolff Olins is one of the foremost) challenged? With their brand manuals and protectionist policies, branding agencies have created a stifling culture of compliance – to use a favourite Boylan epithet – which has led to the now widely held notion of brands as dictatorial, overbearing, and out of touch with the new era of open networks where the consumer is in charge and where, in order to survive, brands need to communicate with their audience rather than dictate to them. The sort of compliance beloved of branding agencies – and brand guardians – will be increasingly unenforceable in the future; less compliance is the answer, not more.

And yet, admirable as it is to antagonise lawyers and brand control freaks, we are still left with the question of whether Wolff Olins got it right with 2012. My own view is that it did. Undoubtedly some of the momentum of what they proposed was lost as a result of being caught between LOCOG's genuine desire to have a truly participatory Games, and the need to enforce sponsor's rights: Visa-only cash machines at Olympic events, and restricting the choice of food and drink to sponsors' brands only, is not participatory. Nor are designated car lanes for officials to whizz about in. This is dictatorial, and the antithesis of what Wolff Olins proposed.

Ironically, as we get closer to the Olympics there are signs that LOCOG realise that the brand protectionism has been over zealous. But this softening has come too late, and the notion of the 'people's games' has been lost.

In one regard at least, the Wolff Olins' plan has been an unqualified success. In the famous logo, with its lack of rounded edges and its stubborn reluctance to please, they have created a truly dissonant symbol. It has a brutality that makes it hard to love, but also hard to ignore; with its palette of buzzy, migraine-inducing colours, and its angular formation, it is a bit like an elbow in the retinas. Perhaps, inadvertently, they have created a symbol that fits our anxiety-filled era.

1. The Leveson Inquiry was a government-sponsored public inquiry into the culture, practices and ethics of the British press following the *News International* phone hacking scandal.

When less really does mean less
The post-graphic design era
2012

Two or three times a year, a longstanding design client commissions me to do some work. He normally pays me £5000, but recently he told me that for the same amount of work he could only afford £400. After some harrumphing and eye rolling I accepted his terms. In other words, I grudgingly embraced the new reality: less is the new normal.

Since the banking crises of 2008, Western nations are learning painfully to adapt to this condition of extreme lessness. Writing about the current American situation, the economist Joseph Stiglitz paints a bleak picture: 'middle-aged people who thought that they would be unemployed for a few months have now realised that they were, in fact, forcibly retired. Young people who graduated from college with tens of thousands of dollars of education debt cannot find any jobs at all. People who moved in with friends and relatives have become homeless. Houses bought during the property boom are still on the market or have been sold at a loss. More than seven million American families have lost their homes.'

Here in Europe, the European Monetary crisis has contributed to the gradual realisation that after years of economic growth we have now entered a period of contraction and reduced expectations, and there's no end in sight. This is a bitter medicine for designers to swallow. We have become accustomed to prospering by catering for the insatiable appetite for consumption that has characterized the last few decades. But what if there is a fundamental change in the way people think about consumption? And what if huge numbers of people are going to learn to live with reduced spending power? This is not mere speculation; there are signs that this process is already underway.

In a post on the Yale e360 blog titled 'The New Story of Stuff: Can We Consume Less?',[1] a report by environmental campaigner Chris Goodall is quoted at length: 'In the past decade, Britain has been consuming less water, building materials, paper, food (especially meat), cars, textiles, fertilizers and much else. Travel is down; so is energy production. The country produces less waste, too.'

It is also noted that even in the United States there are signs that something similar is happening: 'American truck mileage has been on a plateau for a decade now. The number of cars on American highways is also flat. And per capita mileage is falling. As a result, gasoline consumption is expected to be at a ten-year low this year, according to the Department of Energy.'

How can graphic designers adapt to this new world? For some, life goes on as normal. Digital expansion provides opportunities for modest growth and there will always be a need for specialist skills in areas such as packaging, wayfinding and information graphics. But for others, there is only contraction and the fight for survival – studios that once employed ten or 12 people, now get by with two or three interns.

All we can be sure about is that the old way of hoping for big clients with fat fees is no longer viable. P&G recently announced that it would lay off 1600 staffers as part of a cost-cutting exercise. CEO Robert McDonald told Wall Street analysts that he would have to 'moderate' his ad budget because Facebook and Google can be 'more efficient' than the traditional media that forms the bulk of P&G's ad budget.

Even the small clients are vanishing: who needs a designer when you can start a business with a Facebook page, a Twitter account, a crowd-sourced logo, and a fully functional, oven-ready, customer-targeted website downloaded straight from the Internet?

It appears that we are entering a 'post-graphic design' era: a time when pretty much anyone can make graphic design, and when, in a networked and 'template-for-everything' world, communication can be had more cheaply and more easily than at any time in history. In the post-graphic design era, the demand and need for routine graphic design skills will inevitably diminish.

But I refuse to be defeatist. None of this is unique to design. It's a problem shared with many other professions: journalism, publishing, filmmaking, music, and advertising are all facing up to the need for wholesale reinvention in the face of the new lessness. No one knows how designers will earn a living in the coming decades, but the most likely outcome is that for many people, design skills will become the equivalent of owning a driver's licence: lots of people drive, but very few earn a living from just driving – they drive to do other things. In the long-term, I can see design skills becoming a licence – a passport – to do other things. But in the immediate future, survival will depend on adaptability. And as the Darwinians tell us, adaptability is the key to survival.

1. www.e360.yale.edu/feature/the_new_story_of_stuff_can_we_consume_less/2468 (December 2012).

The iPad
2010

When the iPad, the latest piece of Cupertino wizardry, was launched earlier this year, I took the curmudgeonly view that, for once, I would not join the pack-mentality rush to acquire yet another Apple product. Firms that exercise too much control over our lives become disliked and mistrusted, and I've started to worry that Apple is turning into Microsoft.

Not buying an iPad became my tiny act of Apple rebellion. And besides, I had another reason for not adding to my Apple product mountain: I have a fanatical love of books, and to my bibliographic-obsessed eyes, the iPad looked like a threat to books.

But I crumbled, and I'm now an iPad owner. And like most converts, I've become a proselytising zealot. The iPad is a slice of Jobsian genius, and just as I feared, its real value is in its ability to offer a viable alternative to printed media. Reading on an iPad is not like reading on a laptop or a monitor. Jobs' tablet has all the ergonomic versatility and transportability of, well, a book or a magazine. On-screen colours, of course, are ravishing, and the tap and swipe mechanisms are akin to the actual physical processes we use to hold and turn the pages of books and mags. There's none of the restraining qualities of track pad or mouse: the iPad can be read while lying down; you can read it on a train or at a table; and the ability to view in landscape or portrait formats is usability par excellence.

So far, I've downloaded a few dozen books and subscribed to a handful of iPad-optimised magazines. Books transfer well to the iPad screen. I find reading easy and pleasurable. In fact, for novels and books with continuous text, the iPad is as good – if not better – than a run-of-the-mill paperback. The type may not be as crisp[1] as on the printed page, typographic detailing is often dire, and the faux book interface is corny,[2] but all the other features – scrolling, searching, highlighting, rotating, web connectivity, etc – make reading on the iPad a joy.

Magazines are equally well suited to the iPad. But only where publishers – and art directors – have designed specifically for the iPad. *Vanity Fair*, for example, has failed to take advantage of the flexibility and navigational fluidity offered by the iPad. It looks suspiciously like the print version dumped into the tablet format.

Wired, on the other hand, has created a bespoke iPad version. It shows a brilliant disregard for traditional linearity, and by using smart signposting to maintain a sense of place, the reader is encouraged to move through the publication using both the x- and the y-axis. Like driving in a foreign country, it takes a while to get used to, but you soon get the hang of it.

The iPad doesn't mean the end of books and magazines. But these two ancient and venerable formats now have a genuine competitor. From now on, anyone who produces a book or a printed magazine must ask themselves the question – do I have a compelling reason to produce my publication in a physical format? For certain sorts of books – art books, books that are themselves works of art and objects of desire, books we want to last – the answer is yes. For magazines, the response is less clear: we are mostly happy to regard mags as ephemeral and disposable, therefore the iPad seems to offer the perfect platform. Just don't be surprised in the coming months, if your favourite magazine suddenly becomes an app.

1. This was written prior to the introduction of the retina screen on iPad 3.

2. Apple would receive intense criticism for their use of skeuomorphic design.

Google and the tyranny of good design
2006

The Google logo – that scrap of oddball typography – is perhaps the most famous piece of graphic design in the world today. Milton Glaser's 'I "Heart" New York' may have a prior claim, and the Coca-Cola script, the Nike tick (or swoosh) and the Mercedes roundel undoubtedly enjoy greater global 'penetration' (to use the aggressive and invasive language of marketing), but for the web-surfing millions, the Google logo occupies a position of unrivalled prominence.

Google's corporate value is staggering. Despite a recent dip in their stock market rating, Google's financial gigantism places it alongside some of the biggest corporations in the world. Odd then, that it should have a folksy logo that looks more like a school project than the mark of a global corporation. And a logo that changes with astonishing frequency, too.

I began to think about the Google logo (having previously, and with a good deal of superiority, dismissed it as hopelessly amateur) when I noticed clients mentioning it, and telling me how much they liked its frequent graphic makeovers. These comments usually came from hard-nosed business people who'd no sooner allow their own logos to be messed around with than turn up at a board meeting wearing a loincloth. Something about Google's playfulness was getting through to these sober business types.

Even *The Times* recently ran a half-page story on the mutating logo: 'The Google masthead is altered to mark special occasions about fifty times a year, with the chosen subject brought to the attention of millions during its 24 hours of fame.' *The Times'* story was prompted by Google's use of a Braille rendition of its logo to commemorate the birthday of Louis Braille: for 24 hours, the letters in the word 'Google' were replaced by dots.

The article goes on to describe the work of Dennis Hwang. As well as being a Google webmaster, Hwang is also the Google doodler, and the man responsible for the graphic transformations of the logo. *The Times* credits Google founders Larry Page and Sergey Brin as the originators of the idea of a transforming logo: 'They posted a drawing of a burning man to alert Google's then-modest band of users that they would be at the festival in the Black Rock Desert in Nevada, and would not be in to answer the telephone if the website crashed. Mr Hwang has since adapted the logo to mark everything from World AIDS Day to the transit of Venus.'

The Google website gives great prominence to Dennis Hwang's graphic endeavours, but fails to mention who created the original logo. The font is Catull, designed by Gustav Jaeger for Berthold, and is described as 'a display face with a strong calligraphic influence. A large x-height and well-defined contrast make this face most suitable for advertising and display work.'

Catull's calligraphic origins are only faintly discernible in the Google logo: the use of a soft-drop shadow, and the chamfer-effect on the letterforms themselves, turns it into a DTP classic: the sort of hybrid creation that tech-heads choose for the front covers of IT reports. In truth, the logo is weedy, corny and ill-conceived. It's the same with the Google homepage – a brutal display of functionality. Clearly, no graphic designer has been near it. Compare it to the home pages of other large corporations, and its obvious that Google has avoided hiring slick design companies. It looks like they've just gone and done it themselves, motivated by the need for an instantly downloadable page, rather than anything else.

And yet, I think there's something magnificent about Google's lack of design. There's something defiant, almost obtuse about its reluctance to indulge in the sort of oleaginous branding and design that is now the corporate norm. We've reached a point, in the homogenized West, where good graphic design is everywhere. The battle has been won: every business knows it needs good design. It's enshrined in the business schools and embedded in the corporate HQs. Even small businesses understand that good design is good for business. It's a universal truth, like 'customer service' and 'value for money,' and all the other boardroom nostrums that drive modern commerce.

But the consequence of all this is that design has become, more often than not, a badge of mediocrity. The old modernist dream of good design standing for rationality and human values has been flipped. Today, good design is little more than a cosmetic agent, an obscuring agent. When I see my favourite sandwich bar introduce a slick new fascia and smart window decals, a little wave of disappointment runs through me. You don't see the work of sign writers any more; it's hard to find handmade signs and ramshackle window displays. The urban environment is now over-designed. It's all too branded, too inhuman.

So, Google, you might be behaving disgracefully over your willingness to acquiesce to China's demands for censorship, but keep your wonky little logo and your austere, ad-free homepage. In its own small way, the Google chameleon has become a little beacon of insurrection, a symbol of strength in a world in which graphic designers have become the agents of conformity.

The Type Archive
2011

As we crash-zoom deeper and deeper into the era of instant digital typography, graphic designers are becoming increasingly divorced from type's origins in manual and mechanical processes. These laborious and highly skilled practices – designing letterforms by hand, manufacturing matrices and casting pages of metal type – have given civilization one of its most precious gifts: the printed word.

Recently, I had the good luck to have a conducted tour of the Type Museum – now renamed the Type Archive – in Stockwell, South London. My visit made me simultaneously ashamed and inspired: ashamed because I realised that I was guilty of mentally relegating traditional type generation to the dustbin of history; inspired because I also realised that here was something that was worth preserving and which enhances our knowledge of typography even in the digital domain.

It wouldn't be true to say that everyone shares my lazy dismissal of mechanical type technology. The archive receives frequent requests from design schools around the world asking for help in educating students in traditional typesetting processes; academic interest in the collection is growing; and the small team of skilled engineers who work at the archive are still producing matrices for customers around the world. This is not a museum of dead technology – it is a living organism.

The Type Archive houses three major collections: the archive and machinery of the Monotype Corporation; the entire contents of the Stephenson Blake type foundry; and the Robert DeLittle collection of wood type. These magnificent specimens are held in a hotchpotch of buildings previously used as a veterinary hospital that looked after London's carriage-pulling horses. It also tended to the health of the capital's ... elephants.

The archive is run with flair and campaigning zeal by Sue Shaw, its founder and trustee. It also relies on knowledgeable volunteers, such as Ian Chilvers of Atelier Works (my guide on the day of my visit), who devote time and energy to ensuring the collection's promotion and survival. But most importantly, it retains the services of the few remaining skilled engineers who understand the complex processes that allow movable type to be both made and used.

The processes are fiendishly complicated and require a mix of mathematical dexterity and precision engineering. These are skills that take many years to acquire, and unless there are others trained to carry on the work, the skills will die out and a vital aspect of typographic culture will be lost. As a result, the trustees have wisely made their priority the training of apprentices to carry on the work.

As a 'modernist' by instinct, I gravitate towards the new and the revolutionary. But a few days after my visit to Stockwell I had an encounter with a student in Liverpool who was specializing in type design. He had produced a number of digital fonts and was a type enthusiast. As a digital native he had only ever known screen-based type. But he had recently been exposed to metal type and hand setting, with the result that his all-digital practice had become greatly enriched. He told me this with real pride – like someone discovering that they had a famous ancestor.

Living as we do in a dust-free world of iPads and software-generated type, it might seem odd to want to preserve noisy smelly machines that use liquid lead and pressurised air to generate type. But talking to the young digital typographer from Liverpool, and visiting the Type Archive, have made me realise that our storehouse of typographic wisdom will be depleted if we lose our connection with typography's glorious past. Sometimes you have to go back to go forward.

Typography now
2011

Typography has never been more popular. There's even a hit book devoted to the subject – *Just My Type: A Book About Fonts* (2011) by Simon Garfield. The book is aimed at the general reader. At the time of writing, it is No. 1 in Amazon's oddly named 'Humour > Encyclopaedias' chart. The coveted No. 2 spot is currently occupied by *Is it Just Me or is Everything Shit?: The Encyclopedia of Modern Life* (2006).

Evidence of typography's booming popularity surrounds us. Erik Spiekermann has over 100,000 followers on Twitter.[1] The *Helvetica* film can be downloaded from iTunes. Type-based blogs thrive in numberless abundance: there's even one called 'Typography for Lawyers' that aims to show the legal profession the importance of good typography.

Typography, once a subject shrouded in mystery and masonic-like secrecy, has gone mainstream. It is now routine to have serious discussions with non-designers about the qualities of various typefaces. What was once the preserve of the trained practitioner – and the occasional bibliophile – is now a subject of near universal familiarity.

What's going on here? In the non-professional world, the popularity of typography is usually explained by the ease with which typefaces can be used on domestic computers. Drop-down menus allow anyone to do what once required craft skills and, in the days of hand setting, manual dexterity. Blogging software, and the ability to alter typographic layouts on e-reading devices and websites, further promote the notion that typography is a malleable subject that anyone can participate in.

The democratization of a craft that was once the exclusive preserve of experts is not restricted to typography: ordinary people now make credible moving image sequences using mobile phones and affordable editing software. Blogs allow pretty much anyone to publish text and images to a global audience. Increasingly sophisticated music can now be made – and distributed – using free or low-cost software.

But even in the professional world, typography is growing in popularity. How do we explain the blogs, the books, the seminars, the conferences, the research papers? How do we explain the mania for designing typefaces? Perhaps the reason is also related to its demystification amongst a non-professional audience. Think of it like this: as the typography becomes more accessible, the need grows for professionals to do it better and to offer more specialized knowledge, particularly in the online realm. In addition, to stay ahead of the pack, professionals are forced into areas where amateurs can't follow – hence the rise in decorative and fantastical letterforms, as well as the serious academic study of the subject at all levels.

It might also have something to do with the ongoing complexity of the term graphic design. Finding a definition of graphic design that expresses the fullness of the subject is becoming increasingly difficult: most people prefer the catch-all term 'branding'; others see it as an increasingly dematerialised activity that is entirely digital. But as graphic design becomes more fragmented and less homogenized, typography emerges as the one constant that runs through all strands of the discipline.

My guess is that typography fulfils a need that designers of all kinds universally share: a love of craft and making. Despite the rise of user-driven communications (what would the master typographers of old think about Kindle readers being given a choice of fonts and sizes?); and despite the increased dematerialization of the typographic process, there is still a thrill attached to rendering a raw manuscript into a cultured, ordered and typographically sophisticated document.

Oh, by the way, the Kindle version of *Just My Type: A Book About Fonts* is a typographic mess.

1. By early 2013, this figure had risen to nearly 250,000.

Should designers be accredited?
2010

Earlier this year *Design Week* reported that the Chartered Society of Designers (CSD) had filed an application to the UK's Privy Council to approve a system of professional certification for designers. This would allow designers to join the ranks of other 'chartered' professionals such as accountants, surveyors and engineers. In a closely argued article in *Creative Review*, Frank Peters, chief executive of the CSD, laid out his reasons for this move. It's an extraordinary article.

For a start, it reads as if Mr Peters has reheated the manifesto of one of those ambitious 1980s design groups that latched onto the go-go business culture of the Thatcher era. He writes: 'design must embrace and adopt the culture of its new environment and cast off notions of artistic grandeur ... above all it must begin to speak the language of those it will need to work with and ultimately those who will pay for its expertise.'

In fact, the mainstream design industry shook off its 'notions of artistic grandeur' thirty years ago and became hyper-professionalized. And to say that designers 'must begin to speak the language of those it will need to work with' is verging on the insulting. Does he think that designers turn up at client meetings wearing berets and carrying easels? Hasn't he spoken to any designers lately? Hasn't he heard about the new generation of digital designers who are in many cases ahead of the clients he urges us to 'speak the language of'?

In building his case, Mr Peters goes on to berate designers who rely on a 'portfolio of examples of work'. He should take a look at designers' websites. They are groaning with case studies, mission statements, branding philosophies and client endorsements. And besides, as the recent debate surrounding procurement has shown, many clients no longer look at portfolios anyway, relying instead on clumsy point-scoring questionnaires more suited to the purchasing of office carpets than creative services.

I support anything that elevates the status of designers and design, but 'certification' is a waste of time. Design has been professionalized for years: it has strategised itself to the point where creativity is often eliminated; in fact, in my view designers have made themselves too business-friendly, and the consequence of this is that design is widely regarded as something that marketing departments can buy off the shelf and spray onto their products and services. Too much professionalism has led to a decrease of status rather than an increase.

Designers are not 'accountants, surveyors and engineers'. The designers who created 'Cool Britannia', which Mr Peters' mentions approvingly, are exactly the sort of designers he berates for their 'notions of artistic grandeur'. They certainly won't want to join the CSD after reading the views of its chief executive.

But there's a more serious flaw at the heart of the CSD's plea. The debate has shifted from the need for professionalism and certification to the ethical and the social dimension. Here's an area where the CSD could show leadership, yet there's no mention of either in Mr Peters' article. Look at what's happening in America. Designers are being welcomed into the social enterprises that are springing up, and the expertise that designers bring to commercial projects is now being harnessed to make social projects fly.

We will always need designers who can design shampoo bottles and do the layouts for celebrity magazines, but there is a growing need for designers with green and ethical credentials to help build the new world of sustainable development in the post-financial meltdown era. Turning us into estate agents is not the answer.

The benefit of designers as outsiders
2011

For as long as I can remember, I've preached the doctrine of designers getting into bed with their clients. Figuratively speaking, of course. All my professional life, I've advocated – and practised – getting as close to clients as possible. I've signed up to the nostrums that we all spout: we must understand our clients; we must know their businesses inside out; we must form partnerships with them.

There is truth running through all these timeworn pearls of wisdom. Certainly we can't hope to produce good results if we don't understand the fundamentals of our clients' businesses, or grasp who their audiences are. Many designers – especially the big design groups – are so enslaved to this idea that they have spent the last three or four decades turning themselves into clones of the companies they work for.

But is this really the best way to help our clients? I used to think it was. Now, however, I'm coming round to the view that it is better for both client and designer if the designer remains an outsider.

I was led to this thought while delving into the current debate around 'design thinking'. Like most designers, I'm attracted to the idea that designers have a special way of thinking that offers an alternative to the research-based, deductive thinking as practiced in most businesses. But I struggle to define the difference between creative thinking – which is not confined to designers – and design thinking. Are they really any different?

From my own experience as a designer, and being around designers, the nearest I can get to a definition of design thinking is the ability of many designers to do 'what if thinking'. By this I mean the ability to put forward radical, oppositional, and sometimes contrary ideas that fly in the face of logic but which are born out of an intuitive grasp of human psychology and the creative impulse.

In a recent post on the Core77 website, the writer and usability expert Don Norman debunks the notion of design thinking. He writes: 'Design thinking is a public relations term for good, old-fashioned creative thinking. It is not restricted to designers. Great artists, great engineers, great scientists all break out of the boundaries.'[1]

I don't agree with Norman's outright dismissal, but in the article he also makes the observation that within organisations individuals often 'find it difficult to break out of the traditional paradigms, for usually these seem like givens, not to be questioned. Many of these beliefs have been around for so long that they are like air and gravity: taken for granted and never thought about.'

Few would disagree with that. But Norman goes on to note that designers can often break through this rigidity by their outsider status: 'Outsiders bring a fresh perspective, particularly if they are willing to question everything, especially that which seems obvious to everyone else. It helps to be an outsider, where tradition and existing corporate policies do not apply, where it is ok to break with the standard way of doing things and where one's promotion or bonus is not in jeopardy.'

It might be hard to convince the brand managers in large corporations that being an outsider is the best way to help them, but the irony is that many designers are outsiders anyway. There are many reasons for this. For example, the design education system sits apart from mainstream education, and despite the towering importance of design in commercial life, design is still not fully recognised as a 'grown up' profession by government and decision makers. Designers worry about this, but perhaps our outsider status is our greatest asset?

1. www.core77.com/blog/columns/design_thinking_a_useful_myth_16790.asp (December 2012).

Design awards schemes[1]
2006

Design awards. What's the point of them? Worthless beauty parades or an accurate thermometer-reading of the health of design? Mutual back-scratching or an opportunity for great work to rise to the surface? Designers love to win design awards, but we also love to moan about their fundamental unfairness. We've all looked at winners and thought, why? And we've all looked at work that hasn't received any recognition (usually our own) and wondered, why not?

The arguments against design awards are persuasive. Even for those in favour of them, there is an undeniable element of randomness in the allocation of prizes which renders awards schemes mildly farcical – or at best, imperfect. For many, the notion of design as a competitive race with winners and losers – not to mention gold, silver and bronze medals – is unpalatable. And in truth, the notion that one piece of design can be adjudged to be 'better' than another is hard to justify.

For a start, you have to enter to win (or lose). Not only that, you usually have to pay to enter, which automatically wipes out the many possible contenders who can't afford the entry fees. This is not good, especially if an awards scheme's aim is to recognise achievement across the full spectrum of design activities. After all, much good work is done by individuals and small groups, many of whom are unable to afford the entry fees, or allocate the vast amount of time required to prepare and dispatch entries.

So, the playing field isn't even level to start with. But it gets worse. Most design awards are judged by other designers. If you pay your entry money, prepare your work for display, and shell out to have it delivered, how can you then be sure of a fair trial? How can you be sure of impartiality or avoid being the victim of cronyism? You can't. You have to rely on the honesty of design juries, and the transparency and good intentions of the various awards bodies. Perhaps entrants should be allowed the right to vet juries: any juror with a bit of previous for the over-use of Helvetica, for example, could be objected to and sent home as unlikely to look fondly on work that incorporates a script typeface or decorative embellishments.

In defence of awards organisers, they invariably advise jury members about the need for impartiality and the obligation to declare personal involvement. But designers are human beings, and total impartiality is impossible. I was once sitting on a design jury and found myself agonising over a piece of work. I genuinely liked the item, but I wasn't sure if I liked it enough to hold it up to my fellow jurors and say I think this is worthy of our consideration. Until, that is, I found the designer's name hidden in a remote corner of the work. The identity of the designer was officially supposed to be concealed, but there it was, plain for all to see. As it happens, the designer was one of my favourites: my hesitation evaporated and I urged its consideration.

Would design awards be any better if they were judged by members of the public? Or what about allowing clients to judge them? The Design Business Association (DBA)[2] uses clients to judge their Design Effectiveness Awards. As their website says: 'Judges are senior business and marketing professionals who have been chosen for their business experience and acumen. During the judging process, results such as profitability, sales, market penetration distribution, staff morale and market share are measured against the initial client brief.'

But let's not kid ourselves that this has got anything to do with design: why not go the whole hog and take the word design out of the equation completely? There's not much evidence that using the balance sheet to assess design, and allowing non-designers (clients or civilians) to sit in judgement on design leads to anything other than the rewarding of the predictable.

Designers mustn't be ashamed of being experts. Nor do designers need to be reminded about 'appropriateness' and making things 'fit for their intended audience' – it's ingrained in our psyches. But if we stop rewarding design for being design, then we'll slip into a quagmire of sameness and the endless recycling of tried and tested formulae.

Despite their fundamental unfairness, design awards are one of the few outlets open to designers to stake a claim for design. Design will remain parochial and tangential to cultural life until it develops, and surrounds itself with a robust and sophisticated critical discourse. But as there's not much hope of this emerging in the foreseeable future, design awards schemes, with all their warts and snaggle-toothed imperfections, are the best we've got.

1. I wrote a regular monthly column in *Design Week* from 2004 to 2010. During that time, the magazine's editor Lynda Relph-Knight gave me carte blanche to tackle any subject matter. She never once interfered with my copy or requested changes, except on this occasion when she rejected my piece.

2. The DBA (www.dba.org.uk) is a UK organization promoting best practices in the product design industry.

Reduction
2000

Interior magazines and architectural journals bulge with photographs of houses, offices and shops styled in the frill-free rigour of the new urban minimalism. If these publications are to be believed, we have all abandoned excess in favour of a pared-down metropolitan monasticism; we have renounced the superfluous in favour of the essential. Minimalism, or so it seems, is everywhere and not just in the lofts of New York fashion czars. In the manicured room sets that fill the magazines we search in vain for many of the familiar appurtenances of modern living: piles of dust-attracting books, for instance. In the new minimalist credo, books represent unacceptable clutter; they are as intrusive as chintz-covered sofas, old bicycles or Dralon-bound collections of TV listings guides.

It is a nice irony therefore, that we are currently deluged with books on the subject of minimalism. Even the architect John Pawson, undisputed heavyweight champion of minimalism – the King of Clean, the Emperor of Less, the Nabob of Nothing – has contributed to this trend. In fact, with the publication of his book *Minimum* (1996), he might be said to have started the flood tide of literature devoted to the subject. Profoundly influential, his book led to minimalism becoming one of the dominant terms in the 1990s lifestyle lexicon, as well as instigating a lively discourse about minimalism as 'a way of life'.

But the cult of minimalism is not confined to architecture and interior design. Minimalism in art can hold its own (and has done so since the early 1960s) with any of the *-isms* that populate the contemporary art scene. Notions of minimalism infuse music, film and literature, but what about graphic design? Of course, the notion of restraint has always been a favourite battle cry for graphic designers. As designers, we extol the virtues of white space and we remind ourselves that 'less is more'. But is this the full extent to which minimalism pervades graphic design? Is minimalism attainable within contemporary graphic design?

Judging by the number of books devoted to the subject, we might be forgiven for assuming that the answer is yes, and that minimalism is flourishing. Yet in *Minimalism* (2004), an exhaustive survey of minimalist art, the writer and art historian James Meyer defines it thus: 'Minimal work does not allude to anything beyond its literal presence, or its existence in the physical world. Materials appear as materials, colour (if used at all) is non-referential.' This takes us to the nub of the matter; graphic design is by its nature almost entirely referential, and therefore – we are forced to conclude – antithetical to genuine minimalism.

In graphic design, especially in its contemporary practice, every mark, every colour, every font, every reflex, is required to mean something. Graphic design is never allowed to be itself. Everything is symbolism, everything serves an ulterior purpose. Read the design press and observe the way designers speak. They 'create a feel', 'inject a mood' or 'make references to'. They use colour and typography that 'suggests the rising sun', 'evokes feelings of nostalgia' or 'reflects brand heritage'. This is the depressing lingua franca of contemporary graphic design; cliché ridden, repetitive and reminiscent of what the critic and satirist Victor Lewis-Smith, calls the 'Mmmmm lovely' language of TV cookery programmes.

Three recent books deal with the subject of minimalism in graphic design, and while none of them engages in minimalist theorising to the extent found in John Pawson's writings, each raises important questions concerning the nature of minimalism in the current practice of graphic design. In a wafer-thin introduction to her book *Minimal Graphics: The Powerful New Look of Graphic Design* (1999), author Catharine Fishel explains the 'new look' thus: we are, she claims, in the process of rejecting 'a decade of distended, layered, filtered, fragmented, disordered and reassembled graphics' and although she doesn't name them, she presumably has David Carson and the post-*Raygun* school of graphic iconoclasts in her crosshairs. However, the alternatives she offers us in her book are, for the most part, a dull and unremarkable catalogue of professional graphic design that contributes little to the notion of a genuine minimalist aesthetic at work in graphic design.

In fact, many of the items included here would be equally at home in a book entitled *Busy and Really Rather Complex Graphics*. For example, the Microsoft Delivery Bus by cult NY artist Michael Bartalos makes Ken Kesey's Merry Prankster bus (or the psychedelic charabanc from Magical Mystery Tour) look like paradigms of heroic restraint. Bartalos is an important visual artist, but he is hardly a minimalist. And although some of the items featured in Fishel's book make a vague genuflection towards minimalism, the majority of work selected is a bewildering collection of stylistically indeterminate commercial graphic design. If this is minimalism, then it's ersatz minimalism.

The most erudite of the three books is Steven Heller and Anne Fink's *Less is More* (1999). Subtitled *The New Simplicity in Graphic Design,* the book is a worthy investigation into the subject of this ethos in contemporary graphics. In a series of essays, Heller brings his customary rigour to bear on the subject and the book emerges as a booster-ish manifesto for simplicity in graphic design. For Heller, one of the reasons for the current taste for uncluttered design is little more than the workings of the zeitgeist; what he calls 'currents in the wind'. However, he also sees it as a serious rejection of the 'more is more' virus that has infected graphic designers over the past decade.

It is no part of Heller's thesis to claim minimalist status for graphic design. Indeed he avoids the 'm' word – perhaps sensing that it has little currency in graphic design – and talks instead about 'simplicity, economy and reduction'. It is hard to disagree with Heller's fair-minded and perceptive survey of design trends (he seems equally at home discussing Cranbrook-influenced deconstruction and early-20th-century American woodblock advertising), but it is possible to take issue with his choice of work, and to ask whether the examples shown can be legitimately described as representative of the 'less is more' ethos. As with Fishel's book, Heller and Fink confine themselves to mainly American work. My guess is that if these books were compiled from European sources, and the same editorial philosophy applied, both books would be vastly different. Within current European practice, very little of the work included in either of these books would attract the epithet 'minimal', or even, for that matter, 'simple'.

A more adventurous and aesthetically stimulating attempt to define minimalism in contemporary design is made by Alexander Gelman in *Subtraction* (2000). Gelman, creative director of New York consultancy Design Machine, nails his colours to the mast from the outset with an authentically minimalist front cover to his book (if either Fishel or Heller and Fink had included *Subtraction*'s splendid cover in their books, they would have enhanced their arguments greatly, see p.356). Gelman slightly mars his minimalist credentials by resorting to a subtitle. *Aspects of Essential Design* is suitably concise as subtitles go, and it only appears on the spine, but in the spirit of the book he might have 'subtracted' this inessential appendage. However, it should be noted that he refers to 'design' only, thus freeing himself from the restriction of seeking 'subtraction' in graphic design.

Gelman sets out his views in brief but illuminating commentaries appended to each picture selection, and Mel Byars and Baruch Gorkin echo and amplify these thoughts in two short essays. *Subtraction* takes as its premise the Pawson-esque notion that it is what is subtracted, and not what is added, that defines 'design essentialism'. Gorkin notes that it is a '... willingness to give up something known,' that is the hallmark of greatness and Gelman articulates this persuasively through his 'picture thesis'. The book shares more than a philosophical affinity with John Pawson's *Minimum*. Both books feature a B-2 Stealth Bomber, and both offer an invigorating selection of unexpected images. But it's here, in its catholic selection of examples (Japanese wooden slippers, Rachel Whiteread's Water Tower installation, Rei Kawakubo tailoring) that *Subtraction* exposes the lack of genuine minimalism in graphic design. Gelman shows a few items of austere typography, logos and graphical material, but to make his point, he is forced to drift beyond the shoreline of graphic design. And by doing so, Gelman comes much closer than the other two to engaging in minimalist theorising on a par with Pawson and the artists featured in James Meyer's book.

On the basis of these three books, the claim for minimalist status for graphic design appears to fail. Graphic design, it seems, can only fleetingly attain the levels of abstraction and selflessness of a work by Carl André, Donald Judd or Dan Flavin. It is tempting to suggest the reason for this is typography, the basic DNA for nearly all graphic design. With their semiotic intrusiveness and constant, unavoidable assertion of 'meaning', do words preclude genuine minimalist expression? This point is made in the September 2000 issue of *i-D*, devoted to that publication's annual design awards. The magazine's graphics jury (Sean Adams, Janet Froelich, J Abbott Miller and Paul Sahre) picked out *Line Form Color* (1999), an Elsworth Kelly monograph, for an award. The magazine notes approvingly that Kelly's images are not 'marred by typography'. It is as though Kelly's images would somehow be contaminated by typography, their essential minimalism compromised by language.

Sources

The politics of desire and looting. Design Observer, 15 August 2011. See pp.18–20.

Social design. *Design Week*, 6 August 2009. See pp.21–22.

Chaumont Poster Festival. *Creative Review*, July 2010. See pp.23–25.

AIGA conference: the next generation. *Design Week*, 1 November 2007. See pp.26–27.

2012 Olympic logo ate my hamster. Design Observer, 6 June 2007. See pp.28–30.

Wolff Olins: expectations confounded. *Creative Review*, January 2008. See pp.31–35.

Learning to love the unlovable. *Creative Review*, August 2012. See pp.36–41.

When less really does mean less – the post-graphic design era. Design Observer, 29 February 2012. See pp.42–44.

The iPad. *Design Week*, 7 October 2010. See pp.45–46.

Google and the tyranny of good design. Design Observer, 12 March 2006. See pp.47–49.

The Type Archive. *Design Week*, 5 May 2011. See pp.50–51.

Typography now. *Design Week*, 3 February 2011. See pp.52–53.

Should designers be accredited? *Design Week*, May 2010. See pp.54–55.

The benefit of designers as outsiders. *Design Week*, 7 April 2011. See pp.56–57.

Design awards schemes. Unpublished, 2006. See pp.58–60.

Reduction. *Eye* 38, Winter 2000. See pp.61–65.

Essays

Profiles

TDR RIP – an appreciation
2009

In 2007, The Superbrands Organisation, a self-appointed body dedicated to promoting 'the discipline of branding', declared that the British design company The Designers Republic was 'one of the UK's coolest brands'. Two years later, TDR (as the studio is widely referred to by its many zealous admirers) no longer exists. In January 2009, the 23-year-old practice was declared bankrupt.

The reason given for TDR's demise is the loss of two clients, an unpaid tax bill, and a major client's failure to pay its debts. But on deeper reflection, the studio's demise may also have something to do with the way it has helped shape the world of design over the past two decades. To find out how TDR indirectly contributed to its own demise, we have to go back in time and examine the influence exerted by the group and its charismatic founder Ian Anderson.

Throughout the 1980s and 90s, graphic design became increasingly absorbed into the world of business. Nothing new in this, you might think; graphic designers had always looked to industry and commerce as their primary source of patronage. But in the final decades of the 20th century, a boom time for Western economies, the eagerness of designers to align themselves with big business and to be front-line soldiers in the combat zone of consumerism resulted in the intensification of the relationship between design and commerce. As a result, design became less about craft and more about strategy – a trend that has escalated in recent years to the point where the term 'graphic design' is barely used within business circles. It has been abandoned in favour of 'branding'.

Yet while the bond between design and business was deepening, there was an alternative strand of graphic activity that was less business focused. Not every designer wanted to create the communications fodder for global commerce. Many went as far as to reject design's purely mercantile role in favour of a more socially and politically inclined one; others saw graphic design as a tool for self-expression and artistic exploration. None of this was new either; there had always been rebellious and artistically inclined graphic designers –

Grapus in France, Push Pin in USA – and graphic design had boasted an avant-garde wing since the 1920s. But during the last two decades of the 20th century, something happened within design that fundamentally changed it – and one of the primary agents of change was The Designers Republic.

Founded on Bastille Day 1986, TDR was in the vanguard of a new generation of media-savvy designers who championed the use of graphic design as a cultural and aesthetic force that could be enjoyed on its own merits. For the first time in its short history, graphic design became valued for itself and not for the message it was conveying. And most significantly of all, it acquired a small following amongst non-professionals.

Leading this end-of-the-millennium movement within graphic design were big hitters such as David Carson, Tomato, Jonathan Barnbrook and M/M (Paris). Yet arguably none of these designers rivalled the influence of TDR (certainly in Europe and the Far East). Based in the industrial city of Sheffield, in the north of England, TDR inspired a generation to go to design school and learn about graphic design. And they did this through the sheer visual exuberance of their graphic work. No strategy here; it was all about the look. Their witty and confident use of purloined consumerist imagery from Japanese supermarkets, the NASA space programmes, and the hard-edged imagery of the burgeoning digital revolution that was then infusing music, computer games and popular culture, all contributed to the TDR graphic design style.

TDR and their founder Ian Anderson emerged at roughly the same time as rave culture engulfed the youth of Britain. This hedonistic eruption was different from previous outbursts of youthful sub-cultural behaviour. It was a merging of rebellion and materialism that took place within a society ruled over by Thatcher and Reagan. The rave movement didn't demand social justice – it just wanted the right to party and to have a good time. The acid yellow 'smiley face' became this generation's ban-the-bomb/peace symbol.

Anderson and his team produced the vivid colour-saturated graphics for this pharmaceutically-charged revolution. TDR became the graphic laureates of the acid house generation in much the same way that the great psychedelic poster artists had been for the 1960s hippie revolution. TDR design was full of slogans – often interjected into the commercial assignments the group undertook, and permitted by smart clients who welcomed the knowing intervention of the TDR signature. It signalled the end of the era when the graphic designer could only be a mute and neutral conveyor of a client's message. And by juggling with the language and symbolism of consumerism, TDR caught the late-millennial zeitgeist with their ambiguous approach to materialism. We couldn't quite be sure if they were rejecting commercial culture or celebrating it. Slogans such as 'Buy nothing, pay now' seemed to catch the spirit of an affluent generation of MTV-saturated youth who wanted to get off their heads on ecstasy while dancing to trance music but also to own a house with designer furniture, and paid for with a mortgage.

Equally timely was TDR's long and fruitful association with Warp Records – also Sheffield-based, and one of the pioneers of electronic dance music. Many of the album covers that emerged from this celebrated designer/client relationship – for artists such as Autechre [see p.357], Aphex Twin and LFO – are amongst TDR's most lasting contributions to modern graphic design. Within this fertile liaison they created a graphic style that was to propel them to the front ranks of graphic expression, and was to cause a generation to venerate – and eventually emulate – their freewheeling style.

It was hardly surprising that music was to prove a fertile ground for TDR, yet it was their work for the computer game *Wipeout* that was to bring them a reputation and a following from beyond the worlds of music and graphic design. For *Wipeout*, TDR designed the packaging and the in-game look. It was a seminal work in the graphically unsophisticated world of computer games, and its graphic flair hasn't been superseded yet.

While this great body of work flowed out of TDR, Anderson become adept at promoting his studio. He never allowed The Designers Republic to become part of the British, or European design establishment. He carefully cultivated the group's status as geographically – and spiritually – removed from London, the design and media capital of the UK. Anderson's promotional flair was no accident. He had begun life as a promoter and manager of bands, and he knew how to circulate the oxygen of publicity and hype. He was a master of the modern art of spin. He also developed a knack for hiring talent. He attracted brilliant designers to work for him in Sheffield and soon amassed a heavyweight team of talent, many of whom were eventually to leave TDR and set up on their own – but more of this later.

By the early years of the new millennium, TDR was one of the world's most famous design groups, inspiring a following – a fan base – that has never been rivalled for passion and commitment in the design world, before or since. For a generation, The Designers Republic represented the apotheosis of the super creative, non-corporate design group. TDR continued to work for leading record labels and exert an influence out of all proportion to its size.

But it gradually became noticeable that something was lacking. The effervescence had gone. The work continued to have attitude – but it was a less abrasive and less confident attitude than before. There were rumours of the studio taking on corporate work and hiring account managers to run these big projects. The record business, one of TDR's most consistent sources of work, was contracting. It was a period of change and transformation.

I mentioned at the beginning of this article that I thought that TDR was the architect of its own downfall. What did I mean by this? It's clear that the current global financial crisis contributed to the studio's financial woes, but this alone does not fully explain its demise. For me, three key factors also contributed to TDR's undoing.

The first is the simple fact that when TDR started out in 1986 there was no one else like it. Back then, if clients wanted uber-cool pop graphics, TDR was almost the only place to go. But now there are thousands of designers and small studios who can do what TDR did, and ironically, many of them were inspired to become designers by Anderson and TDR in the first place. In other words, TDR spawned its own competitors, and now clients have dozens of TDR-like designers to choose from.

The second factor is that in order to stay ahead of the pack, TDR had to look for new clients. They could no longer rely on cool, design-savvy clients. They had to look to corporate clients for business, and if studios are going to work for big corporate clients they need account handlers and strategists, not just smart designers. Yet what TDR did best – freewheeling visual expression devoid of strategy and brand guideline books – can't be done in a studio filled with account handlers and business managers.

The third factor is Ian Anderson's success at finding talent. Over the past decade a string of small studios has opened up, all run by ex-TDR designers: Michael C Place's Build and Matt Pyke's Universal Everything being foremost amongst them. These studios – and three or four others – have made a better job of carrying on the TDR tradition than Anderson has. Clients who in the past might have gone to TDR now find what they want in these satellite studios. Yet, without Anderson's inspiration, it's doubtful if many of these ex-TDR studios would have the thrived as well as they have.

Ian Anderson has vowed to carry on the TDR studio in some form or other. A few years ago I sat on a discussion panel with him and the late Tony Wilson, the founder of Factory Records. It occurred to me then that there were similarities between the two. Both were showmen; both had created pop culture institutions (Factory and TDR); and both had a nose for sniffing out talent. But as Tony Wilson discovered in the 1990s, maintaining a pop culture institution in the face of savage commercial pressure is not easy. In my view, TDR – like Factory Records – was entirely a creation of its time, and found it difficult to adapt to a changing zeitgeist. If Anderson is to bounce back, he needs to find the vim and vision that made TDR great in the 1980s and 90s. That won't be easy: it's a different world. But it isn't impossible.

Willem Sandberg
2011

Is it possible for a piece of graphic design to worm its way into our hearts and become an object of infatuation? It seems hardly likely – after all, most graphic design is ephemeral and ends up as discarded junk. Yet if human beings can become infatuated with jewellery, coins and rodents (I know people who are smitten with each of these phenomena) it must surely be possible to fall in love with a piece of graphic design?

I should know, it happens to me regularly. But rarely with the impact with which these little books hit me. *Experimenta typographica 11* (1956) and *Experimenta typographica 2* (1969) [see pp.358–359] were lent to me by my friend the designer and collector Tony Brook, and contain the work of the Dutch graphic designer Willem Sandberg. I was aware of Sandberg as an important figure in Dutch design history. He studied psychology in the Freudian hot house of pre-World War II Vienna. During the Nazi invasion of Holland he worked for the resistance movement creating fake ID cards. Later he became the director of the Stedelijk Museum. But before seeing – and holding – these little bibliographic gems, if you'd asked me to name my favourite Dutch designers I wouldn't have included him. I'd have named van Doesburg, Schuitema, Crouwel, Wissing, van Toorn, Martens, and any number of bright-eyed current practitioners.

Today, Sandberg is top of my list. Odd really, because he doesn't even do the sort of rectilinear, hard-edged, graphically-explicit work that I normally like. Yet there's something primal and atavistic in his expressionistic use of type and image that makes me swoon. I get a sense of formmaking coming straight from Sandberg's unconscious: the same primordial sense you get from the work of Picasso, African art and Mayan sculpture. And like a great movie, which hangs around in your head long after you've left the movie theatre, Sandberg's work imprints itself on the soft tissue of memory and refuses to budge.

Graphic editorship
2007

Are graphic design skills transferable? Does being a graphic designer equip a person to do anything other than be a graphic designer? I know half a dozen designers – friends and associates – who are using their professional know-how to launch alternative or parallel careers. I'm not extrapolating a trend here: but there's something in the harsh ecology of contemporary graphic design that is encouraging certain sorts of designers to use their skills, instincts and sensibilities to create alternative ways of earning a living. One of the most interesting examples of this is the publishing venture set up by the British design group FUEL.

FUEL were the most daring and self-aware of the UK design groups to emerge in the post-Brody era. Less fashionable than Tomato or The Designers Republic, they had an arty hauteur that made them graphic design outsiders. In the early 1990s it was common to see the three FUEL men staring out of photographs wearing sharply tailored matching pinstripe suits and 'fuck you' expressions. They eschewed the mateyness of most British graphic designers in favor of a dash of menace backed up an air of calculated detachment. Or to put it another way, they conducted themselves like junior members of the Brit Art movement, a connection that remains active today: on their website they list Tracey Emin, Juergen Teller and Jake and Dinos Chapman as clients, and their studio is in the same East London street as the home of the dapper Godfathers of Brit Art, Gilbert and George.

Damon Murray, Stephen Sorrell and Peter Miles formed FUEL in 1991 (Miles left in 2004). They produced graphic design for a variety of clients including MTV, Levi's, Diesel and the Sci-Fi Channel, and yet the trio declined to follow the path of growth that so many other design groups chose at that time. Instead they put their energy into producing self-initiated books and films. The most ambitious of these projects was *FUEL 3000* (2000), a hefty tome that acted as a manifesto for their brutalist, non-ingratiating style. The book was an emotionally glacial mix of images and text that navigated a course through the 21st century media world of instant gratification and glassy-eyed fixation with the surface of things. In twenty years time, *FUEL 3000* will be seen as far more emblematic of its era than most of the boosterish eye-candy design books published at the same time.

FUEL's interest in personal authorship had started at the Royal College of Art where their eponymous magazine, with its quixotic use of vernacular motifs and crude default typography, seemed like a rebuke to the seductive design of their style-besotted contemporaries. Yet when Rick Poynor wrote about them in 2000, in an essay entitled 'Power to Translate' (reproduced in his book *Obey the Giant*), he commented '... FUEL certainly didn't regard themselves as exponents of "graphic authorship" – a term they had not heard until the late 1990s, when they reacted to it in conversation with derisive laughter.'

My guess is that the derisive laughter was an admission that FUEL knew – even then – that they were not indulging in pure graphic authorship, rather that they saw themselves as editors. As they told the British journal *Design Week*: 'editing text has much in common with art directing in terms of deciding what to take out and what to leave in, and it's all problem solving, whether its for a client or a personal project.'

A talent for editorship has led them to become publishers and to establish FUEL Publishing. As they also told *Design Week*: 'Half of the business now is publishing, so the books have to pay for themselves. Obviously each book is a huge undertaking and financial risk, so there's a rigorous process from the initial idea to the possibility of realization before we develop individual titles.'

Looking at FUEL's small, carefully nurtured backlist, it appears that they have entered a new phase. Detached scowling and graphic obliqueness have been replaced by a warmer, less austere sensibility that has allowed them to produce books with surprisingly broad appeal. FUEL's books have a cultural reach that lifts them out of the design ghetto and into the world of book chains and the review pages of broadsheet newspapers. Their two surveys of Russian criminal tattoos[1] [see p.360] have become cult hits; a book on English football match-day programmes, from the era before David Beckham and the merging of football and fashion, offers a guide to an ignored stratum of British graphic design; and a book pairing Andy Martin and the eccentric 'performance poet' and broadcaster Ian McMillan shows what happens when publishers make inspired commissions. Their latest volumes include a return to Russia and a book inspired by an entry they found on Design Observer.[2]

Murray and Sorrell's realization that they possessed the transferable skills and instincts to publish thought-provoking books with editorial depth, has allowed them to create a publishing venture that offers a fresh take on visual culture. It's a venture that their design background – especially their early explorations into self-publisher – has equipped them well to undertake.

1. At the moment of publishing there are three volumes in this series.

2. *BibliOdyssey: Amazing Archival Images From The Internet* by PK. FUEL Publishing, 2007.

Hideki Nakajima
Japanese graphic master
2002

Last year, alongside the designer Malcolm Garrett, I took part in a design seminar in Seoul. An audience of Korean students, academics and working designers politely received our presentations. (This doesn't mean that we were any good, Korean people are far too cultured and well-mannered to do anything other than respond politely.)

The seminar's third and final speaker was the Japanese graphic designer Hideki Nakajima. With a theatrical flourish, worthy of a great Kabuki actor, he asked for the lights to be turned down. In near-darkness he held up a book, its slim spine facing the audience. The book glowed supernaturally (the spine had been printed with a strip of luminous ink). A round of wild applause erupted. I looked at Malcolm and we both realised we'd just been upstaged.

But Hideki Nakajima is no design seminar show-off. His character is like his work: restrained, introspective and disciplined. Ask young Japanese designers about him and you'll quickly see how highly he is regarded. They talk about him with a sort of quiet awe. And this is fitting because he is a remarkable and visionary designer: a graphic design Zen master.

Nakajima is the son of a Kimono tailor and grew up surrounded by traditional Japanese design motifs: these motifs awakened his embryonic sense of design and pattern. As a boy he liked to 'stay at home and draw', and it was here, in front of the family television set, that he encountered the second big influence on his visual development: Ultraman.

This monster-fighting figure occupies an important position in Japanese pop culture. The programmes were made by a company founded by Eiji Tsuburaya, the special effects genius behind the early *Godzilla* films. Ultraman's appearance was inspired by Russian avant-garde art; Nakajima refers lovingly to Ultraman's 'metallic texture and colours', and the effect this had on his early aesthetic growth.

Browsing in record shops was also to play a critical role in Nakajima's design education. And it was amongst the record racks that he found the third great visual influence in his life: Peter Saville. Nakajima had a sort of epiphany when he encountered Saville's famous die-cut OMD cover. 'I was influenced (the word "influence" does not fully explain my feeling at that moment) by this record jacket ... it was the most dramatic event of my whole life and changed my destiny.'

Saville was to continue to exert a strong spell over Nakajima, a spell that was only broken when the Japanese designer paid homage to the English designer with the design of two Ryuichi Sakamoto sleeves: *Playing the Orchestra* and *Jungle Live Mix of Untitled*. In these sleeves it is plain to see that the fusion of East and West that makes Nakajima's graphic work so compelling. His expression is unequivocally Japanese but there is an equally unequivocal Western ingredient.

Nakajima recognises and embraces the relationship. 'I believe my design work,' he argues, 'should be considered as a western art. I don't want to compete with Japanese Orientalism, even if foreigners detect traditional Japanese influences in my work. It is similar to a Japanese fashion designer using kimono patterns in a Paris collection, it would be a violation of the rules.'

The English designer Hal Udell lives and works in Japan. He is a sharp-eyed observer of Japanese culture and design trends. 'From a European perspective,' he notes, 'we might see two sides to Japan; the understated, modest side which seems a reflection of the respect and understanding of Japanese tradition and nature, and the hyper-developed, in-your-face side, with its heart in technology and pop-culture inspired by the West. But, it is where these two sides meet, blend and are re-interpreted that the real essence of the Japanese way of thinking exists.'

Nakajima puts the case for his interest in western graphic design bluntly; 'Although many Japanese designers of my generation are influenced by Japanese advertising designers, I have a sympathy with British design and believe it is of the highest quality in the world.'

However, he acknowledges that minimalism is the most salient Japanese characteristic found in his work. You can see this again and again in Nakajima's work for Ryuichi Sakamoto [see p.360], a composer with pronounced minimalist tendencies.

Nakajima is best known in the West for his work with Sakamoto. His CD covers for the great Japanese composer/performer are amongst the most successful collaborations between a musician and a designer.

The relationship with Sakamoto is clearly central to Nakajima's aesthetic life. As he says; 'I first worked [with Sakamoto] on his photo book *N/Y (NO/YES)* (1996). I have worked on the design of his record jackets ever since. I have also to mention Norika Sora, Sakamoto's creative director. All the work is collaboration between the three of us. We have a love of minimalism and a desire for no barriers between the music and the design.'

But is not just sleeve design that Nakajima excels at. His work for *Cut* magazine is a good setting to track his 'western' design sensibility being used to good effect: Bauhaus lettering; Hollywood movie typography; lettering made from wood, acrylics and metal. It's bravura magazine design of the highest order. The book *Revival* (1999) is a collection of 57 typographic pieces 'directed' by Nakajima.

Nakajima seems reluctant to embrace the Internet as a design medium ('I have difficulties with the web'), nor does he use a computer ('my assistants use computers to complete my work based on my hand-designed ideas'), but he is an enthusiastic filmmaker and has made several music videos and commercial films.

Many UK graphic designers revere the Japanese graphic design scene, but in Nakajima's view, it is far from healthy: 'Nowadays in Tokyo, graphic design is getting popular and there are lots of designer-wannabes.' But in his opinion this has not resulted in meaningful and vibrant design: 'Advertising design is the mainstream in Japanese design. I don't know why, but graphic design is considered as humble. For my work, it is valued more in foreign countries than here in Japan. I think there is a design rate like a currency rate. This design rate could be raised if there were ten great designers in the country. I don't want to [be the one who has to pull] the rate up, but I would like to contribute.'

Peter Saville
Creative director of Manchester
2004

Manchester was one of the great power capitals of the Industrial Revolution. Its wealth came from cotton imported from America ('the colonies') in the 18th century. Writing about the city in the 1840s, the young Friedrich Engels said: 'If anyone wishes to see in how little space a human being can move, how little air – and such air! – he can breathe, how little of civilisation he may share and yet live, it is only necessary to travel hither.' The city has a long and noble tradition of political radicalism. Engels' disgust at the conditions of Manchester's poor was to fuel his co-authorship (with Karl Marx) of *The Communist Manifesto* (1848).

Since the end of industrialisation, Manchester has festered in the shadow of its vanished past. The devastation caused by an IRA bomb in 1996, which ripped out much of the Victorian heart of the city, created an opportunity for the city authorities to rebuild its centre. Today, this great northern British city is famous for rain, one of the world's best known and richest football clubs,[1] iconic pop music, a booming new commercial and cultural life and a television soap opera called *Coronation Street* that has entranced Brits for the past forty years.

To promote their rejuvenated city, Manchester City Council turned to the branding experts. A body called Marketing Manchester was handed the task of turning Manchester into a 'brand'. Its response was to mount a lacklustre campaign built around the feeble-sounding phrase 'We're up and going'. The paucity of the campaign angered a group of vociferous Mancunians. Calling themselves The McEnroe Group (after the tennis player's famous utterance 'You cannot be serious'), they dismissed Marketing Manchester's efforts as 'dull, mediocre and worthy of a cycling proficiency badge,' and challenged the city council to do better.

The McEnroe dissenters comprised a number of local movers and shakers, including Factory Records founder and local TV personality Tony Wilson, and Manchester-born designer Peter Saville. The group stung the city council into a volte-face. One of the outcomes of which was the appointment of Peter Saville to the role of Manchester's creative director.

Saville's famous insouciance and legendary aversion to deadlines make him an unexpected choice for this task. Despite being the crown prince of British graphic design, a sulphurous whiff of risk and danger always accompanies him. Yet he never seems short of clients. He takes a predictably confident and grand view of the task facing him in the city of his birth: 'Manchester has no longer got to compete with Liverpool and Sheffield,' he notes. 'It has got to compete with Bilbao, Barcelona, Lille and San Diego.'

Saville is already making a mark on the city. The 'Peter Saville Show', a dazzling retrospective of his 25-year career, has moved from London to Manchester, and to coincide with his exhibition, he has been given eight billboards situated throughout the city, on which to leave a Saville-esque impression. The city-wide installation is titled 'At Home', and Saville has chosen to fill the boards with visual ephemera from his 'estate'. It's a curious word to use, with its hint of mortality and artistic pretensions, yet it's part of Saville's genius (and perhaps his only genius) that he has always cleverly appropriated art world tropes, attitudes and terminology, both in his work as a graphic designer, and his life. But he is guilty of grandiloquence here. He's actually talking about a few pages from his scrapbook.

So, what will Saville do for Manchester as its creative director? He has no track record in creating 'branding' on this scale. And how do you brand a city, anyway? Happily, he is not short of advice. A local radio presenter called Pete Mitchell is reported saying that Manchester has now moved a long way from the minimalist industrial style of Peter Saville's early work for Factory Records. 'Whatever Peter Saville does,' he states, 'it needs to include more colour. It also needs to emphasise Manchester's rich musical heritage.'

A more pragmatic note is sounded by Councillor Pat Karney, a 'city centre spokesman', and part of Marketing Manchester. 'The main thing is to brand Manchester as an international city,' notes Karney. 'This isn't art for art's sake. We are a global economy and the main aim is to bring jobs to the city. We want to see real benefits. I think brand Manchester needs to emphasise that this is an entrepreneurial city with some of the best people in the universe.' Ray Makin, chairman of the

Manchester Civic Society sounds an appropriately dissenting note: 'Why does (Manchester) need branding? It's a great place that is known worldwide for a variety of reasons. To try and pick a bit out and say "We'll make it that" is belittling.'

Manchester's tradition of political radicalism mixed with healthy northern British truculence, will not make Saville's task easy. He is facing the most severe test of his career. His detractors dismiss him as a designer who never gets his hands dirty with 'real' work, but Saville's new task will involve him stepping out of his normal habitat of London-based record labels and chic fashion houses, and into the stew of local politics, civic pride and tribal allegiances. He has the confidence, talent and insolence to pull it off. Whether he can become the arbiter of Manchester's visual style and emulate what Milton Glaser did (unofficially) for New York in the 1970s, is another matter.

1. At the time of writing, Manchester United was the richest club in the world. Ironically, that accolade is now accorded to that club's great rivals and city neighbours, Manchester City.

Bruce Mau
2010

I've seen the future of graphic design. It is short, portly and dressed from head-to-toe in black. I am referring to the Canadian designer and theorist Bruce Mau. Thanks to an invitation from the design group Thoughtful, I attended a recent talk by Mau in Liverpool, where he is consulting on the redevelopment of Everton Park. The talk was a revelation.

The first thing that struck me was the audience. There was a smattering of design students and a few Converse-shod designers, but most were besuited professionals – the sort of people you might find attending a conference on health funding or urban redevelopment. They listened to Mau with rapt attention. He achieved this without ever resorting to business speak or brand gobbledygook, and by discussing design in a way that was fresh, convincing and visionary.

He began by saying that he no longer views design as being about 'the object' (logos, chairs, houses). In Mau's opinion, design doesn't even have to be visual; rather it is about designing outcomes: outcomes that can relate to anything – health, the reclamation of public spaces, even the well-being of nations.

In a way, this view of design is similar to the purely business-centred view that states that a logo, for example, doesn't have to be a 'well-designed' object, just so long as it delivers the desired outcome. In other words, it's ok for a brand identity to be visually impoverished as long as it achieves the stated business objectives.

Nor, it must be said, is Mau saying anything new. The notion of design helping to solve social and environmental problems has been around for a while, especially in the USA. But crucially, Mau has developed a methodology – and acquired a portfolio of successful projects – that lifts him out of the realm of speculative think tank musings into the realm of doing. His project for Guatemala poignantly demonstrated his credentials and brought a lump to my throat.

Asked by the Minister of Education to help build a new vision for Guatemala – a nation emerging from 36 years of civil war – Mau went about it like any half-decent branding agency.

He proposed various initiatives and even started a national movement centred on changing the name Guatemala (meaning 'bad place') to Guate Amala (meaning 'place I love'). So far so conventional. But Mau showed how his thinking differs from the normal consultative branding process when he described being introduced to the Vice President of Guatemala as 'the man who was going to redesign Guatemala'. Mau protested that this was not what he was going to do: he was, he said, the man who was going to help Guatemala *redesign itself*.

When he talks about community involvement, which he does frequently, Mau is not advocating a lazy focus group abdication of responsibility. Quite the opposite. For him, the role of the designer is to design responsibly. But, he argues, this can no longer be done in isolation, it has to be done with the support of the communities involved.

In Mau's view the world has become so complex and so threatened by environmental apocalypse that we have no choice but to design nature if we are to avoid disaster. 'Our only chance,' he says, 'is that we design our presence in the natural world.' This, he stresses, is not megalomania or designer hubris. Rather, it is about responsibility and obligation. Of course, this is not the language normally used by designers. Yet it was clear listening to Mau that it might have to become the way designers think.

Storm Thorgerson
Infinite regression
2007

The notion of record covers as works of art, as epic visual statements, is mainly derived from the great album covers of the 60s and 70s. Today, in the age of the music download and CDs designed to be racked in supermarkets alongside hair gel and toothpaste, we are less likely to encounter epic cover art. Of course there is still great cover art being made: you just won't find it in your local Asda.

Many of the best covers from the 60s and 70s are the work of the design studio Hipgnosis, and their co-founder Storm Thorgerson. For many people, when they talk about great cover art, they're really talking about Hipgnosis covers. Yes, there were great LP sleeves before Hipgnosis, and there have been great covers since they disbanded in 1983, but Hipgnosis' best sleeves are the embodiment of what record sleeve art should be: iconoclastic, disturbing, and turbo-charged with psychological weirdness. Hipgnosis raised the bar of cover art – and then they set fire to it.

Storm Thorgerson, along with Aubrey (Po) Powell, and a floating army of brilliant collaborators, perfected the enactment of highly-charged, photorealist psychodramas on a 12" cardboard square. With their lavish artwork for the gods of millionaire rock – Pink Floyd, Led Zeppelin, and a dozen others – Hipgnosis did something new in sleeve design: they brought the meticulousness and technical perfection of advertising to the world of album covers for the first time. Prior to Hipgnosis, record covers were often graphically (and typographically) crude; the great psychedelic covers of 60s America, and the garish fantasies of Krautrock, had introduced outré imagery into music packaging, but it was Hipgnosis who combined startling imagery with the presentation standards of the best commercial art and design.

When we look back at the finest Hipgnosis covers (take your pick from a dozen or so contenders) we also see that unlike much of the work from that period, Hipgnosis covers have – mostly – not dated. Slick execution, conceptual depth, and a sense of access to a cinema-of-the-interior, mean that

Hipgnosis' covers hold up to scrutiny, even by contemporary eyes sharpened by heightened visual awareness of visual art and design in general. On the other hand, if we look at the contemporaneous work of Roger Dean[1], we cringe at the bell-bottomed, tie-dyed, outdatedness of it, but with Hipgnosis, and the work of Thorgerson, we see a sharp modernity that hasn't diminished with age.

But who is Storm Thorgerson – this Dorian Gray of album cover art – and what does he do? Let's deal with the 'who' question first. For the purposes of writing this essay, I went in search of the real Storm Thorgerson. I talked to him on the phone a few weeks before the publication deadline (he was having acupuncture at the time); I read his extensive writings on his own work (the book *Eye of the Storm*, 1999,[2] is especially revealing in this respect); I pored over his extensive back catalogue of well-known and less well-known album covers. But the only thing I learned about Storm Thorgerson was that the more you look at his work, the further he recedes. Come to think of it, that's what happens on one of his most famous sleeves: 'The cover for Pink Floyd's *Ummagumma* album is about infinite regression,' he tells me from his acupuncture session [see p.361].

This comment alerts me to the idea that perhaps it is possible to build a psychological portrait of Thorgerson through his work. There are themes that recur with compulsive regularity throughout his forty years of sleeve design: burning people, eyeballs, deserts, underwater scenes. But then he lobs a spanner into my theory by telling me that, 'All I try to do is represent the music. This is a difficult thing to do. I've only got a small surface to work on, and I can't really represent forty minutes of music. I don't have duration. I only have a moment to represent the music. I have to use shorthand.'

Does this mean he is a mere interpreter? A translator of other people's ideas? Unlike a lot of sleeve designers I know, he seems to listen to the music more than is usual. As he writes elsewhere: 'Since music is our province we listen a lot, playing it time and time again so it soaks in and the design process can work osmotically as much as deductively. We talk to the musicians as much as they permit to glean their thoughts not on design but on the music. We play the music; we talk; we scribble; we listen; we talk; we scribble words thoughts jottings lyric lines; things we were told; themes and preoccupations. Always the music and slowly ideas emerge, feelings become verbalised and notes are made. From this maelstrom designs begin to take shape and are then fused with our own visual interests, modified and amended and materialised as rough drawings.'

If we disregard the eccentric punctuation and spelling, this reads like a professional graphic designer responding to a brief: conventional graphic designers do what Thorgerson does; they research, ask questions and then deliver a 'solution' to their clients. But these 'solutions' will be devoid of personal expression, since professional graphic design is about eliminating the self in favour of the unmediated delivery of the client's message. And that's where the comparison between Storm Thorgerson and the professional graphic designer ends: Thorgerson's work is brimful of personal expression and he's driven to anger when he's thwarted in the fulfilment of these ideas by record company personnel, managers and visually illiterate rock musicians (ask him what he thinks about Kiss or Mike Oldfield).

So, just when we think we are close to defining him, he runs away (recedes) yet again; on the one hand he's a traditional 'problem solving graphic designer' trying to 'represent' the music on behalf of the bands who commission him, but on the other hand, he's an artist-manqué who can't endure not getting his own way.

This sense of Thorgerson having more than one identity is heightened by talking to him. During a second telephone conversation, following his acupuncture, he is warm, friendly and happy to discuss his work at length; he does so with a mixture of breathtaking arrogance and disarming humility. Unexpectedly he starts talking about 'fans'. It's not clear whether he is talking about his fans, or the fans of the bands he works for: 'I take the fans very seriously,' he says. 'I go to conventions and gigs and I meet them. They seem pleased to meet me, but I think they really want to meet the bands.' What starts off as self-aggrandisement ends in the admission that he's not the main attraction. The bands are.

Just as he jumps between arrogance and humility, he also jumps between the personal pronoun and the collective pronoun: you never know whether you are getting the regal 'I' or the democratic 'we'.

None of this helps build a clearer picture of Thorgerson. So, let's try to answer the 'what' question. What does he do exactly? Throughout our telephone conversation, he refers to himself variously as 'a graphic designer', 'an art director', 'an artist.' He is clearly all of these things, but just as the conversation is about to end, he provides a description of himself that, for me at least, defines his role in the sheer theatricality of his sleeve art: 'People call me a surrealist,' he says, 'but I don't think I am. Well, maybe I am. But what I do is set someone on fire or build a statue and photograph it. Actually, I think what I do is performance art.'

Of course, performance art! That's what he does. Most of Thorgerson's work is an elaborate enactment of some sort of quasi-dramaturgical performance. Nobody hangs about doing nothing in his images; no item appears randomly; no landscape is chanced upon; no lighting effect is accidental. In other words, Thorgerson's work is an immaculately choreographed performance. Nothing is left to chance. And as a performance artist, Thorgerson never fakes it. Everything he does, he does for real. It's what gives his work its scale and impact. It's emotional appeal. In *Eye of the Storm* he writes: 'In terms of a technical ethic my basic inclination has been to do it for real. That means constructing or finding, arranging or positioning whatever actual ingredients are demanded by the design. Though the idea for the design is the first and crucial step, it is stillborn without adequate, if not superb, realisation. And that is when we do it for real. Whether it is building a large metal ball, or hanging people upside down from a great height. Or squashing naked youths into small wooden boxes. Or putting people on tall poles, or immersing hapless swimmers in icy rivers, or submerging dancers underwater for unreasonable periods. Or constructing an armchair the size of a generous house, or making a teddy bear robot, or a model hot air balloon. I don't fake it. I organise the making or finding of these "real" or hyper-real ingredients, which I then relocate to some extraordinary and particular spot to be photographed, and then rendered as a finished image.'

But to do work on this scale, to 'perform' at this level, you need expert help. And this brings us to one of the key aspects of Thorgerson's modus operandi: he is a collaborator. Since the earliest days of Hipgnosis, he has surrounded himself with top people; with excellent photographers, designers, retouchers, digital manipulators, set builders and prop makers. This lifts Thorgerson into a different category from most sleeve designers. Today, much of the evocative sleeve art we see is made on an Apple Mac by one person working without external ingredients. The reason for this? Money. To do what Thorgerson does costs money, and as the traditional record business stares into the abyss of oblivion, budgets are melting like an ice sculpture in Death Valley.[3]

'I have budgetary struggles,' Thorgerson confirms, 'but it just means I have to box clever. I'm not in the mood to give up.' Clearly he's not. He continues to work for bands – young bands like the Scottish group Biffy Clyro, and older bands in thrall to the great rock mythos of which Thorgerson is part of. How long the record business can accommodate his Cecil B deMille-like aspirations is an interesting question, especially since he has always been quick to bite the hand that fed him. As he tells me, one of his most famous covers, Pink Floyd's *Atom Heart Mother*, which uses a photograph of a cow in a field [see p.361], was in fact a 'serious critique of the record business. Pink Floyd liked the idea, I think they liked the cover more than the record,' he chuckles.

So, I offer you 'Storm Thorgerson – Performance Artist'; a man with the drive, ego and vision to render his interior life visible through collaboration and negotiation. As you browse through his work, you will inevitably find yourself drawn into the search for Storm Thorgerson: his work is too full of psychology and strange quirks for us not to want to know more about him. But watch out, just as you think you've nailed him, he bursts into flames and recedes into the desert.

1. Since writing these words, my views on Roger Dean's work have softened. I still find much of his work overwrought, but he remains a superb and imaginative draughtsman, and a startlingly original artist.

2. *Eye of the Storm: The Album Graphics of Storm Thorgerson* by Storm Thorgerson. Sanctuary Publishing, 1999.

3. For the album *August Everywhere* (1999) by Blinker The Star, Thorgerson commissioned an ice sculpture of a swan and photographed it in Death Valley. The shoot was fraught with difficulty, yet Thorgerson resisted the easy option of doing it 'on the computer.'

The French designer Toffe and the 'nuclear moment' 2005

His personal and professional nom-de-plume – Toffe – suggests a character played by Jean-Paul Belmondo in a light-hearted French gangster movie. In fact, his real name is Christophe Jacquet and he's a French graphic designer. His work, a well-kept secret in international design circles, fizzes with daring thinking and unexpected imagery; but it is his recurrent use of provocative and often jarring juxtapositions that is the most appealing aspect of his graphic design. His best work is a bittersweet mixture of 'ugly' computer default settings and 'beautiful' decorative touches; he mixes ranged-right system fonts (usually Times New Roman) with elegant filigree line work; he fuses 19th-century typefaces with hybrid digital fonts. His work has the aesthetic and conceptual heft that comes from being created by someone with iron hard inner convictions.

Toffe is an important, if somewhat enigmatic figure even within the French design scene. As Etienne Hervy, the editor of French graphic design magazine *Etapes*, notes: 'He is regarded by French designers as a one-off, a kind of curiosity. Someone who is somewhere else – in an intellectual sense. But there is a strong group of young designers that follow him and occasionally work with him on big projects, usually after being impressed by him during one of his workshops or visits to their school. If you disregard big stars such as M/M (Paris), or before them Grapus, he's one of the few French designers to have this kind of court – the word is too strong, but I'm not sure what the right English word would be.'

Toffe's work defies easy categorisation. It is undeniably French, yet it seems to look beyond Gallic culture for added resonance, finding it at least partly in universal digital culture. His work is recognisably postmodern in its eclecticism and its lack of reverence for cultural and graphic design conventions. But this is only half the picture: his eclecticism is not promiscuous, it is calculated and suffused with intellectual purpose. 'We can consider his work as postmodern design,' notes Etienne Hervy, 'but the French design scene did not really explore this area because Grapus had another response to modernism. In my opinion, this is a really important point about French design.'

Toffe was born in Paris, and still lives there. 'I live in the south of the city,' he explains. 'My studio is also my home. The area is cosmopolitan with lots of babies and families.' He went to the Ecole Nationale Supérieure des Beaux Arts de Paris to study painting and sculpture. 'It was very formal,' he recalls. 'Students received a classical art education. Emphasis was on drawing from the nude, and no graphic design was taught at all. But while I was there I discovered the Apple Mac computer. This was in 1984. A friend had an early Mac Plus – it was so new it even had American voltage. This was a nuclear moment for me. I decided to become a graphic designer on the spot.'

Evidence of Toffe's momentous encounter with the computer is still vividly present in his work today. The distinctive aesthetic flavour of early graphics software packages – bitmapped lines, vectorised paths, default typographic formatting, and the effortless repetition of graphic shapes – are all recurring motifs in his design: 'I use a lot of default settings in my work,' he says. 'I like people to see the nature of the machine I have used.' [see p.362] The little grey Apple box, the runt-like ancestor of today's sleek ergonomically sculpted iMacs, ignited within Toffe a deep-seated passion for the digital – or what the French more poetically call, 'numerique'.

'I was immediately enchanted with the computer,' he says. 'It gave me a sense of power. It did for me what the Internet does now. It meant that people all over the world were using the same machine. I was using the same machine as someone in America. I used MacPaint and MacWrite. I recently met Bill Atkinson, the guy who created MacPaint and I thanked him profusely. What really excited me about the Mac was the "undo" function. You can't undo a drawing or a painting. I found this psychologically stimulating. I was also obsessed with repetition. I had been making repetitive sculptures – bas reliefs – and this seemed to be a bridge for me between art and graphic design.'

After art school Toffe made personal work using the computer. He produced prints of bitmapped graphic doodles using a dot matrix printer. But because he could only generate A4 sheets, everything had to be laboriously assembled by hand,

and on top of everything, he found it hard to sell any work. 'I was told my work was too experimental, too new,' he recalls. 'And of course I could never repeat what I'd done, because everything was hand assembled. But I told people that I was a graphic designer and I began to do logotypes and theatre posters for friends.'

I first met Toffe in France in February 2005 at the International Poster and Graphic Design Festival of Chaumont [see pp.23–25]. An exhibition of his work was one of the event's main attractions. The show – a retrospective of his print and digital output – was held in an imposing church (Chapelle des Jesuites) in the town centre. It was a remarkable exhibition in a remarkable location. The church's seating had been removed and replaced with stacks of industrial-sized, moulded polystyrene pallets, which were used to display the work. Resembling vitrines from a futuristic museum, the white polystyrene units (inhuman and repetitive) were placed next to the carved white stone (organic and formal) of the church's grand interior, making yet another robust Toffe-ian statement of opposites.

The notion of contradiction was further enhanced by the show's striking poster: Toffe's name was rendered in isometric letterforms constructed out of liner renderings of the polystyrene trays which were then superimposed over a mound of dead fish. The Christian symbolism of the fish carried a hint of playful provocation; here was a show held in a fully-functioning, consecrated Catholic church, yet which featured entirely secular work including heavily bitmapped pornographic images, and a large amount of material produced for an Algerian – and therefore Islamic – audience.

Seven months after Chaumont, Toffe is sitting in my studio in London talking infectiously about his work, his family (his wife is a photographer and he has a 16-year-old daughter) and French colonial history. Listening to him talk on a swelteringly hot day, with his rich French accent and his only occasionally faltering English, it becomes clear that he has chosen graphic design as a mode of personal expression rather than as a comfortable career option. He has none of the hectoring desire to champion art over design so often found amongst designers who regard self-expression as their sine qua non. In fact, he is disparaging about contemporary art, dismissing the recent Venice Biennale, which he attended, as an 'art supermarket.'

His pantheon of heroes reveals his preference for artistically inclined design: 'I am influenced by constructivism. By Rodchenko, El Lissitzky, and the others. When I look at Rodchenko and El Lissitzky, I'm glad I call myself a graphic designer. There's a big problem in France. You have to be graphic design or art, you can't be both. This is shit. I am happy to say that I am a graphic designer.' He also confesses to a love of Paul Rand and Giotto.

Yet despite his convivial and unaffected manner, it is not easy to imagine him working with corporate clients: 'If I do a commercial job,' he says, 'it is always 50% me, 50% the client. I don't want to have to change what I do to make clients happy. This is very important for me. I won't become technical or functional just to please a client. I want to be just like I am when I'm with my friends: my bad habits, being stupid or drunk. I want to be automatic. I have to keep the same response, the same reflexes, no matter who I am dealing with. In my mind, there is no difference between doing a job for a corporate client or doing my own show at Chaumont. So yes, I will work for corporate clients, but I prefer cultural clients.'

Many of the bigger European nations creak under the weight of their colonial pasts. The French occupied Algeria from 1830 onwards, finally withdrawing in 1962, after a decade of guerrilla warfare. Today, Algeria is an Islamic state, and French rule has bequeathed a troubled cultural legacy, as well as many unhealed scars. Under the auspices of the French government, The Centre Culturel Français d'Alger is dedicated to 'the renewal of a dialogue between the two banks of the Mediterranean'; and is committed to 'contemporary thought and creation, artistic gestures, risk-taking and discovering ideas.' This cauldron-like arena is where Toffe, and his studio, have produced some of their most significant work. 'There is a very complicated relationship between France and Algeria,' he notes. 'The director of the Cultural Centre, Aldo Herlaut, is an interesting man. He asked me to do the Centre's visual identity. In my studio, I worked with an Italian designer called Gianni Oprandi, he was one of my students and I've worked with him on other projects. Together we made a style manual for all the centre's communications. Also we did many other individual projects, including posters and leaflets.'

The visual identity for CCF is one of Toffe's most compelling graphic statements. As is customary, it bristles with internal contradictions. It is a stew of Arabic and European signs and tropes. It is a genuine hybrid: nothing is authentic; everything is artifice. Yet it is rooted in French typographic tradition and the noble grammar of Arabic ornament. And like the polystyrene pallets in the church, it contains some unlikely and provocative gestures. 'The use of a hexagonal motif might have been regarded as dangerous,' he notes. 'The French ambassador thought it was dangerous. It might have been seen as the Ka'bah, the cube-like shrine in the courtyard of the Sacred Mosque in Mecca, toward which Muslims face in daily prayer. In fact, it's a graphic representation of the shape of France. To make it acceptable, I used a nice French blue for the octagon shape. I also adapted the classic French typeface Normandie. It predates the French occupation of Algeria in 1830. It's like Mistral and Banco – typically French. Of course, I didn't use it straight, I doctored it. I hope the identity is provocative, and not colonialist. But I can't help my French heritage. I can't just throw it away.'

At a time when Islamic fundamentalism is a powerful global presence, and when there is great concern in the west about the depiction and reporting of Arabic culture, Toffe is untroubled by notions of sensitivity. He plunders Arabic lettering with cavalier abandon: its essence gleefully extracted and used as abstract decoration. As he explains: 'We developed an approach using vector drawings to create a wire-like line that we could use to make abstract Arabic lettering, without it being readable. The motifs used in the CCF identity are based freely on Arabic lettering – we kept the movement of the line. Arabic typography is like handwriting. It flows. I don't think they find it disrespectful. They treat it like a gift. They view it in the same way they view cakes and delicacies, which are very important in Arabic culture. Eating, nice colours, icing, these are things that give pleasure.'

Another striking piece of graphic design produced under the CCF banner is Toffe's book devoted to the French poet Jean Sénac (b.1926). Sénac was a protégé of Albert Camus, but the relationship became strained by Sénac's fervent support for Algerian independence. Sénac, a homosexual, became an

Algerian citizen and his love for his adopted nation runs through his poetry. He was murdered in Algeria in 1977.

Toffe's Sénac book is a tour de force of graphic expression. It is laden with his trademark signs and symbolism. It is also a bravura display of the designer as editor. No conventional editor would ever produce a book like this. It is clearly the work of a visual artist engaging fully with the book's subject matter, and using the rich rhetorical language of graphic design to impart a layer of visual commentary that adds to the accumulated pleasure of handling and studying this volume: 'The Sénac book project was very important to me,' explains Toffe. 'When people pick up this book they say, not "who is Jean Sénac?" but "what is this book about?" Half of it is actually about my studio. It was an open brief, we were free to do what we wanted. The book wasn't economically successful for me, but you don't remember that when you look back.'

'When you consider the Sénac book,' notes Etienne Hervy, 'it's about two people, but the great talent of Toffe is that his contribution to the book is that he succeeds in integrating his artistic creation into the design process of the book. To be honest, I consider it's all about personal conviction. He is the real "point" of all his work. What might be presumed to be graphic design arrogance, comes over in the pages of this book at least, as inspired and visionary thinking. The book is a dazzling artefact made all the richer by an intrusive design presence.'

Face to face. Toffe is arrogance-free. He is charming, modest and delightful company. But in his professional life he has a steely hardness that might easily be interpreted as arrogance. As Etienne Hervy, a long time admirer says: 'He has the generosity you often find in egocentric people. He does great design because he knows he is one of the best. This kind of arrogance is a French speciality that you also find in Grapus, M/M (Paris) and Labomatic. It's not a literal arrogance, more a conviction that designers can make great things by the use of their personal expression.'

Julian House
Self-initiated House music
2005

The British graphic designer Julian House is best known for his album covers for Primal Scream, Stereolab and Broadcast. House has an attentive following amongst graphic designers attracted to his idiosyncratic, image-laden work. His admirers might be surprised to learn that he has recently added music making to his repertoire. It is perhaps stretching definitions to say that House has become a musician, but with the help of sampling technology and an array of digital audio tools, he makes striking and compelling audio assemblages that have strong stylistic parallels with his collage-based graphic design.

To date, House has released two CDs of music (under the name The Focus Group), and started a record label called Ghost Box to release music by himself and other like-minded individuals [see p.363]. Visitors to the Ghost Box website can buy a range of CDs with ravishing House-designed booklets.

I worked with Julian House for seven years at Intro, the studio I co-founded in 1988 (I left in December 2003). I gave him his first job after he was enthusiastically recommended to me by one of the designers at Intro. Interviewing him, I found him diffident; he didn't seem robust enough to survive bruising encounters with clients or the demands of a busy, deadline-driven studio. Nor was I convinced by his work, either. It contained not much more than a few flashes of promise. But I liked him enough to offer him a job. I sensed an inner core of strength beneath the diffidence, and he had a quirky intelligence and a stock of arcane knowledge that distinguished him from run-of-the-mill design school graduates.

It took six months for the full extent of his talent as a designer to emerge, and another 18 months for him to develop into what I considered to be a near-perfect example of a contemporary graphic designer: a strong individual 'voice', coupled with an equally strong desire to please and accommodate his clients. When he was asked recently by Rick Poynor in an interview if he regarded design for music as an area for self-expression, House replied: 'I would never say, "This is my vision that I'm bringing to the band." It is a two-way process, a collaboration. Their responses to some of my ideas often focuses it in a way that maybe I would not have done.' Designers who are insistent on their own vision without compromise, and who reject all client contributions, are no better than designers who offer total compliance. Graphic design is the art of 'collaboration', and all great designers understand this.

House began his career with an ambition to be an illustrator. You can see this clearly in his best work: a curious melding of unlikely imagery and expressionistic typography. His aesthetic touchstones are the 60s and 70s international avant-gardes; Pop Art; comics; old text books; pre-digital British TV graphics; East-European movie posters; and visual arcana of all kinds. Music critic Matthew Ingram, writing in *The Wire*, describes House as 'an exacting collector of the tainted British parochial. Obsessed by the twilight world of Diana Dors, Donald Cammell, Joe Meek and Delia Derbyshire, he crafts both exquisite visual collages in thrall to European modernism (the moiré effects from the covers of Penguin books, Lettrism and Polish movie posters) and divinely wrought soundscapes that hark back to an eternal past.'

Despite his interest in the crafts-based visual culture of the first half of the 20th century, House is entirely dependent on his computer. He uses all the standard digital tools, but rarely in the way they were intended to be used. Quark Xpress is deployed to manipulate imagery, for example. The results are unpredictable, jagged, and prone to extreme and unexpected elisions, yet at the same time, startlingly beautiful. House's primary design tool, however, is Google's image search tool, which allows him to trawl the murky margins of the Internet for oddball imagery. Much of House's work is the transformation of 72dpi web detritus into sharp, contemporary graphic design. He is a collagist in the grand tradition, but what makes him unusual is that he is an audio as well as a visual collagist.

And there's another thread running through House's music; it's the aesthetic thread that binds together his audio work and his visual work. House is a collector of library music, a fact noted by Mathew Ingram in his review of *Hey Let Loose Your Love*, one of the two albums House has released to date: 'Pieced together from the mustiest samples – children's exercise records, vintage BBC drama, clunky Brit jazz and (most pertinently) library records ...'

The cult of library music is centered around records made in the 60s and 70s, often by elite session musicians making off the shelf music for TV, movies and advertising. Some of this music is superb – beautifully crafted and emotionally charged. This is music that deftly defines the times it was made in, often more resonantly than the chart-based pop music of the time. And of course, it comes with the warm analogue glow of vinyl.

A sizeable cult has grown up around library music. For DJs, remixers, record collectors and pop-culture vultures of a certain age (thirty-forty-somethings), it provides the aural equivalent of 'dipping the madeline'. The cult has its most visible focus in the activities of DJ and record collector, Jonny Trunk. Trunk is the curator of a mildly salacious website devoted to errant Brit audio/visual ephemera ('music sex nostalgia' – as he proudly announces on his home page). He also runs a record label (Trunk Records) devoted to unearthing neglected music from Britain's recent past: usually misfit sounds that recalls the 1970s Britain of damp Sundays, sexual inhibition, and a nation with only three TV channels. Trunk is about to publish a book devoted to the album covers of library music.[1] Designed by FUEL [see pp.76–78], it shows a remarkable array of graphically inventive covers. Free from commercial inhibitions and the need to promote the careers of pop stars, these covers are closer to the sleeves for avant-garde classical music than the pop sleeves of the time: in fact, they look as if Julian House designed them.

For House, library music's allure is plain to see. Here is music that invites appropriation. It is made to be 'used'. It is House's audio equivalent of Google image search – a seemingly unending source of material waiting to be crafted into something new and vibrant.

1. *The Music Library: Graphic Art and Sound* by Jonny Trunk, Damon Murray and Stephen Sorrell [Eds.]. FUEL Publishing, 2005.

Neville Brody
2011

In 2009, I was asked to interview the graphic designer Neville Brody in front of an audience of 900 people. In a taxi on my way to the theatre, I was grilled by an inquisitive cabbie. In an attempt to deflect his questions, I told him I was on my way to interview Neville Brody. That'll fox him, I thought. 'Neville Brody,' he said. 'Wasn't he the guy who designed *The Face* in the 1980s?'

I've heard it said that the definition of celebrity is someone whose name is recognised by the drivers of London's black taxis. If this is true, then Neville Brody is a rare phenomenon: a graphic designer famous beyond the confines of graphic design.

Until recently, graphic design was an activity that most people had heard of but few were able to define. Today, however, thanks to the ubiquity of the home computer, anyone who can choose a font from a drop-down menu is able to create basic items of graphic design such as newsletters, posters and even websites. In other words, if you've got a PC you can produce the sort of graphic communication that was previously only done by art school trained graphic designers.

And yet, as with a great many subjects that have been democratised by new technology – music, photography, filmmaking – the amateur soon discovers that there is a vast difference between what he or she can do, and what the professionals can do. We only have to look at the great masters of graphic design to see that when done well, graphic design can possess all the invention and dignity of a work of art. Most of the 'great masters' of graphic design are Swiss, German or American. But we can boast a few top drawer Brits – and one of those is Neville Brody.

Brody was born in London in 1957. A childhood love of art propelled him to undertake a Fine Art foundation course at Hornsey College of Art, a notorious hotbed of student unrest in the 1960s. Brody was full of ideological and political fire, but he soon discovered that Fine Art didn't accommodate his need to spread his 'message' of rebellion and opposition. Graphic design, on the other hand, offered him the tools and skills to enable him to speak to a mass audience, and so in 1976 he began a three-year degree course in graphics at the London College of Printing.

But Brody's taste for experimentation, and his refusal to become a conventional commercial designer with a cosy, well-paid future in advertising, meant that he was branded by the school as 'uncommercial' – back then, a lack of commercial savvy was considered a great sin. The 1970s was a boom time for designers: the corporate world had recently woken up to the fact that packaging, corporate identity, and visual presentation of all kinds, were key drivers in business success. It was the start of an explosion that was to result in the 1980s earning the not always flattering designation – the Designer Decade.

None of this appealed to the young Brody. His interest in punk rock was beginning to influence his attitude to design. At one point he was almost thrown out of the college for designing a postage stamp with the Queen's head placed sideways – an almost treasonable offence in British philatelic circles. Brody completed his education without being awarded a degree; he spent the next few years earning a pittance.

Brody's reluctance to join the design boom engulfing commercial design, his infringement of Royal protocol, and his failure to gain a degree, were all to return in unexpected and zironic ways: in the 1980s, as the art director of the style magazine *The Face* [see p.364], he became for many the personification of the Designer Decade. He recently received a Special Commendation from Prince Philip in the Royal Consort's Annual design prize; and in the summer of 2010 was appointed head of the Visual Communication course at the Royal College of Art – for many, the pinnacle of academic posts in British design education. But more of this later.

After leaving college, Brody worked firstly for a small design group called Rocking Russian (run by Alex McDowell, now one of Hollywood's most in-demand art directors, working on films such as *Fight Club*, *Minority Report* and *Charlie and the Chocolate Factory*). Next came a spell at Stiff Records, the pioneering indie label that signed Elvis Costello, Ian Drury and the Blockheads and Madness. But Brody's big break came when he was appointed Art Director of *The Face* magazine. For a generation, *The Face* was both style bible and arbiter of cultural taste. Nick Logan who had been editor of the *New Musical*

Express in the 1970s, and had launched the spectacularly successful glossy pop mag *Smash Hits*, launched *The Face* in 1980. Brody joined in 1981, after waging a campaign to persuade Logan to hire him.

The 'look' of *The Face* turned Brody into a design star to rank alongside the other 80s style stars of fashion, architecture and music. His use of striking typography and his bold handling of images, brought a new dynamism to both the world of magazine design and the larger world of visual communication in general. Clients queued up to hire the boy wonder. In a period of frenetic activity, Brody designed covers for *City Limits*, *New Socialist* and *Arena*; created the visual identity for a prominent London property agency; designed the Red Wedge logo, numerous record sleeves, and a proposal for a new CND logo.

Brody was riding a wave of success, but he was not behaving like other successful designers. It became fashionable for designers of the period to build big design companies with blue chip clients. Designers were rushing to join the new service based economy of the booming 1980s. But not Brody. As the design critic Rick Poynor has written: 'From the outset, Brody was concerned with ideas and he was precociously forward in explaining the elements of critique in his work. It's easy to take this for granted now, but it was virtually unheard of, in either Britain or America, for a young designer to dwell on his own motivations, agenda and putative "graphic language" in this way.'

The rapid formation of a recognisable Brody style – or 'graphic language' – was to culminate in period of recognition and accolades that was previously unthinkable in the career of a graphic designer, not to mention one who had only just turned 30. In 1988 Thames & Hudson published the first of two volumes of Brody's work, and as if that wasn't enough, he was invited to stage an exhibition of his work at the Victoria and Albert (V&A) Museum. The exhibition subsequently toured Europe and Japan, and Brody's status as the first international superstar of graphic design was cemented.

But like Icarus flying too close to the sun, Brody was scorched by his proximity to the sun of publicity. If celebrity is admired in artists, fashion designers and architects, it is frowned upon in graphic designers. Clients, for the most part, want their graphic designers to be docile and above all, compliant. Generations of designers had been raised in this orthodoxy: like journalists they must never become part of the story. The designer is hired to convey the client's message: not their own. Disinterested objectivity is what is required, and Brody had defied this unspoken edict. He was now more famous than many of his clients, and his punishment was to see them abandon him en masse. Brody entered a period of emotional turmoil and financial collapse. The only work he could pick up was from foreign clients, and for most of the 90s he worked quietly and without attracting much attention.

Slowly, however, throughout the 1990s, Brody reinvented himself. He launched a studio under the impersonal name Research Studios. He became an early pioneer of web design, and opened small satellite studios in San Francisco, Paris, Berlin and New York, staffed mostly by former employees. He produced work for Kenzo, Adobe and Dom Perignon. He designed on-screen graphics for Michael Mann films and for the *Mission Impossible* series. In 2006, he was commissioned to redesign the establishment's house journal, *The Times*. For this task, Brody went back to his roots and created a new font – Times Modern. It was to become the first new font used by the paper since 1932 when Times New Roman was introduced. In 2010, Brody's studio undertook one of their most ambitious projects to date: the redesign of the BBC's website. The rehabilitation of Neville Brody was nearly complete.

Until recently it would be accurate to say that Brody's career had two main phases: the early years leading up to his establishment as a bona fide star of design, followed by a lengthy period as a relatively low-profile, professional designer working with mainstream clients on increasingly complex and demanding projects. But now, in the second decade of the 21st century, Brody's career has entered a third phase: his early revolutionary instincts are no less in evidence, yet rather than exercising them on the margins, he has dragged them into the heart of British cultural life. The rebel now has a seat at the high table.

In 2010, the designer who had once been admonished by his tutors for irreverence towards the Queen in the matter of stamp design, was awarded a Special Commendation at the

Prince Philip Designers Prize 2010. Formed in 1959, the scheme has celebrated over fifty years of innovation in design. The 2010 prize was won by the product designer Bill Moggridge. Special Commendations were awarded to Dame Vivienne Westwood, John Makepeace and Neville Brody.

As if this wasn't enough, Brody has been appointed Head of the Department of Communication Art & Design at the Royal College of Art. The student rebel who left academia without a degree now heads a department in one of the world's leading art and design schools. Dr Paul Thompson, Rector of the Royal College of Art, welcomed Brody with the words: 'Neville Brody is both an eloquent advocate and a superb practitioner. His design talent traverses so many different media – traditional print and typography through to online, motion graphics, and packaging. He is one of the most influential designers of his generation and perfectly captures the interdisciplinary ethos of the Department of Communication Art & Design.'

And yet, while most designers would be content to bask in the reflected glory of a high profile appointment and official accolades, Brody remains one of the design world's fiercest critics. He recently curated the Anti Design Festival [see p.365], which he described as a 'response to 25 years of cultural deep freeze.' He saw the Festival as an 'attempt to unlock creative fires and ideas, exploring spaces hitherto deemed out-of-bounds by a purely commercial criteria.'

The Anti Design festival ran concurrently with the official London Design Festival, but whereas the latter event champions design as a great British export and as a key driver in modern commerce, Brody chose to demonstrate how, via exhibitions, talks and multimedia events, design was also defining an alternative culture of opposition and critical enquiry: 'We have forgotten why we are here,' he said. 'We have lost touch with what makes us tick, what drives us. That fire of creative possibility has started to die, and it is time to re-light it. The Anti Design Festival was born out of a need for change. A need for something new, ugly, scary and dangerous. We welcome no-use, no-function and no-fear. We welcome anarchy, without the stereotypical.'

For some, Brody is a 1970s–80s radical, spouting agit-prop rhetoric and recalling the shouty days of anti-Thatcherism. Yet for others, he is a glowing example of the creative individual who refuses to settle back with pipe and slippers. Now in his fifties, the mature Brody appears more combative, more critical, and more active than most designers half his age.

The design critic Rick Poynor sums up Brody's value when he says: 'Enough time has passed for it to be possible to revisit his 1980s work without worrying about passing questions of fashion. I believe that when future assessments are made Brody will emerge clearly as one of the most considerable designers of the period, working anywhere.'

Philippe Starck
2009

Philippe Starck is a bona fide genius, and his current BBC2 series, *Philippe Starck's School of Design*, is a brilliant advert for design. There, I've said it, and it feels good. Of course, I realise my assertion is heresy. Amongst vociferous designers it has become obligatory to savage the show. The design writer Stephen Bayley said it shared the same genetic code as *Opportunity Knocks*.[1] And in the normally civilized pages of *Design Week*, Starck has been called 'an idiot' and the 'worst type of stereotypical designer'.

Designers will debate the merits and demerits of Strack until the cows come home tinkling their Starck-designed bells. Yet despite occasional bouts of buffoonery, the great Frenchman emerges from the show as the portly embodiment of good sense and design wisdom, and I can't help wondering how many of his critics could survive the scrutiny of a TV crew and ratings-hungry producers?

It's true that a great deal of what Starck stands for today – 'democratic design' and his insistence on products having a 'reason to exist' – is contradicted by his past. I'm thinking of luxury yachts and his beautiful, yet surely inessential, Perspex 'ghost chairs'. But designers are allowed to change their views, and beneath the Asterix-like bluster, and the occasional and forgivable infelicities with the English language ('You. Are. Dead.'), Starck makes some razor sharp points about sustainability and the importance of 'generosity' when designing a product.

His decision in the opening episode to send his 'pupils' on a shopping trip to choose essential and non-essential items was super smart. Nearly all the 12 candidates failed this simple test, thus proving at a stroke their unpreparedness for the bigger task of actually designing something worthwhile. If some of the candidates had listened to what Starck told them at this point, they might have lasted longer.

But reality shows rarely have anything to do with reality. They are entertainment just like any Saturday tea-time ratings smash. And it was here, in the game show aspect of the series, that Strack's attempt to award a six-month internship to a young British product designer was at its most vulnerable to criticism and ridicule.

Yet the fault clearly lay not with Starck, but with the programme makers and the vapid conventions of reality television. It is obligatory in these shows to shamelessly manipulate the action to create phoney tension and faux drama. Starck's candidates were prompted to parrot the usual insincerities about self-belief and the will to win. Simple tasks that would hardly tax a foundation year design student were ramped up into TV melodrama.

The show wasn't helped by the inability of the candidates to explain their thinking. With the exception of one individual (the eventual winner), the wannabe Starckers were woefully inarticulate. But unlike the show-offs and fame junkies that clog up *The Apprentice*,[2] each of Starck's candidates seemed genuine in their desire to be a designer – even if some of them are going to have to reconsider their career options.

In the end, I watched the show for Starck. His moralistic approach to design was refreshing and unexpected. Mercifully, he isn't the sort of identikit designer spouting management guff-speak. Starck is a visionary – and with that comes a lot of messy baggage and an industrial-grade ego. But he's not an idiot and nor – thank God – is he a stereotypical designer. Although I can see a bit of Hughie Green[3] in him.

1. *Opportunity Knocks*, hugely popular talent show from the early days of British television.

2. *The Apprentice*, 'reality' game show where contestants compete to win a job with the show's host, the British businessman Lord Sugar.

3. Hughie Green, eccentric presenter of *Opportunity Knocks*. He came to typify a certain sort of 'Americanised' showman presenter. He also devised the format for *Opportunity Knocks*.

Paul Graham
Poet of the mundane
2008

'This work embraces "amateurish" things like blur, colour casts, camera shake, red-eye, bad-flash technique. Many of these pictures would make a professional photographer shudder. I don't set uplights. I don't diffuse, bounce or soften the flash, there's no colour correction – some of the pictures are even out of focus, for chrissakes!' Paul Graham is talking about the portraits of young adults in his book *End of an Age* (1999). He talks about his work with the same revealing honesty with which he makes his photographs.

Graham describes the 'young adults' in *End of an Age* as being at that moment 'when one has left childhood, but has not quite integrated fully into adulthood'. His subjects seem unaware of his presence. They don't look at the camera. They look into the distance – into the imminent world of adulthood, mortgages, careers, parenthood and the uncertainty of the new millennium that awaits them. Some of the subjects are engulfed in the synthetic, hallucinatory colour of nightclubs. Others are set against the colourless walls of cheap bars and apartments. This is social documentary photography with the added bite of psychological insight. These are people we see every day – in the street, in shops, on trains and buses – but we rarely give them more than a glance. In the poetic setting of Graham's photographs we view them with a stark clarity that reminds us how little we really see.

In an interview with the artist Gillian Wearing, Graham says this: 'It's strange how work always ends up having a degree of self-reflection in it no matter what you do.' The reference to self-reflection is ambiguous: does he mean that he is reflected in his pictures, or does he mean the act of taking pictures causes self-reflection? Either way, Graham's pictures are psychologically revealing. Despite their apparent detached objectivity, we can see that he doesn't patronise his subjects, nor does he set out to be ingratiating: his photographs look like the work of someone searching for deeper truths.

Paul Graham was born in 1956, in Stafford, England. He studied science at Bristol University, but after graduating in

1978, became a photographer. He currently lives in the USA. Graham held his first exhibition in Bristol in 1979, and since then has produced a number of important books and taken part in numerous exhibitions. Along with Nan Goldin, Thomas Struth, Andreas Gursky, Philip-Lorca diCorcia and a handful of other leading photographers, he is widely regarded as one of the pre-eminent figures in contemporary art photography.

Graham is a poet of the mundane. He infuses his pictures of dismal interiors and gloomy landscapes with an unexpected lyricism. In our daily lives we frequently encounter the sort of scenes Graham photographed for his 'New Europe' project: overflowing ashtrays; discarded piles of valueless coins; holes in the ground. Yet we rarely view these glimpses of the mundane as being in the least poetic. But when Graham photographs a hole in the ground he invests it with resonance and meaning. How does he manage this?

Perhaps we need to ask ourselves the big photography question: what exactly are we responding to when we look at a photograph? Are we responding to the subject matter? Are we responding to the photographer's technical accomplishment? Are we responding to the photographer's intention? Sometimes, of course, we are responding to all three, but mostly we are attracted to photographs because of their subject matter. Advertising knows this, as do the fashion and porn industries: all you need to do is shoot that which is desirable and you will hit the jackpot. As viewers we are seduced by ingratiating images: we don't care about the technical accomplishment of the image, and we don't give a hoot about the photographer's intention, all we care about is the desirability of the subject.

But photographers have always challenged this orthodoxy. August Sander photographed country bumpkins in ill-fitting suits; Diane Arbus photographed society's rejects – the shunned and the freakish; Dorothea Lange photographed the down-trodden poor of Depression-era America. Here was subject matter that was disturbing and uncomfortable, but the photographs were artistic triumphs, and searing examples of the photographers' artistic intent.

When Robert Frank, the Swiss-born photographer, produced his famous book *The Americans* (1958), [see pp.282–283], he caused outrage. He didn't photograph the heroic America of

Monument Valley, or the lordly skyscrapers of New York or Chicago, instead he photographed poor African Americans, dreary luncheon counters, and lonely roads leading to nowhere. When he went to photograph that great achievement of American industrial might, the Hoover Dam, he photographed the postcard rack and not the dam.

It would have been easier for Frank, Sander, Arbus and Lange to have photographed the heroic, the grand and the conventionally beautiful. But their photographs would have lacked the pure fire of artistic intent.

Graham defines one of his 'intentions' as the 'process of visual discovery.' He states: 'I'm a firm believer that photographers are like poets of the visual world, and like poetry they should refresh our visual language, or it withers and dies.' In his series 'Television Portraits', Graham refreshed our notion of the portrait. As with *End of an Age*, it's a language that has been adopted by fashion brands and editorial photography. The cool casual detachment of Graham's images has, paradoxically, become the default setting for a postmodern generation of apolitical, self-absorbed, style-obsessed tribes.

In Graham's pictures of television watchers, we don't see the TV sets, we only see the sitters watching the blue-eyed rectangle in the corner – a less self-assured photographer would have shown us the flickering screens as well. Few of the watchers seem captivated by what they are looking at; television it seems is an anaesthetic, an opportunity to blank-out, to forget. Only the children seem absorbed. They have a rapt stillness. They sit upright, as alert as meerkats.

Graham's Northern Ireland opus, *Troubled Land* (1987), show his sublime gift for making photographic treasure out of everyday subject matter. Northern Ireland occupies a unique position in the British psyche. Today, peace reigns in the Province for the first time since the 1960s, but the legacy of our own domestic 'war on terror' lingers on; to this day you won't find metal litterbins in railway stations in the UK mainland (a legacy from the time when the IRA used metal bins to deposit bombs at railway stations and other public sites.)

Here, Graham strays into photojournalism territory. Not that you'd mistake his pictures of the scarred topography of Ulster for photojournalism. As Robert Capa famously reminded us, photojournalism requires that the photographer must be in the thick of it: 'If your pictures weren't good enough you weren't close enough.' But as ever, Graham takes a step back, shunning the obvious drama, removing himself from the newsworthy action, he is able to imbue his pictures with an intimacy and a human scale that photojournalism, with its urge to tell the whole story in a single image, only rarely achieves.

The viewer has to work at Graham's Ulster pictures in a way that no photojournalist would demand. Take his photograph 'Roundabout, Andersonstown, Belfast' (1984), [see pp.366–367]. The composition is nicely balanced; the colouring is muted and flat. At first glance it is an almost subjectless photograph, but gradually we see discomfiting details: armed soldiers are running across the roundabout; the lights have been removed from the tall street lamps; a row of suburban houses strive to keep the world at bay with net curtains, those impenetrable barriers common to British life; a man and a youth go about their business oblivious to the running soldiers; a steel roadside fence in the extreme foreground carries the initials IRA, and other Republican slogans. Blink and you might miss most of this.

In his book *The Ongoing Moment* (2007), Geoff Dyer quotes the critic Hilton Kramer's curt dismissal of William Eggleston as 'the banal leading the banal.' Graham has acknowledged his debt to Eggleston, and banality is a charge that might be levelled against his 'Unionist Coloured Kerbstone at Dusk, Near Omagh' (1985) and 'Republican Coloured Kerbstones, Curmon Road, Belfast' (1984). Ostensibly, they are pictures about nothing. But to think this is to miss their exquisite framing, their ominous brooding atmospherics, and the almost subliminal political statements made by the thin, snaking lines of kerbstones painted with the tribal markings of Loyalists and Republicans that appear in both pictures. Quietly declarative, they catch our eye, yet, like the running soldiers, we hardly notice their deeper meaning.

Graham's Ulster pictures are compelling artistic statements because they are not ingratiating. Graham doesn't seek to flatter. He tells the truth, and the truth is rarely ingratiating. Holes in the ground and bleak housing estates in trouble-torn Belfast are not inviting. Graham asks us to look at his subject matter – subject matter we normally avoid, or fail to see – with freshly opened eyes. He helps us to do this by avoiding showy technique and by daring to record life as it happens in front of his eyes. And ours.

Barnbrook Bible
A graphic autobiography
2007

Jonathan Barnbrook's new book, *Barnbrook Bible* (2007), ranks amongst the most ambitious personal projects undertaken by any graphic designer. It is a 330-page monograph bursting with dazzling refinement. Throughout the entire book there isn't a clumsy or unrefined typographic gesture – not a line that hasn't been weighted to perfection. The effect is like being in a Parisian patisserie – everywhere you turn there are mouth-watering options.

But the *Barnbrook Bible* is more than a big fat designerly monograph. It is a work of semi-autobiography expressing the author's well known political views, and his aesthetic and professional philosophies. It therefore invites judgement by more demanding criteria than if it was just another graphic design book. And so the big question is: does Barnbrook's magnum opus represent a species-jumping leap for graphic design, or is it the outpourings of a massive ego shot through with political anger and a fondness for typographic cartooning?

The *Barnbrook Bible* – which took five years to complete – is a comprehensive re-engineering of the designer's back catalogue, beginning with his student work and coming up to date with his *Adbusters* involvement. The book eschews a conventional structure; instead, it is a fast-flowing river of textual and visual rhetoric. There is a solemn precision to all Barnbrook's work. He produces finely tooled graphic wizardry that distinguishes him from almost all other graphic designers at work today. He can mix a dozen fonts (each designed by him) on a single page – sometimes even changing typefaces mid-sentence – and it still looks coherent and exquisitely judged [see p.368].

The spectre of religion hangs over this book. It begins with the odd-sounding note of the title, and continues inside with Barnbrook's extensive use of religious symbolism and typographic conventions associated with English religious texts; Eric Gill's stark red-and-black typographic creed lives on in Barnbrook's design. The aesthetic flavour of Barnbrook's work is acutely English. It is the flavour of gravestones in rural churchyards, of dusty prayer books and the vivid lustre of stained glass windows. This iconography links Barnbrook to a traditionalist view of Englishness that is increasingly rare in multicultural Britain, and more commonly associated with reactionary conservatism.

Which brings us sharply to Barnbrook's political commentary. Barnbrook is a political radical: American foreign policy and global corporatism are his main targets. Most of this work is self-initiated and self-funded. Much of it is briskly effective and to the point – but there is also a callowness to it. Morphing Ronald MacDonald and Osama Bin Laden into a single iconic character is witty and diverting for about three seconds; although perhaps it has a higher purpose which is to infuriate corporate America and Al Qaeda supporters – in which case, bravo to that.

This occasional callowness means it's easy to dismiss Barnbrook's political work as typographic cartooning (planes flying into perpendicular barcodes, for example), yet the sheer brilliance of his execution prevents us from doing this. In the past, revolutionary and oppositional movements have distinguished themselves by shunning formal graphic design because of its links to political and corporate power, and turned instead to more anarchic modes of graphic expression. Barnbrook, however, brings the gloss and ultra-refinement of cosmetics advertising to the task of exposing US bombing statistics. It's an astonishing conjuring trick that he pulls off repeatedly.

The final component in this book is Barnbrook's text. There are essays by Alice Twemlow, Teal Triggs, Kalle Lasn, Emily King and three paragraphs by David Bowie (one of Branbrook's clients), but the book mainly consists of Branbrook's own extensive writings which appear on nearly every page. He writes engagingly about font creation, his discovery of film-based work, and the conduct of the modern designer. His chapter on working with Damien Hirst is a rewarding read.

I said earlier that this was a work of semi-autobiography. It is more accurately a work of 'professional' autobiography, by which I mean that Barnbrook mainly confines his autobiographical observations to his work, and only fleetingly touches on personal matters. Nevertheless, he opens himself up to critical scrutiny in the way that all good autobiographers do. There's no self-love, no self-aggrandisement – just an old-fashioned obsession with right and wrong, good and evil, black and white. This occasionally manifests itself as sourness and personal bitterness; his dismissive response to objections to the Mason typeface is a good example of this.

I've recently got to know Barnbrook. Prior to meeting him I'd imagined him to be a stern moralist unlikely to be good company. Yet in the flesh Barnrook is an engaging, modest and uncensorious individual with a sly wit and an eccentric affection for Luton Town Football Club[1] – just about the most unfashionable football club in football-mad Britain.

Something of the dour moralist (Alice Twemlow identifies it as a mixture of 'anger, bitterness and melancholy') lingers in the pages of this book. But something else also emerges: an inspirational notion of sacrifice and self-denial. Barnbrook could make a great deal of money if he harnessed his ability to aestheticize everything he touches. Had he wanted to, he could have launched himself as the supreme stylist of his generation. Instead, he chose to follow his own path of dogged opposition to everything he despises. This seems to me to be brave – heroic even – in an age when we deny ourselves nothing, and refuse to make any personal sacrifices unless we are well paid.

Barnbrook is a throwback to an almost medieval notion of ascetic denial. He just does it with enough graphic flair to fuel a small power station.

1. Luton, a dormitory town of London, and the place of Barnbrook's birth.

Felice Varini
The theatre of space: here and now
2008

Felice Varini was born in 1952 in the town of Locarno, on Lake Maggiore in the Italian-speaking south of Switzerland. 'I had a wonderful childhood in both town and country,' he says. 'On the one hand, lakes, rivers, mountains, and on the other, the busy little tourist town of Locarno.' Today, he lives and works in Paris.

We meet in the East London studio of designer Jonathan Ellery on a cold January morning. All the surrounding streets are cordoned off with police crime scene tape. There had been a stabbing the night before. It's a long way from Varini's idyllic Swiss childhood, yet he manages to bring a glow of southern European warmth to London's grim ambience. He is friendly and relaxed but you sense a sharp analytical brain; you sense that if he thinks he is being misunderstood, he will let you know.

It's an intellectual sharpness that can be seen in his work: Varini's dramatic works of art are pieces of visual theatre that depend on meticulous planning, faultless execution and a singular vision [see p.369]. It's no coincidence that he started off as a theatre set designer. A Varini artwork is an event that takes place in space: you witness it like you witness a theatrical performance – viscerally.

Talking to him it's hard to equate the man with the severity and technical perfection of his work. He is devoid of art world rhetoric, and talks freely in good if faltering English about Sarkozy (he doesn't approve) and property prices in Paris (he doesn't approve). The way Varini speaks about his work is at odds with the way art critics write about him. If you want to find out about Varini's work you have to plunge into a murky pool of impenetrable art theorising. These texts may appeal to professors who run PhD departments in art schools, and the sorts of people who read the gallery reviews in *Frieze* and *Art Forum*, but for the general reader they are discouraging.

Sitting round a table looking at layouts for this book,[1] I'm hoping that Varini will talk about his work with more clarity than the art theorists manage. I began by asking him about his education: 'Education is a big subject,' he says. 'I would rather talk about the influences I encountered as I grew up. I was very attracted by everything I identified as being artistic: this includes the workshop of a sculptor almost next door to where I lived, the paintings I discovered in the public places of Locarno, the churches filled with all kinds of iconography – the primitive icons acknowledging favours received and the more evocative religious historical paintings, too – plus the sculptures scattered over the town, among them those by Jean Arp.'

One of Varini's formative influences was the work of the Argentinian born painter, sculptor and theorist Lucio Fontana. His first encounter with Fontana was at an exhibition in 1962 at an avant-garde gallery in Locarno, a gallery that was to prove critical to Varini's development as an artist. 'Fontana, whose work I could not understand at all,' recalls Varini, 'enabled something to start moving within me. I subsequently discovered the great events of abstract art in works of Malevich, Mondrian, Pollock, and it is certainly because of what I began to perceive and interpret at those moments, that my work took form.'

Varini's recurring use of geometric shapes links him to Malevich and Mondrian, and his uninhibited use of space is Pollockian, but an even bigger formative influence was his early work in the theatre. It was while making and painting theatrical scenery in Geneva (from 1972 to 1978) that Varini became aware of what he calls 'spatial volume and the benefits of treating it as such.' And when he later moved to Paris to work as an artist he discovered that the canvas and the atelier were too restricting: 'I could scarcely see myself shut up in a studio turning out canvas after canvas,' he notes. Instead, he began to think of architecture and urban landscapes as his new canvas. 'The space, volume, materials, and the light these places of all kinds offered,' he explains, 'were and still are a rich variety of reality off which I can make my pigments ricochet.' From then on, Varini's field of action was to become architectural space and, as he puts it, 'everything that constitutes such space.'

It's easy to see why graphic designers are attracted to Varini's work. Designers expend lots of brainpower making two-dimensional space look three-dimensional. The surfaces of posters, the pages of books, even the screens of computers and TVs are depthless, and so when designers need to create a sense of a third dimension, they have to use graphic tricks and illusions. Colour can suggest distance; perspective can be used to suggest farness or nearness. But Varini does the opposite: he uses his artistic genius to make three-dimensional space look flat. By going out into the physical world, and painting two lines on two different surfaces so that when viewed from a certain point the two lines appear to be on the same plane, Varini is creating a thrilling illusion. But for Varini, it's not a trick. It's a way of seeing and understanding space. Just as graphic designers are masters of two-dimensional space, Varini is a master of *tri-dimensionality* – to use a favourite word of the art philosophers.

I wondered if Varini felt any kinship with graphic design. After all, he is Swiss, and elements of the geometric design of the Swiss graphic masters are plainly visible in his work. 'It's true that in my youth in Switzerland, I soaked up graphic design,' he says, 'which at the time seemed to me natural and obvious; it was only at the end of my adolescence that I realised its quality and its importance. This has without doubt shaped me, in the same way that we can be shaped by our mother tongue.'

For many people who see Varini's work only in reproduction, it is often assumed that his work is graphic trickery; coloured lines and shapes added digitally to photographs of architectural space. If this was the case, then anyone with basic Photoshop skills could make a Varini. 'A graphic designer would have no difficulty in doing it,' he agrees. 'The tools are available to everyone. I use them too in the preparation period. But what is fundamental to what I do, is the experience of space and the physical confrontation between the viewer and my painting, and that is impossible to reproduce artificially.' As he says on his website: 'These spaces are and remain the original media for my painting. I work "on site" each time in a different space and my work develops itself in relation to the spaces I encounter.'

Like other fastidious artists, Varini's preparation is meticulous: you sense that the journey is as important as the destination. 'First, I use a method which enables me to face reality,' he explains, 'which consists of using one or more points of view which I place in the given spaces, and by means of which the shape or shapes appear. Once I have decided on the modus operandi, I begin installing the apparatus – projectors, lasers or whatever. The projections are made in darkness, then a tracing is made on the different types of material which make up the chosen space, and finally I turn to painting.'

According to mathematics professor and art critic Joël Koskas, 'A work of Varini is an anti-Mona Lisa.' How are we to interpret this remark? When I put it to Varini, he says: 'I'm not sure what he means? Perhaps he means that I am free from the framework of the traditional picture and that I adopt a non-academic attitude. If this is what he means then I am in agreement with him.' But if Varini is not 'academic' then is he perhaps a trickster, or an illusionist in the tradition of Escher and Arcimboldi? Varini is adamant that illusion has nothing to do with his creative intentions. 'What is referred to as illusion is neither my subject nor my question,' he says. 'What I am looking for is to produce paintings, derived from geometric positions which, by virtue of their encounter with architecture, break out producing a quantity of totally abstract forms beyond all narrative or symbolism.'

But for the viewer, the thought that Varini might be creating optical illusions is unavoidable. For a start, most people know his work only as photographs, and we have long since learned to mistrust photographs. Yet even when we accept that Varini's work is physically executed in real spaces, we also see that there is a problem with what we are looking at: the problem of viewpoint, or to put it another way, the problem of *from where to look*.

If we approach a 'real' Varini work we find that there is always one vantage point that shows the work in a particular way – the way that it is usually photographed. But if we move to another position, we see the work in yet another way. Does Varini consider that there is only one viewpoint from which to view his work? On his website he has this to say: 'The vantage point is carefully chosen: it is generally situated at my eye level and located preferably along an inevitable route, for instance an aperture between one room and another, a landing ... I do not, however, make a rule out of this, for all spaces do not systematically possess an evident line. It is often an arbitrary choice. The vantage point will function as a reading point, that is to say, as a potential starting point to approaching painting and space.'

But then in an apparent contradiction of the above, Varini points out that the viewer will struggle to find the vantage point: 'This point is so precise that it is almost impossible to check with the naked eye,' he says. 'It can be found using a camera or video. Hence, each view, taken from any vantage point, will be correct in my opinion. The painting will exist in the totality of views one can have of it. I use the point of view as a point of departure, and not as a conclusion.'

Clearly the camera with its ability to maintain a constant viewpoint, and with its ability to flatten space, is crucial to Varini's work, but in fact, the camera is secondary. For Varini, what matters is the physical space and his intervention into it. 'My painting is created directly where it is exhibited,' he says. 'That is the only place where you are in the presence of my work. The photograph remains a photograph. I never take it myself, I call on a professional photographer. I work very often with André Morin, a photographer from Paris. Then, the photograph of the work is released to the media. These photographs are never sold as works of art or as documents. I should mention however, that there was a time when I sold them. That enabled me to earn a living. But at that time, I confused the work with the image of the work derived from it. That is behind me, it was a stage on my journey.'

Today, if you want to own a Varini he will give you the equivalent of a musical score which will enable you to make your own version. 'At the moment of sale,' he says, 'I provide the purchaser with a certificate and a description of the work, specifying the conditions for it to be put on show. That consists of noting that my paintings appear in a specific space for a solo or group exhibition. When the exhibition is over, the piece can be bought and shown in another space, provided it matches the characteristics defined in the certificate. This aspect of the work can be carried out as many times as one wants, if the characteristics of the location allow. We can compare this to what happens in musical and theatrical performance. With a score or a script, we can interpret or perform.'

But why buy when you can do what unscrupulous plagiarists do and simply 'make their own Varini'. Varini is sanguine and generous about his imitators: 'It pleases me to find influences which might be directly derived from my work in the work of other artists,' he says. 'It confirms me in what I do, and can even enrich me. On the other hand, I find it intolerable to be faced with works claiming to be artistic, which are nothing more than unacknowledged copies pure and simple of what I produce day after day. It is heartbreaking to see artists without any real personal agenda, who, for one reason or another, adopt such an attitude.'

It is lunchtime so we walk to a nearby restaurant. All around us the police crime scene tape marks out the urban contours of this corner of London. It's as if Varini had placed them there and we are walking through one of his artworks. Except, the colours are dismal and the atmosphere is heavy with chilly menace. Not like a Varini work at all, really.

1. *Felice Varini*. Browns/ Howard Smith Paper, 2008.

Vaughan Oliver
Minotaurs in suburban England[1]
2010

A chic café next to the Royal Festival Hall on the banks of the river Thames, London. It's mid-afternoon and Vaughan Oliver is talking about blood, sex and death. He pulls photographs from his bag like doves from a magician's hat. It's the work of the 4AD dream team, united again; photographer Simon Larbalestier and designer Vaughan Oliver.[2] They are working on a collector's box set of five Pixies albums: a loving homage to the Boston rockers. No new songs, but all the artwork and imagery is new.

Larbalestier has been living in Thailand. It shows in his pictures. He has been patrolling the murky zones of sex, religion and body politics. We look at sutures, crucifixes and shards of indeterminate anatomy. His images of eroticised Catholicism have a newfound Oriental inflexion. Plaster saints in terrifying close-up; bleached bones; Bangkok sex-tourist neon.

Oliver lives in Epsom, Surrey. Suburban England. Home of insurance brokers and people who make the daily half-hour trip to London on crowded, commuter trains. Unspeaking, they read newspapers and dream of retirement and long days of golf in damp English afternoons. Epsom is a long way from Thailand; it's a long way from Oliver's native Durham in the coal-hard northeast of England; it's a long way from Boston, Massachusetts.

Oliver says proudly that the Victorian artist and illustrator Aubrey Beardsley lived in Epsom. Beardsley is the patron saint of English weird. The first superstar of English graphic art. A consumptive who coughed blood into his handkerchief and saw his own death in the red stigmata on the white linen. Dead at 26.

Oliver produces more pictures. He spreads them out on the café table: a tabletop movie of dark beauty. The staff in the café, who have accents from France and Eastern Europe and probably have university degrees in difficult subjects, glance at the images; a waiter with dreadlocks piled up on his head, does a double take. A Pixies fan? A Vaughan Oliver fan? But he doesn't linger. He looks away and serves brownies and tea to people with time to kill before attending afternoon poetry readings or Gamelan workshops at the Royal Festival Hall.

Vaughan Oliver explains his new role as art director and image editor. A grandee of graphic design now, he has others do the work while he watches and edits. Under his attentive gaze an army of student helpers, many of them born after the release of arguably the Pixies' most famous album, *Surfer Rosa* [see p.370], work with Oliver to forge a new Pixies' iconography. He watches, ever vigilant for the happy accident or the unintended collision, as the typography for all five Pixies 4AD albums is warped, twisted and distressed and as entirely new styles and forms emerge from the eager hands of his students.

Oliver, the wizard of the image-meld, pushes Larbalestier's photographs up hard against ghostly fragments of Pixies' graphic mythology. Pictures of abandoned gloves and rosary beads (stills from an imaginary Tarkovsky movie) are slammed against a new Pixies visual lexicon created by the students.

But why a book? Why a box set? Why all this physical-world matter? After all, we live in the age of the audio download – a super-convenient data stream of invisible ones and zeros that arrive in our laptops, cell phones and iPods within seconds of being summoned. No waiting. No hanging about in record shops. No browsing through inky music papers. No delayed pleasure. Only instant demand and instant gratification. All the music we ever need held in a zippy piece of 21st century product design smaller than a cigarette packet. Soon we'll have an implant in our brains and all the data in the world will be streamed into our heads, where it will float about like the messages heard by clinically insane serial killers. But why a book? Why a box set? Why all this physical-world matter?

Because we love the real world touch of paper, ink and cardboard. Because you can't scratch an MP3 file; it never gets dust on it; it never develops the patina of age. Even some of my CDs, bought in the first wave of digital technolust of the 1980s, have turned tobacco yellow. But an MP3 file? It's just audio vapour. A keystroke away from deletion.

A Pixies box set is like experiencing them playing live. It has heft and dimension. You can feel it. You can touch it. Like Minotaurs in Epsom, it's real. Not imagined.

1. In 2009, I met the designer Vaughan Oliver to discuss writing a short text for inclusion in a deluxe Pixies box set called *Minotaur*. Oliver didn't like my text, and it wasn't used. It was subsequently published on Design Observer.

2. 4AD, an independent British record label with a cult following, founded by Ivo Watts-Russell in 1979. Vaughan Oliver was responsible for the majority of 4AD sleeves. Many of the photographs were taken by Simon Larbalestier.

Six things you should know about Herb Lubalin 2013

Prior to writing a book on Herb Lubalin (1918–81),[1] I had a rather lowly opinion of him. Of course, I recognized that he was a significant American typographer and designer, responsible for some high quality typographic logos and a handful of era-defining typefaces. I was aware of his role as a founder of ITC, and as a pacesetter in the photomechanical typesetting revolution of the 1970s. I was also familiar with his editorship of *U&lc* magazine, which had been an important ingredient in my education as a tyro graphic designer in the 1970s. But that was about the extent of my appreciation.

In fact, when I analyzed it, I realized that I had formed a view of Lubalin that was mildly dismissive. He wasn't known as a great design thinker, and unlike Paul Rand or Milton Glaser, he hadn't survived the critical reassessment that took place in the 1990s in the pages of publications such as *Eye*, offering a revisionist view of graphic design history. Plus, I was further encouraged to dismiss him because he was the darling of a set of backwards looking designers who thought that graphic design was about visual puns and graphic trickery (the 'smile in the mind' school), and who regarded theorizing about graphic design as wasteful navel gazing.

Yet the more I delved into the life and work of Herb Lubalin, the more interesting he became. Far from being the slight figure of my estimation, he emerged as a sophisticated and surprisingly progressive designer. Gradually, I became seduced by the typographic poise and power of expression that he brought to every project that bore his name.

It is against the backdrop of this journey from skepticism to admiration, that I offer you six things that you should know about Herbert Frederick Lubalin. If you are already a fan, the list will only serve to add to your appreciation. If you are a doubter (as I once was), you might find yourself inspired to take another look.

1. The correct way to pronounce Lubalin. His name is pronounced *Loo-baa-lin*, with the accent on the *baa*. Like most Brits, I had always referred to him as *Loo-b'lin* (accent

on *Loo*), and it took many months of interviewing Lubalin family members and former colleagues, to break the habit. Even Lubalin had problems with people mispronouncing his name, which is why he devised a simple typographic device to aid correct pronunciation.

2. He was colour-blind and ambidextrous. An inability to distinguish colours is a severe handicap for a graphic designer, yet Lubalin seems to have negotiated professional life without being greatly hampered by this impairment. In fact, it could be argued that his colour blindness contributed to his genius for incisive black and white imagery. His ambidextrousness, however, was seen as a sign of virtuosity. He was famously known to sketch all his ideas on 'tissues' that were then passed to lettering artists to turn into highly polished artwork. So great was his virtuosity that he could draw with his right hand while signing cheques with his left hand.

3. He was a key figure in the 'creative revolution' that transformed American advertising in the 1960s. After Doyle Dane Bernbach, Sudler & Hennessey was the most important agency in the creative revolution that took place in mid-century American advertising. Herb Lubalin worked at S&H from 1949 to 1964. During that time he became one of the pioneers of expressive typography ('word pictures', to use his phrase, see p.371): his print ads for leading pharmaceutical companies radicalized advertising at a time when press ads featured people in evening dress standing next to gleaming new Cadillacs. But although he became a partner in the firm, and hired many of the smartest brains of the 'new advertising' movement (George Lois, Helmut Krone, amongst others), he ultimately rejected a career in advertising in favour of graphic design. Later, he outlined his objection to advertising: his opposition was partly moralistic ('I don't particularly like to advertise products and help clients sell products that I have no particular use for. And very often I turn down a product because I just think it detrimental for people to buy certain products'), and partly creative ('At an agency there are no individuals ... and all those who stick to it become anonymous').

4. He was a generous acknowledger of the contribution made by his employees and partners. As with many graphic design studios – especially those run by celebrated designers –

the question of authorship arises: the 'who did what?' question. In the case of Lubalin, the matter is further complicated by the fact that, as has already been noted, he only ever produced 'tissues' – sketches done with a cheap Pentel pen and then passed over to highly skilled lettering artists such as John Pistilli, Tom Carnase and Tony Di Spigna. This methodology made authorship questionable. Was Lubalin the sole author of his work, or was he part of a team? In interviews he always paid humble tribute to his many collaborators. Their names frequently appeared on studio promotional literature, and in the case of Ernie Smith, Tom Carnase, Tony Di Spigna and Alan Peckolick, he also made them partners. For Ernie Smith, however, there was no doubt about the central role Lubalin played in the studio's creative output: 'The art director who got a Lubalin tissue couldn't take credit as the designer,' he said. 'You tightened it up and refined it; but the idea, the major spatial relationships, the elegance, was built into it. Once Herb made the tissue, the ad or booklet was designed.'

5. He rejected Swiss modernism in favour of a more humanistic 'graphic expressionism'. Unlike Paul Rand or Lester Beall, Lubalin rejected the 'Swiss Style'. It wasn't that he didn't appreciate Swiss rigour, or that he knew nothing about it, it was just that he thought it was unsuited to the exuberant mainstream American imagination. As he told *Idea* magazine: 'The American people react to ideas. We are a concept-conscious society.' So rather than pursue European minimalism, Lubalin gave birth to a new conceptual typography which he called 'graphic expressionism'. In an essay he wrote in 1979 for *Print* magazine he said: 'Graphic Expressionism is my euphemism for the use of typography, or letterforms, not just as a mechanical means for setting words on a page, but rather as another creative way of expressing an idea, telling a story, amplifying the meaning of a word or a phrase, to elicit an emotional response from the viewer.'

6. He was a designer with a political conscience at a time when it was not fashionable to have one. Herb Lubalin was never a shout-out-loud political revolutionary, and he didn't go on protest marches, but he frequently used his talents to support causes that appealed to his liberal sensibilities. He designed a number of left-leaning publications (often, it

must be admitted, for reasons as much to do with the artistic freedom these small magazines gave him as for their political complexions). He co-designed *The McGraphic* which has been described as a pro-McGovern/anti-Nixon/anti-Vietnam War publication. In the pages of the various magazines edited by Ralph Ginzburg and art directed by Lubalin (*Eros, Fact, Avant Garde*) he pushed the boundaries of what was acceptable to the conservative authorities of 1960s America. As an employer, he hired African American women at a time when this was not common. And for *Ebony* magazine, he produced one of the most effective advertising campaigns, exposing discrimination amongst US corporations, reluctant to spend ad dollars in a magazine for black readers. This was a man with a political and moral view of the world that was not common amongst prominent graphic designers of the period.

1. *Herb Lubalin: American Graphic Designer (1918–81)* by Adrian Shaughnessy. Unit Editions, 2012.

Michael C Place
Building a reputation
2004

He's a big guy. If you put him in a dinner jacket he could pass for a nightclub bouncer. But you only have to be with him for a few minutes to spot the telltale signs of intelligence and sensitivity. Michael Place is a calm-mannered Yorkshireman. He's confident, likeable and unexpectedly modest for someone who was, for nearly a decade, a key member of one of the most famous design groups in the world.

A farmer's son, Place grew up in the North Yorkshire countryside. Like many designers he enjoyed drawing at school, and this led to a foundation year at Scarborough Art College, where his aptitude for technical drawing was noted. 'They saw me using a Rotring,' he explains, 'and so I was encouraged to do graphic design.' Someone should write a thesis about the link between early training in technical drawing and graphic design – it's a recurring theme in the personal histories of many British graphic designers. Or alternatively, the importance of the Rotring in British graphic design.

After York Art College, Place moved to the graphic design course at Newcastle College of Art and Design. The course had a strong practical focus: 'They wanted to equip students for the real world,' explains Place. 'There was a big emphasis on advertising. They taught you how to hand-render Times, that sort of thing.' But none of this suited Place, he was more interested in record sleeves: 'I was a big fan of Vaughan Oliver and his work for 4AD. And I liked Malcolm Garrett's work.' Place's interest in album covers didn't go down well with the tutors, and he failed the course. 'I've since heard,' says Place, 'that I'm now held up as a successful product of the course.' The irony of this makes him chuckle dryly.

In 1990 he did work experience at *I.D.* magazine in London, and this was followed by a two-week stint at The Designers Republic, or TDR, in Sheffield [see pp.70–74]. He then returned to London to work for maverick designer, musician and record label owner Trevor Jackson. Jackson's company Bite It worked on early-90s dance music acts like Stereo MCs, and helped pioneer the sharp graphic look that was to characterise the best dance and club culture design of the 1990s. Place is generous in his praise of Jackson: 'Working for him was great. Scary, a steep learning curve, but I came out of it with a lot of confidence.'

Place had clearly made a favourable impression on The Designers Republic founder Ian Anderson: one year after his stint at TDR, Anderson got in touch and invited him to join the Sheffield design group. I wondered what qualities Anderson had seen in Place that singled him out. After all, Anderson couldn't have been short of willing candidates, there must have been many designers who would have given a vital organ to join TDR: 'I think he liked my type treatments,' reckons Place modestly. 'I spent a lot of time on the PMT camera with chopped-up type.'

The first year at TDR was, according to Place, a 'learning year'. But by the end of it he was given the freedom to work in his own style and to pursue his own vision without interference, a position he has not retreated from since. 'It was incredible,' he recalls, 'a unique situation. I was given lots of freedom with almost no intervention. And it was great to be designing the sleeves of bands I was a fan of. And also working for a company that I was a fan of.'

For the first two years of Place's time at TDR he worked without a computer. Place is amongst the last wave of graphic designers to have trained in the old pre-digital ways, and I think it shows in his work. There's an old-fashioned fastidiousness about his design that can be traced back to the laborious preparation of mechanical artwork. You can also see it in his use of elaborate printing techniques, indicative of someone who has created artwork without the aid of 'do-everything-for-you' pre-press software. 'Yes, it has stood me in good stead,' he agrees. 'I learned a lot by having to mark-up type and create my own typography effects.'

Place found a congenial home at TDR: 'I was happy to find a company where I could design in my own style.' To keen observers of the UK design scene, TDR has always appeared to occupy a unique position amongst contemporary design groups. Ian Anderson is famously uncompromising. To the outsider there seems to be no watering down, no dilution of the TDR end product. I asked Place if this was an accurate assessment. 'I suppose it is,' he says. 'Clients come because they buy into the TDR style. They get what they're given, and they're happy. But it didn't always work. There were some who rejected this approach, and some who were frustrated by it. I don't believe in the designer always being right, but at TDR it was a case of this is what we do, take it or leave it. Funnily enough, it was the foreign clients who were most comfortable with it. Especially the Japanese.'

After nearly a decade, Place quit TDR. The split seems to have been amicable. There is no hint of a falling out – no smoking gun. And anyway, Place seems too nice a guy to go in for messy bust-ups. Anderson must have felt the same way; he gave Place a computer as a leaving present. Place's departure was brought about by his wife being offered a high-powered job with Sony Playstation in London, and Place hitting that moment, familiar to many designers, when they look at their boss and say, I can do this on my own.

Place now runs Build from his home in South London. How does he feel about swapping Sheffield for Clapham? 'Build is an interlude before I go back up North,' he states without hesitation. 'London is not a career choice. I'm here because my wife Nicola has got a great job and while she's doing that I'm building up Build.' We talk a bit about the North/South divide in design. Despite his passion for the region of his birth, Place is not a sitcom caricature Northerner. 'I'm pro the North,' he states, 'but I'm not going to fight anyone over it. The South is good too. I like London, and it is definitely easier to do experimental or cutting-edge work here than in the North. But even that is changing. Because of email and the Internet it doesn't matter where you're based now.'

I wondered which designers excited Place. 'I'm so focused on what I do I don't notice other designers,' he states. 'This was easy to do in Sheffield, where the design scene was really small. But also because I was a workaholic. Weekends, all-nighters, I did them all the time. The sort of work I do, taking details to extremes, means I have to be totally committed and I can't have too many distractions.' It has become fashionable for designers to trot out the I-don't-look-at-other-designers line. In most cases, I suspect it is used as a distancing mechanism, a way of freeing designers from accusations of plagiarism; or a way of asserting their imagined superiority over other designers. But in Place's case it seems genuine. It has a ring of authenticity to it. 'I like architecture,' he states, 'and bits of packaging, instruction manuals, you know, non-designed things'.

Place has run Build for the past two years. I asked him to talk about the work he is doing currently: 'I'm working on all sorts of things. I'm doing identities for two big arts and music events, and I do everything for a New York label called Record Camp. It's like a Factory Records situation; I get to take care of every detail. I really like that. I'm also doing a Build book with a Hong Kong publisher. It's a no-holds barred production, 120 pages, and everything created specially for the book. I'm really pushing the boundaries with it.' He's also just completed a Siemens project for Wieden+Kennedy. It got rejected in the end, but it gave him a taste for doing big ticket work. 'I don't see why you have to be boring just because it's a global brand,' he says earnestly. 'But I won't dilute what I do, and I'll never put out anything that I'm not totally happy with.'

Despite this zero-compromise attitude, Place is ambitious for Build and wants to be successful. 'I want eventually to employ people, but on my terms,' he states. 'I want bigger jobs. But I want to stay a designer. I don't want to become an art director, instructing someone to do a Build design.'[1] Was there a danger, I wondered, that he might be forever stigmatised as an ex-TDR designer? Might Build be regarded always as a junior TDR? It would be hardly surprising if this was the case since for nearly a decade Place was a co-author of the TDR look. 'Well, I know what I did,' he says in his customary calm and considered way. 'I know that a lot of people think Ian does everything, and I never begrudged him that, it's his company. But I know what my contribution was, and I think most people who know me understand that it is my style. It's what I do.'

1. In 2006 Nicola Place joined as Build's business director and project manager. They recently hired a designer and studio assistant to join the team. For a recent example of their work, see p.372.

Sources

TDR RIP – an appreciation. *Etapes* 166, March 2009. See pp.70–74.

Willem Sandberg. *I Heart Design* by Steven Heller. Rockport, 2011. See p.75.

Graphic editorship. Design Observer, 16 December 2007. See pp.76–78.

Hideki Nakajima – Japanese graphic master. *Creative Review*, May 2002. See pp.79–81.

Peter Saville – creative director of Manchester. *Voice: AIGA Journal of Design*, 2004. See pp.82–84.

Bruce Mau. *Design Week*, 3 June 2010. See pp.85–86.

Storm Thorgerson – infinite regression. Foreword to *Storm Thorgerson*. Browns/Howard Smith Paper, 2007. See pp.87–91.

The French designer Toffe and the 'nuclear moment'. *Eye* 58, Winter 2005. See pp.92–97.

Julian House: self-initiated House music. Design Observer, 4 August 2005. See pp.98–100.

Neville Brody. Unpublished, 2011. See pp.101–106.

Philippe Starck. *Design Week*, 5 November 2009. See pp.107–108.

Paul Graham – poet of the mundane. Foreword to *Paul Graham*. Browns/Howard Smith Paper, 2008. See pp.109–113.

Barnbrook Bible: a graphic autobiography. Design Observer, 30 July 2007. See pp.114–116.

Felice Varini – the theatre of space: here and now. Foreword to *Felice Varini*. Browns/Howard Smith Paper, 2008. See pp.117–122.

Vaughan Oliver – minotaurs in suburban England. Design Observer, 9 November 2010. See pp.123–125.

Six things you
should know about
Herb Lubalin.
*Ultrabold: The
Journal of St Bride
Library*, No.13,
Spring 2013.
See pp.126–129.

Michael C Place:
building
a reputation.
Grafik, 2004.
See pp.130–133.

Illustration

The thinking eye
2010

What is the role of the illustrator in 2010? Much of the commercial illustration we see around us is vacuous decoration, a fashionable lingua franca of instant coolness and prettification. When illustration is used by mobile phone companies, fashion houses and advertising agencies, it is usually an attempt to seduce us into thinking that the ordinary is somehow extraordinary: illustration as gloss.

It might be argued that anything that makes the world a prettier place has merit. But illustration is capable of fulfilling a higher purpose. Illustration is one of the ways in which we can be helped to understand the world and how it works. At its best it throws an intellectual spotlight onto the world and its complexities. It also fires the imagination in ways that words sometimes fails to do.

In the 1990s cheap printing and digital reproduction techniques meant that photography became feasible where once it had been prohibitively expensive. Prior to this, illustration had been the pre-eminent way to convey visual information. Hard to believe, but there was a time when cars were advertised with illustrations of cars; food packaging used drawings of food; and magazine profiles of writers, movie stars and politicians were accompanied with hand-rendered portraits.

And when we think of the great illustrators we realise that the best of them wielded an astounding power – the power to create a way of looking at the world that has become *our way* of looking at the world. Our view of 1940s America is at least partly formed by Norman Rockwell; Victorian London by George Cruikshank; Weimar Republic era Germany by Georg Grosz. It extends into the realm of imagination too: Gustave Doré determines our vision of Biblical apocalypse; Erté defines our vision of 1920s luxury and elegance.

The artist Paul Klee wrote a famous book called *The Thinking Eye* (1961). Mulling over this phrase, it occurred to me that here was a near-perfect description of what distinguishes the great illustrators – the ability to think visually. And if illustrators want to reclaim the position of centrality that they once occupied within visual communication, they must rediscover their thinking eye.

Few illustrators embody the notion of the thinking eye better than Brad Holland. From his earliest days as a young image maker in 1960s America, Holland demanded to know why his point of view wasn't as valid or profound as that of a writer's? When he was commissioned to create an illustration to accompany a text, Holland insisted on being given the same brief as the writer. It's hard to imagine many illustrators thinking – and acting – like this today. Some do, of course, and it must be remembered that when Holland's career was at its zenith (during the 1970s), illustration was viewed differently from the way it is today. Illustrators were the stars of visual communication. When they created record covers and magazine spreads for *Playboy* they made huge amounts of money and were lionized by art directors and editors. Many illustrators – such as Holland – used this freedom to create work of lasting merit. And they used their power and influence to insist on a point of view.

Illustrators remained dominant throughout the 1980s, as they had done for over a century. But in the 1990s, with the advent of the Macintosh computer, cheap desktop scanners and smart graphics software, designers and art directors discovered that they could do many of the things that they once employed illustrators to do. As has already been noted, they also found that they could use photography much more easily than in the past, and as design entered the digital era, typography and photography became the principle vehicles of visual communication.

Back then, it was easy to see how photography would benefit from increasing digitalization, but what happened to typography was less predictable. In the 90s typography boomed. Digital software allowed a new radicalism to enter the staid realm of lettering and typographic expression. Suddenly it became possible to do with type what illustrators had done with line, tone and colour. And as typographers emerged from the closet, so illustrators seemed to slip back into the darkened space just vacated. Budgets fell, art directors became shy about commissioning illustration, and worst of all, illustrators themselves seemed to lose confidence and direction.

I caught a glimpse of this failure of nerve when, a few years ago, I was asked to run a workshop for designers and illustrators on the topic of professional practice. During a discussion about how creative people deal with clients, one of the illustrators pointed out that he never met his clients. They sent him briefs by email; he executed the task and delivered the finished work to his clients via email without ever meeting face to face. I thought this was an appalling situation, yet indicative of the way the craft was viewed by commissioners: illustration as instant space filler.

To those who value illustration, its demise in the 90s was a cause for concern. Despite the fact that typography in its higher forms has a mysterious, almost occult-like power, it can never match the emotive richness or expressive potency of the best illustration. But something of this potency has been reclaimed in recent years. Illustration courses are once again popular in art schools and universities around the world. As I noted in my opening paragraph, illustration has re-entered the commercial mainstream – although in a watered-down form. Yet perhaps the most interesting development is the way that certain influential graphic designers have introduced an illustrative element into their work.

This is nothing new. If we look back at the output of sophisticated designers such as Milton Glaser, Paul Rand or Grapus, we see a confident and unforced synthesis of graphic design and illustration. In the 1970s, this was considered normal – a sign of a designer's visual literacy and graphic eloquence. But this trend evaporated during the 80s and 90s as designers became specialists. Many of the more influential designers turned to pure type and eschewed the use of any sort of illustrative elements. Helvetica-driven purism was the norm. Few design groups epitomised this 'type only' stance more that the influential UK designers 8vo. They said: 'We believed that typography, the key building block of printed communication, could be the core ingredient of a graphic solution (unsupported by illustration or photography ...)' [see p.373].

Yet over the past decade or so, this melding of imagery and typography has been revived by a new generation of graphic designers: M/M (Paris), Marian Bantjes, Non-Format, Universal Everything, and numerous other designers have utilised drawn and 'illustrated' elements into their work. They created a new digital art nouveau; a sudden explosion of floating tendrils and whiplash line work. Designers were drawing again – or at least utilising the drawing tools in Adobe Illustrator. Yet none of the names mentioned above refer to themselves as illustrators. They are graphic designers.

This new graphic design and illustration hybrid has contributed to the reigniting of interest in illustration and has added a layer of visual sophistication to much contemporary graphic design. But it is not the only way that illustration is propelling itself forward. We need only look at the way in which the visual styling of Hollywood mega hit *Avatar* bears a resemblance to the 1970s work of Roger Dean and other fantasy artists. It is intriguing to see how illustration is at the centre of the media enterprise that has, in many ways superseded Hollywood movies – computer games. And that's before we think about the rise of the graphic novel.

It is also inspiring to see how illustrators have become reimbued with the entrepreneurial spirit that has always animated artists and the better illustrators. Illustrators are no longer passive – they no longer wait by the phone for their next commission. Instead they are creating books and magazines; self-publishing; staging exhibitions; painting murals; designing and making apparel. Illustration has gone supernova and is in vigorous good health.

But I mentioned earlier that illustration has a higher purpose. What is that purpose? Let's consider the role of illustration in the climate change debate. *Vanity Fair* caused alarm when it ran illustrations showing New York and Washington submerged by rising seas. And I recently saw a series of paintings showing what parts of Northern Europe would look like if the direst predictions surrounding global warming come to pass. These 'artists' impressions' of how the green and fertile valleys of Northern Europe might be transformed into Sahara-like emptiness through climate change were viscerally alarming in a way that no amount of scientific data could rival.

Sensationalist visions of an apocalyptic future may do little to advance the strict scientific discourse surrounding climate change, but as the environmental activist and designer Jody Boehnert has noted: 'The ability of information graphics and illustration to educate audiences makes it an important tool for ecological literacy campaigns about the science of climate change.'

The thirty exhibits in 'En Tube' show that illustration has the power to delight us. Thirty artists from all over the world have contributed images from their archives to demonstrate the endless variety and range of their craft [see p.374]. But they demonstrate something else too: ever since our prehistoric ancestors daubed on cave walls, human beings have felt the need to make marks, draw lines, and use colour to enchant and delight. This urge to illustrate – to illuminate – is part of the fundamental human impulse to communicate. And at its best, illustration can communicate just as effectively as the written word. In truth, it can often do it with more immediacy and greater impact. All you need is a thinking eye.

Graphic design and illustration
Schism and reunification
2009

There was a time when graphic design and illustration used to sleep in the same bed. Look through any design annual from the 1970s and early 1980s and much of the work on show has drawn imagery as its main ingredient. During the fizzy, go-go 1980s, however, something happened to the relationship between design and illustration. Design was promoted to the front line of commercial life: professionalised and strategised, it took ownership of identity and branding within the corporate world. Not long afterwards designers discovered that cheap technology and reduced repro costs allowed them to use photography where once they might have relied on illustration, and they also discovered that new digital tools enabled them to make their own images, collages and visual effects. Illustration on the other hand clung onto the notion of autonomy of expression and refused to learn the language of strategy and branding. It was banished to the sofa.

Since then the craft has had numerous upswings and mini-revivals. Demand for illustration courses is booming, and the best practitioners continue to do remarkable work. Yet perhaps the most interesting development in illustration is the way that a new generation of graphic designers has rediscovered the old model of the designer-illustrator. Pick up any design magazine from anywhere in the world and it will be full of a new sort of hybrid graphic design – typography-based, yet infused with the fluid and expressive qualities of illustration. Look closely, however, and you'll see that the people doing this work nearly always call themselves graphic designers.

This visually rich strand of graphic expression is a reversal of the stance adopted by many graphic designers in the 1990s; a stance that had its most austere expression in the work of groups like 8vo. In their monograph *8vo – On the Outside* (2005), the 8vo partners state their philosophy of purist graphic design '... we believed that typography, the key building block of printed communication, could be the core ingredient of a graphic solution (unsupported by illustration or photography) ...' [see p.373]. The current crop of designer-illustrators have more

142–143

stylistic and temperamental affinity with the pre-digital era when to be a graphic designer usually involved the ability to draw, or at least an ability to commission illustration and a readiness to incorporate it into visual communication. No group exemplified this better than Push Pin during the New York studio's 1960s pomp.

The Push Pin style was also a rejection, this time of the fashionable International Style. Milton Glaser and Seymour Chwast effortlessly combined typographically sophisticated layouts with zeitgeist-defining illustration. Looking at the work of the current designer-illustrators – influential figures such as M/M (Paris), Michael C Place (working under the studio name Build), Kim Hiorthøy, Marian Bantjes and Julian House (working both as a senior designer at Intro, and running his own record label Ghost Box) – we see the same confident melding of typography and imagery. However, unlike the work of Push Pin, with its knowledgeable referencing of art nouveau and art deco, and the more pragmatic examples found in the 1970s design annuals, this new blend of graphic design and illustration tends to be more abstract – fewer winged logos and more amorphous vapour trails; and it is usually a product of the computer rather than the pencil. Yet it is undeniably a digital equivalent of the Push Pin model, and even earlier manifestations such as Abram Games.

Having recently finished a three-year stint editing the illustration magazine *Varoom*, and having looked repeatedly at the nexus between illustrators and designers, I've come to the conclusion that three factors appear to be driving this latest fusion of the two wings of visual communication.

The first is the image making possibilities afforded by the digital tools that are now ubiquitous within design. When I ran my design studio (between 1988 and 2003) I boasted that I hardly ever commissioned illustration. This was partly a reaction against the vapid, Matisse-lite scribblings that seemed to festoon every bank or insurance company leaflet at the time, but it was also to do with the exhilarating realisation of what could be done by visually astute graphic designers with scanners, vectors and the cut-out tool in Photoshop, something that is second nature to the current generation of design school trained graduates.

The second reason is the over-strategized, over-purposed state of modern commercial graphic design. For free spirits attracted to the richly seductive design of past decades, current professional practice with its enslavement to branding theory and marketplace absolutism, can often be dispiriting. On the other hand, illustration at its best seems far less constrained by commercial dogma and the suppression of a personal signature. As the American designer Ed Fella noted: 'Whereas graphic design is more anonymous, all illustration is sold for its particular and individual style.'[1]

The third reason for a rise in designer-illustrators can be attributed to the supremacy of typography – and photography – in branding, advertising and visual communication of all kinds. For most brand owners, illustration is too imprecise and too resistant to strategization to be trusted with delivering marketing messages. It's why many tutors on illustration courses routinely urge their students to learn typography and thus avoid being pushed further down the food chain. The designer-illustrators have responded to this by blending typographic skills with the ability to create illustrative effects, resulting in a new seductive messaging that combines the directness of typography with the sensory appeal of illustration, pattern and form making. The imaginative and ornamental lettering of Marian Bantjes, Alex Trochut, Non-Format, Si Scott, Grandpeople and Yulia Brodskaya can be found in advertising, newspapers, magazines, book jackets, physical environments, and in various digital settings.

The same flair and expressivenesses can be seen in the visual output of M/M (Paris), Michael C Place, and in the digital radicalism of Universal Everything. Yet none of these people define themselves as illustrators. Instead they function like graphic designers and respond to client briefs with problem-solving rigour while simultaneously using the emotional heft of illustration. In Peter Grundy's work, the problem-solving intent of graphic design and the narrative potential of illustration are yoked to create informative and narrative-rich imagery well-suited to modern information-based communication demands. It's no accident that Grundy gets commissions from both Shell and *The Guardian*.

At its simplest level, the re-emergence of the designer-illustrator means that the words graphic design and illustration appear side by side more frequently than they once did on the websites and business cards of designers and illustrators. But it has also coincided with a much bigger change within the visual communication landscape. We are seeing the forging of a new expanded definition of illustration. Today, illustration is any sort of made image – and by 'made' I mean an image that has been created, manipulated, melded or fashioned; it can be virtual or physical; it can be interactive or static; it can be made by a human being or by a computer laden with smart software; it can be model making; it can be found in 3D environments; it can even be made randomly by processing software. The consequence of all this is that illustration is now beginning to catch up with fine art which long since species-jumped out of the canvas into a new frame-free zone where anything goes. It is hardly surprising that designers – and illustrators – are embracing this new freedom with zeal.

Of course, not all the work produced by design's re-marriage to illustration produces meaningful work. Much of what we see falls into the honey-trap of mere prettification and space filling; often pleasant but rarely engaging. Yet what tends to snag the eye in the visual communication firmament is the work that fuses the precision of graphic design with the floating-world abstraction of the illustrator. Design historians will look back on the first decade of the 21st century and see that it was normal for designers to eschew the 1990s fixation with pure typography and photography in favour of marks, splodges, scribbles, and letterforms spouting quasi-organic tendrils. They just might struggle to know what to call the people who were doing this work, but they will identify a significant moment in graphic design's evolution that is hyperlinked to the craft's radical origins in the avant-garde art movements of the early decades of the 20th century.

1. 'Ed Fella: King of Zing' by Alice Twemlow. *Varoom* 01, 2006.

'What's wrong with a piece of straight illustration?' – *Illustrators* The AOI's house magazine 2007

Illustrators was the somewhat underwhelming name of the house magazine of the Association of Illustrators (AOI) during the 1970s and 1980s. It was a slim A4 publication that barely merited the description magazine. In its earliest incarnations it wasn't much more than a souped-up pamphlet, and in fact, its predecessor had been called *Newsletter*. Yet despite its slimness (early issues ran to 16 pages), *Illustrators* succeeded in providing the Association's members with a bustling and readable guide to the artistic and professional ramifications of illustration at a time when the craft was enjoying a strong upward swing.

Published six times a year, a typical issue carried articles on such quotidian subjects as copyright, National Insurance contributions, Trade Unions and agents, with additional coverage given to technical matters including an examination of the merits of transparencies over flat artwork, and the use of an airbrush. At its peak in the late 1970s and early 1980s, *Illustrators* was to feature more commentary, regular interviews with leading, sometimes controversial, practitioners, and frequent nods to the history of the craft.

Three decades on, these modest volumes offer an insider's view of the subject. The editorial tone is energetic and adventurous, and reminds us that there was a time when illustration was regarded as a vital component in publishing, advertising and editorial production. Yet even though the craft enjoyed greater patronage than it does now, the life of a freelance practitioner is invariably precarious, a factor that is acknowledged by the publication's coverage of professional matters.

For young illustrators emerging onto the scene, the magazine provided the only place to find the practical information that they had been denied at art school. Derek Brazell, a professional illustrator, and now an official at the AOI, recalls the benefits the magazine offered to the young illustrator: 'College hadn't really presented us with much of the outside world. It's daunting to step into the unknown and I wanted to know what was going on out there. The AOI magazine gave me an idea of that and also presented many different illustration styles and images which you couldn't find in one place?'

The May–June 1977 issue features a purely graphic cover by Dan Fern – a radical departure for the magazine at this point. However, under the editorship of Rufus Segar, the editorial content remained biased towards professional concerns typified by an article on VAT, followed by a lengthy piece on contracts. The September–October issue from the same year has a two-colour cover by American Jim Heimann, and features a note of cosmopolitanism, in what had been up until then a determinedly parochial journal. In an article entitled 'Talent from LA', editor Segar surveys the West Coast scene and reproduces images by John Van Hamersveld, Everett Peck, Dan Quarnstrom, Philip Garner, Catherine Loeb, Taki Ono, Glen Iwasaki, Johnny Lee, and Brit expat Mick Haggerty.

By 1978 the publication had increased in size to 32 pages. In issue 24, editor Alan Manham interviews Michael Peters, one of the key entrepreneurial figures in the emergent British design scene of the time. Peters had fused graphic design with strategic business thinking to form one of the first ultra professional British design groups. He and his designers were lively commissioners of illustration. 'Illustration solves many more problems for (designers) than photography,' observes Peters. 'With photography you know the answer you want before you've even taken the photograph. With an illustration you have the opportunity of combining your talent with someone else's, and to come up with a very surprising picture.'

This edition of the magazine also carries a first attempt to record the history of the AOI; it's a tale of stoicism, planning meetings in Soho pubs, late-nights putting the first editions of the house magazine together, heavy handed Union tactics, reluctant publishers and the perennial search for new members. There is also a profile of Luck and Flaw in their pre-Spitting Image incarnation, a letter from Quentin Blake and a five-line obituary recording the death of Norman Rockwell.

Illustrators 27 features another long interview with a designer: Milton Glaser gives terse well-rehearsed answers to Brian Grimwood's questions. When asked what he is doing, Glaser unexpectedly replies: 'Right now I'm designing supermarkets, which is one of the most interesting things I've ever been involved in. I redesigned Sir James Goldsmith's magazine *Express* last year. So he asked me if I would apply some intelligence to his supermarket chain in America.' In the same issue, Rufus Segar contributes a scholarly and copiously illustrated profile of Eric Fraser.

Under the editorship of Wendy Coates-Smith, a new, more cerebral editorial stance is evident. The cover of *Illustrators* 30 trumpets this new direction. Beneath the masthead (which changes with every issue) sits the stark legend 'Violence Issue', accompanied by a Ralph Steadman drawing of a nightmarish fly tearing at human flesh. Inside, there is a lengthy and well-researched article on Steadman who had recently completed his pioneering work with the pharmaceutically emboldened prince of gonzo-journalism, Hunter S Thompson. At this time, Steadman had a legitimate claim to being the most famous illustrator in the world, and this profile must have ranked as a substantial coup for the magazine. The issue also features a detailed account of the work of Sue Coe, written by Coates-Smith. Coe's brutal, politically charged work offers a less ostentatious view of human nature than the abattoir musings of Steadman, but they are no less unsettling.

Alongside Coates-Smith's efforts to raise the intellectual temperature of illustration, the magazine contained its customary pages of parish council jottings. AOI chairman Bob Norrington strikes a vicarly note when he writes: 'Performing valiantly on the high wire for a second year our treasurer Ken Kirkland has, without the aid of a safety net, kept our balance magnificently although, of late, this state of affairs has existed only in theory which means a lot of people owe the Association an awful lot of money.'

Illustrators 32 (1980) has a profile of NTA – the famous illustration collective that included George Hardie, Malcolm Harrison and Bush Holyhead. NTA were the hip kids of their day. Their work, frequently done for skin mags like *Knave* and *Club International*, fizzed with a disciplined power; it had a precision and polish that has resulted in it remaining sharply contemporary to today's eyes. Bush Holyhead (interviewed by

Terry Dowling) and George Hardie (interviewed by Dan Fern) talk lucidly about life as professional illustrators. When asked what his attitude towards working in advertising is, Holyhead replies with timeless accuracy: 'It pays very well, doesn't offer much freedom and is generally more the art directors job than the illustrators.'

According to illustrator Ian Wright, NTA were the hottest studio in town. But in *Illustrators* 33, they incur the wrath of a disgruntled correspondent who expresses his strong disapproval of NTA: 'Surely, there must be a certain proportion of tongue-in-cheek in these interviews? Some of the dialogues, big-time "in" talk, will make any illustrators worth the name, cringe! What is wrong with doing a good piece of straight illustration? Yes experimenting is also a good thing, in fact a necessity, but, not at the expense of good drawing.' The tension between the old and the new, between the experimental and the established, remains a constant factor in attempts to publish a contemporary magazine that chronicles the creative zeitgeist.

By 1981 the magazine had graduated to full colour covers, although the text pages remained steadfastly mono. Issue 39 was entitled *Radical Illustrators* and was edited by Robert Mason. This issue is perhaps the most famous edition of the magazine, and is still talked about reverentially by illustrators who remember its impact on the genteel Brit illustration scene of the time. It featured a colour photograph on the cover [see p.375] – by George Snow, who co-edited and designed the issue. According to Mason, 'The cover model was the illustrator Robert Ellis, whose work was featured in the magazine. It was meant as a parody of women's magazine covers, as I remember. It was intentionally provocative to use a photograph, as opposed to the usual illustrated image.'

The tone is dark and anarchic; the layout is messy and disregards the niceties of the 'grid' in favour of headlines that slip drunkenly about the page. Cheap typesetting adds to the fanzine atmosphere. Was the punk and post-punk DIY culture an influence, I asked Mason. 'Well, yes I guess it was inevitable,' he replies. 'We were all out at gigs, listening to Joy Division, Wire and The Fall. George Snow (actually a Merle Haggard fan) was the designer so he'd be better able to talk about that.

Obviously everything was pasted up physically. I did the centre spread (Under the Influence, see p.375) at the last minute as we didn't know what else to put there – and the punky look of that is simply to do with my rudimentary design skills! Which is of course what the punk ethic was about. Funnily enough I still approve of the content of that spread – a range of influences from Fra Angelico to David Cronenberg can't be bad. I wish my current students would explore as widely.'

Radical Illustrators features the work of Ian Pollock, Edward Bell, The Brothers Quay, Terry Dowling, Anne Howeson, Russell Mills, Carolyn Gowdy, Sue Coe, Andrzej Klimowski and Shinro Ohtake. It contains articles on do-it-yourself publishing (by Jake Tilson) and a history of the underground press (by George Snow). Today, Mason is ambivalent about the issue. He regards it as 'juvenilia', but he is also aware of its impact: 'It was amazingly influential among younger illustrators and "the business" alike,' he recalls. 'A bit of a Frankenstein's monster, really. Many art directors, who initially reacted against it, subsequently were happily commissioning illustrators whose work would never have emerged without *Radical Illustrators*. Saying that, I'm fully aware that this issue wouldn't have appeared without the inspiration that Stewart Mackinnon, Sue Coe and Terry Dowling – a couple of years' our seniors – provided.'

The inevitable backlash appeared in the letters page of *Illustrators* 40. A writer accuses the group of hypocrisy, and quotes George Snow's remark that 'We can't wait for the dullards of *The Sunday* supplements to wake up.' The angry correspondent goes on to point out that Pollock, Howeson, Mason, Snow and Mills had all worked for *The Sunday Times*: 'Is this what you call sticking your necks out and taking "greater chances than other illustrators?"' she asks. 'You are more commercial than radical. Anyone who is surviving in this climate as a freelance illustrator can't be radical and has no right to set themselves up as hard-done-by martyrs ...'

Controversy was again courted in issue 41 (1982). This time the theme is erotica. In his introduction, editor Bruce Wilson references Gilles Deleuze, Georges Bataile and Maurice Blanchot; he calls feminism 'the most important movement of our time'; and notes cryptically that 'the meat joys, released over a decade ago have dissolved into a liberal, soft hedonism.

The latest crowd of vermouth drinkers are still there, of course, conspicuous, with their sleek unfriendly, virtuoso images.'

The issue moves onto less elevated ground in an interview with Roger Watt, the then art director of *Men Only*. (There's an interesting history to be written on the role of illustration in late-20th century porn mags; without their patronage, here and in America, illustration would be the poorer). Watt states his criteria as a commissioner of illustration plainly enough. 'I have to commission illustration on the basis of what I am given in the way of manuscripts, and they've changed. We used to have a lot of social comment, a lot of deep thinking writing, which were marvellous for illustrations, science fiction stuff (Chris Achilleos or Chris Fosse for example). Now there's a slight downward trend and, although we aren't dropping our standards, the illustration content has a far larger acreage of female flesh, if I can put it like that. Consequently I'm trying to use illustrators now whose primary quality is that they can draw very highly finished, believable ladies.' A range of 'believable ladies' are shown in a 'highly finished' state by artists including Mike [sic] Brownfield, Jennifer Euchas, Celestino Valenti and the aforementioned Achilleos.

Coverage is not restricted to the heterosexual domain. Elsewhere in the issue we find an investigation into the ways in which illustrators were finding work in the burgeoning early 1980s gay scene. The work of Ian David Baker, Oliver Frey and Sue Dray is discussed with seriousness and sensitivity. Robert Mason conducts an interesting interview with Anne Yvonne Gilbert (best known in certain circles for her cover image for the Frankie Goes to Hollywood 12" single *Relax*). Gilbert is an articulate interviewee, and many interesting threads emerge during the discussion: the difference between gay and straight reactions to erotic imagery; the use of photography as source material for fantasy imagery; the role of Christian ritual in the psyches of murderers. She also provides the cover image – a rather chaste depiction of a feminine-looking man floating Ophelia-like in water with a violin.

By issue 48 (1984) colour pages appear regularly, and although the focus on practitioners is maintained (this issue contains articles about Edward Bawden, an investigation into British illustration and the Third World, Ian Pollock on illustrating Shakespeare, and an obituary of Barney Bubbles), the tone is beginning to change with an increasing bias towards purely professional matters. However, there is still space for articles about less well-known talent. Issue 51 (by now full colour throughout) features a profile of Flavio Constantini written by British anarchist Stuart Christie, a review of Ambit's 100th birthday by Sarah Culshaw, and a study of Frans Masereel by Robert Mason.

Increasingly however, flicking through volumes from this period, more and more pedestrian work appears: the sort of worthy run-of-the-mill stuff that has dated horribly. In the late-1980s, *Illustrators* is beginning to resemble a contact book. A section called Index is advertised as a 'special pull-out centre section in full colour for illustrators and agents to advertise their work.' Here illustrators are invited to buy space to advertise their wares. A useful service no doubt – but one senses that this is some sort of turning point for illustration. Some of the intellectual heft is being drained out of the craft. As the Thatcher decade turned us all into raging Gordon Gekko's, it seems that illustration also signed up to the new service-sector mentality that we were told was our only hope of survival.

Issue 69 carries the words Last Issue! It has an illustration of a Phoenix on the front. Inside it explains that the mythical bird's appearance on the cover is 'not unconnected with the end of *Illustrators* magazine and the start of something new, or, to put it optimistically, death and rebirth.' The rebirth was an A2 folded black and white printed newsletter called *Despatch*. This was followed by *The Journal* and now, *Varoom*.

Another time, another place
2004

John Berry and Martin Aitchison produced illustrations for the Ladybird series of learn-to-read books in the 1960s and early 1970s. The studied realism of their paintings, especially Berry's frequent depictions of Britain's nascent technological revolution, was a departure from the patriarchal and often saccharine tone of children's book illustration. Berry and Aitchison depicted a nation on the cusp of profound cultural change: a nation about to get modern.

A recent exhibition in London of their Ladybird work has excited a nostalgic reappraisal of these two octogenarian artists. A generation of British children were weaned on their work, and amongst many British designers and illustrators, Ladybird books from this golden era enjoy an unrivalled cachet. It's not hard to see why. They are beautiful things: typographically sophisticated, and bristling with a laudable social and pedagogical intent. They were conceived by writer and teacher William Murray as a tool for the promotion of literacy. A note to teachers and parents spelt out their purpose: 'The full-colour illustrations have been designed to create a desirable attitude towards learning – by making every child eager to read each title. Thus, this attractive reading scheme embraces not only the latest findings in word frequency, but also the natural interests and activities of happy children.'

For anyone who grew up in the late-50s or early-60s, the appeal of Berry and Aitchison's work today is principally nostalgic. But even for those born later, the duo's work captures a widely recognisable moment in recent British history: the transformation of Britain from a dowdy, war-ravaged country, into an affluent, technologically-enabled modern state. In 1964, the then Prime Minister Harold Wilson famously spoke about a new Britain forged in 'the white heat of technology': Berry and Aitchison recorded this transformation in their Ladybird illustrations. They were the Norman Rockwells of 1960s Britain: for sizzling turkeys and home-made apple pies, substitute automated car factories and police cars next to high-rise blocks; for mawkish over-romanticizing, substitute emotional detachment. The writer Michael Bracewell sees comparisons with more modern figures; he correctly likens their work to the 'claustrophobic portraiture of Sam Taylor-Wood, or the enigmatic Englishness of Martin Parr's photography.'

John Berry studied at the Royal Academy School of Arts in the 1930s, and had a distinguished career as a society portrait painter. He painted Lady Astor, the young Queen Elizabeth and Prince Philip, Diana, Princess of Wales and George W Bush. But he also worked in advertising, and this manifests itself in what Bracewell calls the 'visual immediacy' of his Ladybird illustrations. It is said that Berry 'could do anything, provided he had a photograph to work from.' You can see this in his sparsely elegant portrait of a railway worker: the man dominates the frame in a way that is clearly influenced by commercial photography. He has the demeanour of an airline pilot, and in his uniform, with its hint of Pierre Cardin-like modernity, he cuts a strikingly modern figure. Behind him we catch a flash-frame of contemporary railway architecture; it is new and sharp, and has doubtlessly replaced a piece of crumbling Victoriana. Berry's paintings look like an advertising campaign for Harold Wilson's 'white hot' new Britain. There's nothing messy or distracting in his world; everything is hygienic and clean. To contemporary eyes, accustomed to the advertiser's view of a sanitized and wart-free world, it is a surprisingly modern vision.

But Berry stops short of ad land spin: he always retains an element of Anglo-Saxon restraint; his skies are an optimistic blue, but they are not cloudless, they have a familiar grey-tinged turbulence that renders them authentic. His painting of two policemen in a car is like a still from a 1960s new-realism British TV cop show. These are modern policemen, not the friendly Bobbies traditionally encountered in children's literature. They are anonymous bureaucrats keeping order in a modern metropolis. A modern building, an office block, looms over them. It is white and clean and surrounded by strategically planted trees. Berry's best work records the rise of a new Britain created by town planners and urban developers. In another painting, an eerie depiction of a car descending into an underground car park, no human beings are present and the car appears driverless. It is an almost Ballardian view of modernity, and I was reminded of Paul Valery's remark that nothing is as mysterious as clarity.

In contrast, Martin Aitchison's work is less technologically-focussed; it is cosier, more humanistic, but no less revealing in the way it captures the rhetoric of life in 1960s Britain. Aitchison studied in Birmingham and at the Slade in London. He planned to become a painter, but as he noted in a recent interview, 'After the war, my attitude changed, and I began illustration and advertising as a freelancer.' He was employed by the publishers Hulton as a contributor to the popular children's comic *The Eagle* (1950–69), where he illustrated *Luck of the Legion*.

Aitchison shares Berry's visual immediacy, but their styles are different. You can see it in their handling of policemen. In Berry's hands they are shadowy Robo-cops, while under Aitchison's gentler scrutiny, they become benign public servants anxious to please. In one of Aitchison's scenes a youngish copper instructs an attentive girl in road safety. Behind him another policeman bundles a drunk into the local police station, while others go about their civic business calmly. In another painting, a friendly motorcycle cop with leather gloves and an implausibly neat uniform, talks to some children. They are by the seaside and the impression is of a scene from an Enid Blyton story. Compared to Berry's techno Britain, Aitchison's Britain is still cloaked in the pre-war hegemony of traditional patriarchal values.

Aitchison worked from real models rather than photographs. It shows in his two portraits of children investigating family heirlooms. The first of the two paintings was done in the mid-1960s, the second in the early-1970s. Profound changes have taken place in that short period. In the former scene the children are dressed in the clothes of bourgeois certainty. They look like the children from the 1945 film *Brief Encounter*: the girl is dressed as a mini-version of her mother; the boy in the middle-class uniform of shorts, white ankle socks and T-bar sandals. But by 1972, when the later portait was painted, both children are dressed in the casual attire of youth. They wear dungarees and trainers, and they both look more confident and less reverential as they sift through family relics.

Looking at Berry and Aitchison's work, forty years after it was first published, we see the beginnings of political correctness, we see mild attempts at social engineering, and we see a new honesty and realism in the images presented to children. But we also see history. As we increasingly become a society of the visual, and because we have come to mistrust the authoritarian lessons of history, we turn to the footprints of popular culture and mass imagery for our understanding of the world. Berry and Aitchison's Ladybird work seems as effective as photography, television programmes, films and historical texts in its depiction and illumination of a period in our recent past. In some ways, it is more illuminating, because it deals with life, work, play and childhood in a realistic and largely unpatronising manner. Their work allows a generation to interpret its collective past, without the sentimental fudge that accompanied children's literature since the Victorian era.

Sources

The thinking eye.
Catalogue for
Chaumont Poster
Festival, 2010.
See pp.138–142.

Graphic design and
illustration: Schism
and reunification.
Eye 72, Summer 2009.
See pp.143–146.

'What's wrong with
a piece of straight
illustration?' –
Illustrators – the
AOI's house magazine.
Varoom 4, 2007.
See pp.147–153.

Another time,
another place.
Eye 52, Summer 2004.
See pp.154–157.

Introductions

136 points of reference 2005

Graphic designers have two definitions of graphic design. One definition is personal and hidden, concealed in the way spies hide their true allegiances; the other is the 'official' definition, the one we give to our clients. To make our clients happy we talk about 'delivering messages', 'solving problems' and 'expressing brand values'. But we don't really mean any of these things. We are paying lip service to the notion that graphic design is a service industry where the designer is a hired hand eagerly relaying the client's message without any personal coloration and leaving no fingerprints or tell-tale DNA traces. Yet, in our hearts, we know that graphic design is really about committing acts of personal creation. In fact, we become graphic designers in the first place because we like the idea of doing work that we can claim authorship for – even when we do it in the service of others.

Some graphic designers are happy with the notion of being the client's mouthpiece – although this is a view usually held by designers with not much interest in design, or designers who are only interested in making money. There are also designers who regard graphic design as a public service. They believe that design can be created for the well-being of other human beings rather than merely to seduce them into buying things. Yet here's a funny thing: I never met a graphic designer, no matter how service-minded, no matter how keen to do work with social value, who liked being told how to design something, or who was happy when asked to change his or her work.

There's an inner core of stubbornness in most designers that makes us seem, as a breed, difficult and obdurate. This stubbornness comes from inner aesthetic convictions – we have our favourite typefaces, colours, images, etc., and if we are prevented from using these hard-wired preferences we become unhappy. Graphic design is easy to change (especially in the digital era where nothing is fixed), and as a consequence, clients are rarely shy of demanding alterations to a designer's work, or about expressing opinions which are no more than mere whims. The outcome of this cavalier attitude to graphic design is that designers live perpetually under the threat of creative death. This makes us insecure and unyielding and stubborn, and in turn often makes us unloved by our poor deluded clients, who think that when they hire us they acquire our obedience as well as our talent.

The notion that graphic design is about acts of personal creation is not incompatible with doing good and effective work. Graphic designers may like to do things their way, but this doesn't make them anarchists. It's a rare designer who doesn't want to please his or her clients, and designers like working to briefs. In fact, to be a designer, you need a brief (even if it's a self-authored one), and if you don't need a brief then you are not a graphic designer. Good designers listen, ask questions, do research and take metaphorical thermometer readings of the task in front of them. But, they want to execute the brief in the way they think best, and they want to do it with their voice, their signature.

What is this voice, this signature? Surely we are talking about art world subjectivism here? Perhaps. But it is also the element we bring to our work to make it our own, and when it is missing from graphic design the result is nearly always mediocre.

Acquiring a voice is not automatic. Designers are not born with it, it has to be earned. I found my own voice as a designer when I learned to incorporate reference points into my work. Sometimes these reference points were out in the open, obvious and shared. Yet on other occasions they were hidden and arcane, only visible to me. It might be a colour reference to the way Coppola lit *The Conversation*; it might be a typographic allusion to the way Robert Frank gouged letterforms into the emulsion of his photographic prints; it might be a graphic replication of the way Sergio Leone framed a face. But by using reference points – often from areas other than graphic design – I found a way of working that seemed, paradoxically, deeply personal and at the same time deeply impersonal. Which feels like a pretty good definition of graphic design to me.

This is a book about reference points (*Points of Reference*, 2005, see p.374). It is the hallmark of the genuinely talented that they can reveal their reference points and not be diminished by this act of revelation. Only the terminally second-rate try to conceal their reference points.

Lawrence Wiener is a sort of patron saint of graphic design. He looks a bit like a saint. With his long beard and melancholic demeanour, he looks like a flagellant from the medieval Coptic Church, or a desert dwelling ascetic from a Jodorowsky movie. In truth, he's a sharp-brained conceptual artist from NYC who uses typography with the unforced adroitness of, well, a graphic designer.

Martin Parr is the master of the unflinching gaze. His shadow-free, ring-flash aesthetic is the signature look of postmodern image making – at once brutally honest and at the same time entirely dependent for its existence on the photographer's unerring eye. He cites Brandt, Cartier Bresson, Robert Frank and the British photographer Tony Ray-Jones as key reference points in his development as a photographer. Parr also references the postcards of John Hinde, with their 'saturated colour', which he encountered when he worked at Butlins in the early 1970s.

Erik Spiekermann wanted to be a folk singer as a young man, but it's hard to imagine Erik Spiekermann as anything other than a typographer. He calls himself an 'information architect', which is sharp and modern sounding, but in truth he's the digital era descendent of typo-craftsmen like Peter Behrens, Edward Johnston and Paul Renner. His identity for the city of Berlin and his work for the Berliner Verkehrsbetriebe are unavoidable reference points for any designer who wants to call themselves modern.

Alan Fletcher attended four different art schools. At the Royal College of Art his contemporaries were Peter Blake and Joe Tilson. Later, in the US, he was taught by Paul Rand and Josef Albers at Yale. In LA he worked as an assistant to Saul Bass, before returning to Britain to set up Fletcher/Forbes/Gill, which would eventually become Pentagram. His 2001 book *The Art of Looking Sideways* is a celebration of reference points on an heroic scale.

Record covers made out of shower curtains; Lee Marvin; and the 'enchanted domain of pop' 2003

In the pre-MTV era, the pop album cover was a rich storehouse of visual invention. The great album covers of the 60s and 70s embodied the pop ethos of rebellion, hedonism and escape. They were big and sumptuous and hallucinatory, but then so was the music. More importantly, sleeves from this golden era were powerful cultural signifiers. In fact, they were art.

The great album covers of the past qualified as art because sleeve designers were not asked to think about 'marketing' or 'image building' or any of the other constraints of present day sleeve design. Furthermore, designers were greatly assisted in the creation of this body of work by the existence of a generation of avid record buyers who longed for gestures and tropes that would offend their parents and teachers. Oh, and mind-altering chemicals also played a part.

The great album covers were canvasses smeared with symbolism and obliqueness. It wasn't always clear what this graphic semaphore was telling us: often it was deliberately ambiguous and fragmentary, wilfully misleading, even. Well, that's art for you.

If you 'got it' – if you cracked the code – you entered the 'Enchanted Domain of Pop': a place where the remit of family, school and society did not run. But as with all enchanted gardens, you enjoyed the sensory bombardment for a fleeting moment, and then the flowers wilted, summer ended, and you were ejected, a saddened and bitter figure. Well, that's life for you.

Of course there had been interesting album cover art prior to the golden era of the 60s and 70s, but you had to look to jazz and avant-garde music to find it. There were many good examples: Andy Warhol began his professional life drawing jazz covers in the style of illustrator David Stone Martin; Sun Ra, in his famous East Village house, produced hand-crafted sleeves made from old shower curtains (if you want to give a contemporary record industry executive a heart attack, suggest producing a record cover made from shower curtains); Blue Note was the epitome of stylistic and graphic cool.

The era of album-covers-as-art ended with the arrival of the marketing men (they were nearly always men) during the 80s. Someone left the door open and, like Lee Marvin's character Walker in *Point Blank*, they just walked in and pistol whipped pop into submission. These pony-tailed Walkers ushered in the era of the commodification of pop. In the debased language of marketing, music became just another item of 'fast moving consumer goods'. It was the start of focus groups, of radio stations with playlists selected by computers, of record shops that equated the selling of music with the selling of toiletries.

The pony-tailed Walkers instigated the music video which overnight supplanted the album cover as the principal visual expression of recorded music, and they commissioned marketing campaigns (of which album covers were merely a constituent part) that told you exactly what the music was like, in other words, they told you what to think. (This last sentence is my definition of marketing: it explains why marketing is a great contemporary evil. But this is my personal prejudice. You should ignore me. I'm saddened and bitter.)

The 80s also saw the 12" album cover replaced by the compact disc, which became the primary carrier for recorded music. At a stroke, the Sahara-like canvas of the album cover was lost to designers and artists, and replaced by what the music writer Ian Penman called the world of 'hi-sheen graphix … hi-budget campaigns and CD hygiene …'

I first noticed Rune Grammofon sleeves when tiny ads appeared in *The Wire*. (Thank God for *The Wire*. It has become a sort of *National Geographic* for musical improbability.) The ads had an aesthetic bite that made me want to know more. Everything about them was interesting: the sphere-shaped blobs of colour; the deft use of microscopic sans serif typography; the reluctance to tell the viewer much about what was being advertised; even the names of the bands cast a dark Nordic spell: Deathprod, Supersilent, Chocolate Overdose.

Looking at the first Rune Grammofon sleeves, designed then as now, by Norwegian designer Kim Hiorthøy, was like being back in the 'Enchanted Domain'. Like seeing, for the first time, Bowie in a dress on the cover of *The Man Who Sold The World*. Like seeing your first Big Youth album cover. Like seeing Barney Bubbles' covers for the Stiff label. Or the Elektra sleeves of William S Harvey. (If you don't know who William S Harvey was, you should either pay more attention to the credits on album covers, or you've got a lousy record collection.)

The enchantment that Rune Grammofon offers is of course a postmodern enchantment. Nowadays, we don't feel the same sense of wonder that was possible in the 60s and 70s; today we know too much and we understand too much. But we enjoy Rune Grammofon sleeves for their many fine qualities and for their 'differentness', yet because of our 'knowingness' they can never match the cultural and aesthetic impact of *Trout Mask Replica* or *Closer*, or for that matter Hawkwind's *In Search of Space*. But that's postmodern life for you.

As with all great labels that adopt a house style – or at least adopt a consistent visual approach – Rune Grammofon sleeves act like a visual manifesto. They don't tell you what the music is like, but they hint at the label's sensibility. Their freshness and directness alerts the jaded palettes of record buyers and album cover fans to the existence of something interesting. The use of Digipaks rather than the non-ductile imperviousness of the Perspex jewel case, signals a radical awareness, and the tactile quality of the cardboard echoes the sleeves of treasured vinyl record collections. Even more eye catching is the provocative use of 8pt sans serif typography on the front covers. The copy-right line in the same font and size as the album title! You knew you are not looking at a Hawkwind album cover, that's for sure.

Like many genuinely talented people, Kim Hiorthøy is a modest man. You can see it in his Rune Grammofon work. He's also charming and principled. I once asked him to contribute to a vanity project for a so-called 'cool brand' that I was involved with. Most of the designers I know would have jumped at the chance to see their work in this setting. Not Hiorthøy. He wrote me an articulate and heartfelt note explaining his reasons for declining my offer, and I felt ashamed for having asked him.

Hiorthøy is reluctant to be drawn on the motives behind his work for Rune Grammofon. 'The purpose of cover design is to thicken the plot,' he notes. 'The purpose of cover design is to get more people to buy the record. The purpose of cover design is to overthrow the government and introduce totalitarian regimes. The purpose of cover design is enlightenment.' Well, that's as good a definition of sleeve design as I've heard.

Hiorthøy shares another attribute with many highly talented practitioners in the visual arts: his influences are clearly visible in his work, yet at the same time transubstantiated into something new and personal. Only the terminally second-rate bleat about originality. In Hiorthøy's work we can plainly see the influence of American art from Warhol to abstract expressionism to Eames, yet his work is unmistakably European, Nordic even. You can detect the chromatic influence of Matisse in his use of flat bright colours, and of Arp in his use of spheroid shapes [see p.376]. Digital squiggles hint at the laptop modernity of many of the musicians who record for Rune Grammofon.

But look for yourself. You'll see other things, other influences, other thumbprints. It's one of the great joys of Hiorthoy's work: his sleeves are like Rorschach tests for the visually astute.

Hiorthøy, like all good artists, is continuously expanding his range of expression. He does this because like all good artists he has not been made slow and lazy by the disease of self-satisfaction. As he says: 'I think some of the best designers are those who are able to tell stories. I would like to, I am just rarely able to do it, I am not that good a designer.' I think he is a good designer. But don't take my word for it. See for yourself.

Space and structure
2011

The archeologists have exhaustively sieved the graphic design soil: not much has escaped zealous bloggers, Flickr hoarders, and design historians. We only have to look at the websites, exhibitions and growing library of books cataloguing graphic design's brief history to see that not much has avoided detection.

Occasionally, however, something goes unnoticed. This is usually because it doesn't come from the canon of recognized design practitioners – or because it doesn't quite fit into the pattern of the times from which it sprang. *Form*, a quarterly magazine published in Great Britain between summer 1966 and autumn 1969, is one of those misfit artefacts [see p.377].

The magazine has received scant attention from graphic design's cool hunters. It was featured in 'Clip/Stamp/Fold', an exhibition devoted to radical magazines from the 1960s and 70s, which was organized by a group of History and Theory PhD candidates from the School of Architecture at Princeton. I missed the show when it came to the Architectural Association in London in 2007, but I noticed the front cover of *Form* numbers 1 and 10 on the accompanying website: www.clipstampfold.com. They looked different from everything else on view: most of the other magazines, with one or two exceptions, had the Roneo-ed, free-form approach that was the inevitable consequence of hours spent with glue and scalpel in an era before computers and graphics software.

The first time I saw *Form* in the flesh was in 2008 when I was shown copies by the designer Mason Wells of the design group Bibliothèque – one of the most enthusiastic archaeologists of UK modernism. Wells discovered the first four issues of the magazine in New York and immediately recognized an affinity with the bulletins published by Ulm School of Design (Hochschule für Gestaltung – HfG Ulm). There is indeed a similarity between the two publications (a debt freely acknowledged by Philip Steadman, *Form*'s designer, founder and co-editor), yet what struck me even more forcibly was the sheer improbability of finding a UK publication from the 1960s, designed in the austere style of Swiss and German modernism. It just wasn't terribly British.

I found no mention of *Form* in any of the standard textbooks. I noted from the colophon that the magazine boasted three joint editors and that one of the trio – Philip Steadman – was also the publisher. I also noticed that no designer was credited. After some digging I discovered that a Philip Steadman had written a book on Vermeer (*Vermeer's Camera: Uncovering the Truth Behind the Masterpieces*, 2001). The writer's biography confirmed that this was the same Philip Steadman who edited and published *Form*.

Today, Philip Steadman is Professor of Urban and Built Form Studies at University College London. He trained as an architect, and has taught at Cambridge and the Open University. His biography describes him as: 'The author of several books on geometry in architecture and computer-aided design. In the 1960s he co-edited and published *Form*, an international magazine of the arts, and co-authored a book on kinetic art. He helped to produce four computer-animated films on the work of Leonardo da Vinci for an exhibition at the Hayward Gallery in London in 1989. He has also contributed to other exhibitions, films and books on perspective geometry and the history of art.'

I emailed him and received a warm reply thanking me for taking an interest in *Form*. He mentioned that he hadn't had any approaches from the graphic design world, but that he had occasional contact with people who were interested in the magazine from an art perspective. I told him that I wanted to write about *Form* and he kindly agreed to be interviewed.

Professor Steadman lent me the other six volumes of *Form* which until then I hadn't seen. They confirmed my view that *Form* is an important component in the history of British graphic design: I say important because it seems remarkable that it should have emerged at a time when pop art and the psychedelic style had invaded Britain. But for the young Steadman, steeped in modernist thinking, to design the magazine in the Swiss style, was entirely natural: as an architectural student in the 1960s, modernism was what he was taught – 'it was just the received wisdom,' he notes matter-of-factly.

Steadman is untrained as a graphic designer. He acquired a love of printing and typography while at school, and apart from a spell working on the short-lived magazine *Image*, and a stint on *The Sunday Times Colour Magazine* in its early glory days, he has not worked as a graphic designer. But clearly his training in architecture and his strong interest in the visual arts – especially art with a geometric focus, not to mention concrete poetry and kinetic art – has equipped him with a sense of space and structure that resulted in page layouts and front covers with poise and confidence.

His lack of formal training is revealed in the occasional typographic infelicities that can be found in *Form*. As a publication, it cannot be compared to the finest specimens of modernist editorial design from Europe – *Neue Grafik*, for example – but it had a discipline and purity that makes it wholly unexpected in the contemporaneous UK publication scene. To illustrate just how untypical *Form*'s design and layout was, Steadman struggled to find a printer who held Helvetica – hard to imagine considering that typeface's subsequent ubiquity. In fact, the Cambridge-based Steadman had to 'send to London' to get the magazines' headlines set in Helvetica. Further evidence of *Form*'s unusualness can be seen in the use of good quality art paper – a somewhat lavish gesture for the time – and in the use of the 'wasteful' square format. This was not a typical 1960s publication.

But it's the content that really distinguishes *Form* from other journals of the period. Steadman and his two co-editors were writing about subjects – most notably the rise of French postmodern thinking – that simply weren't being dealt with anywhere else in Britain. In an interview with one of the editors of 'Clip/Stamp/Fold', *Form*'s co-editor Stephen Bann said: 'We thought of *Form* as a kind of neo-modernist publication, I suppose, devoted to the early avant-garde as well as to the classic American avant-garde deriving from it (Black Mountain [College], etc). I was especially keen on work by contemporary literary figures – people like Thomas Bernhard, Robert Pinget and Ian Hamilton Finlay – who have now achieved a great reputation. I also included possibly the first English translation of an essay by Roland Barthes in issue number one.'

Browsing through the ten issues of *Form* is like a switch-back ride through the 20th-century avant-garde. The dazzling array of names forms a dramatis personae of radicalism: Theo van Doesburg, Roland Barthes, Gertrude Stein, Josef Albers,

Walter Gropius, László Moholy-Nagy, Kurt Schwitters and Ian Hamilton Finlay. The subject matter ranges from kinetic art to structuralism; from Marcel Duchamp to American photography, by way of neoplasticism and Russian unofficial art.

The regular feature titled 'Great Little Magazines' allowed *Form*'s editors to write about many of the 'little' magazines that had inspired them: *Secession*, *G*, *Mecano*, *De Stijl* and *Kulcher*. This is subject matter that you'd struggle to find in one place today. But in the 1960s there was a small but dedicated audience eager to support a magazine that surveyed this terrain – a fact corroborated by the discovery made by Steadman when he closed the magazine after ten issues: 'I wrote to all the subscribers at the end and said I'm afraid we've run out of money and we're going to have to close. Lots and lots wrote back and said "Oh we'd have paid much more for it."'

Erik Kessels on show
2008

Erik Kessels is an ad man. Not that you'd guess this when you meet him. He uses words like 'authenticity' and 'honesty'. He is excited by the role of the 'amateur' and the 'untried' in image making. He enthuses about old photographs found in flea markets. It's hardly stereotypical adland conversation material.

But then there's nothing stereotypical about Kessels or the work of his Amsterdam-based ad agency KesselsKramer. For many observers of the visual communication scene, KesselsKramer is one of only a handful of advertising agencies producing work that rises above the level of consumerist drivel.

KesselsKramer campaigns are often witty and irreverent, almost anti-advertising. Their campaign for the cheap backpacker's hotel, Hans Brinker, in Amsterdam, has gone down in advertising history for its dogged honesty. Writing in *Graphis*, one writer noted: 'The Hans Brinker budget hotel campaign has the hotel promoting itself with slogans like: "Now even more dogshit in the main entrance!" or "Now even more noise!"'

Erik Kessels is the creative director of KesselsKramer, but what comes across clearly in talking to him is that he brings the same quest for authenticity to his work for the Hans Brinker Hotel that he brings to rooting around in flea markets looking for the hidden histories in abandoned piles of yellowing photographs. Others surf through this stuff – the detritus of countless lives – but it takes Kessels' eye to see the mystery and quiet dignity in these abandoned archives and turn them into books and exhibitions.

Yet, unlike so many people in advertising and design, Kessels is not a frustrated artist. He's not fighting a wish to be free of clients. He is a willing inhabitant of the modern communication world, and is equally at home creating campaigns for global corporations, as he is sifting through pictures of long-forgotten Belgian cycling groups, and shots of 1980s Russian domestic eroticism. When I suggest that he is unusually optimistic for someone working in the creative industries, he worries in case I'm implying that he is complacent. No one who has Kessels' eye for weird connections, and the sheer oddity of human behaviour, could be complacent or self-satisfied. Kessels is neither.

Sources

136 points of reference. Foreword to *136 Points of Reference* by Jonathan Ellery, Browns Editions, 2005. See pp.162–164.

Record covers made out of shower curtains; Lee Marvin; and the 'enchanted domain of pop'. Essay written for the Rune Grammofon compilation *Money Will Ruin Everything*, 2003. See pp.165–168.

Space and structure. Introduction to *U:D/R 02 Space and Structure: looking at* Form, *a quarterly magazine of the arts (1966–1969)*, Unit Editions, 2010. See pp.169–172.

Erik Kessels on show. Foreword to *Erik Kessels*. Browns/Howard Smith Paper, 2008. See p.173.

Essays

Music

Tony Wilson
The postmodern mythmaker
2007

Tony Wilson, founder of Factory Records, died on Friday 10th August. He'd been fighting cancer for some time. Wilson had many claims to fame: he was a successful television presenter; a music industry impresario of flawed and maverick genius; a professional Mancunian; a witty and literate man who wrote a classic pop autobiography;[1] and he was one of the shrewdest patrons of graphic design there has ever been.

Tony Wilson was the Colonel Tom Parker[2] of British postmodern pop. Just as the Colonel had used fairground astuteness to turn Elvis into the first electronic-age pop star, Wilson deployed his Cambridge education to turn Factory's roster of acts – Joy Division, New Order, Happy Mondays, Durutti Column, and others – into the first wave of postmodern pop stars. Wilson knew how pop myths were made, and he spun them around his bands, around the doomed Factory empire, and around his own career. He did it with style, wit, and a lot of black Armani suits. As a myth builder par excellence, Wilson used all the media-age tools at his disposal, but none more effectively than graphic design.

I met Wilson in 1994. He was charming, unreliable, and totally unlike the other record company people I dealt with at the time. Wilson never let you forget that he'd graduated with a degree (third class) in English from Jesus College, Cambridge. He never missed a chance to tell you that he knew his Goethe from his Boethius. In the two-page foreword to his book *24 Hour Party People* (2002) he manages to weave in references to Voltaire, the Balfour Declaration and Mark Twain.

By the time I got to know Wilson, the Factory dream was over. So too was Madchester and the frazzled acid house hallucination that Wilson provided with an ancestral home in the shape of The Haçienda. He was about to launch Factory Too, in collaboration with London Records, part of the music industry conglomerate PolyGram. Designer Peter Saville, newly returned from LA, had created the logo – two words set in Rotis that hinted at ennui and a lack of conviction on the part of both designer and label boss.

Wilson phoned from his Jaguar and announced that he was coming to see me. He wanted my studio to design *A Factory Sample Too* (the original Factory label had also been launched with a double 7" EP: *A Factory Sample*), the second coming of Factory was to be celebrated with the release of another EP. Accompanied by Yvette Livesey, his partner in life and business, Wilson briefed us on the project. But there was something missing: the bands were dreadful, and Wilson's patter, although as effervescent as ever, rang hollow.

Nevertheless, he was a thrilling client, full of praise and enthusiasm: in Matthew Robertson's excellent survey of Factory's graphic legacy,[3] Wilson explains his attitude to graphic design: 'Why was packaging important to us? Because the job was a sacred one. Music had transformed our young lives, children of the 60s all. And now we were in the privileged position of putting out records ourselves. Does the Catholic Church pour its wine into mouldy earthenware pots? I think not.'

I worked with him off and on for two years, mainly on his music industry festival, In The City.[4] But getting paid was always difficult, and I realised I was doing the work because I was in thrall to the Factory myth, the Wilson myth, and the role that graphic design played in that mythos.

In his book (which he writes in the third person) Wilson describes meeting Peter Saville for the first time: '... a sort of 20-year-old Bryan Ferry look-a-like with searingly intelligent eyes turned up at the Granada canteen to see Wilson over a cup of GTV coffee. Peter showed Wilson a book on Jan Tschichold. He showed him the Penguin Crime Covers from 1941, the constructivist play posters from the 1920s and the cover of the 1965 Hoffmann-Laroche catalogue (the Swiss chemical boys who did so much for the neural pathways in the second half of the century in question).' Wilson recognised Saville's genius. But he also recognised graphic design's potential to be spun into the fabric of the Factory legend alongside the music, the drugs, the guns, and the deaths. Nor was it only Saville's cool postmodernism that Wilson championed. He also recognised the more rigorous genius of 8vo, and the anarcho-weirdness of Central Station Design.

In their book *On The Outside*, 8vo quote Wilson as saying, 'The problem with 8vo is that they are bigger than the music', but as they point out, it didn't feel like that to them. In Central Station, Wilson found a graphic sensibility – the antithesis of Saville and 8vo's – to match the ramshackle pharmaceutical grandeur of Happy Mondays, who ironically would become the agents of Factory's demise.

The last time I saw Wilson was in 2005 at a seminar in Manchester about record sleeve design. He was the host. The audience, mainly made up of young Manchester designers had been attracted by a panel that included Ian Anderson from The Designers Republic and Ben Drury, the Mo'Wax designer. Wilson presided over the discussion. He did it with his usual flair and well-practised exhibitionism. But I noticed the audience growing restless with his anecdotal references to Factory's glorious past. And although I was still in awe of his louche and foppish charm, the locals took a more critical stance: it was not uncommon to walk down the street with him in Manchester and for locals to roll down their car windows and shout abuse at him. It never seemed to bother him: quite the opposite.

As a keen pop culture anthropologist, Tony Wilson will have known during his last days that nothing improves a reputation like a premature death. He will have known that his greatest act of mythmaking was his own death. Anthony H Wilson, RIP.

1. *24 Hour Party People: What the Sleeve Notes Never Tell You* by Tony Wilson. Channel 4, 2002. A 'novelisation' by Tony Wilson of Frank Cottrell Bryce's screenplay for the film *24 Hour Party People*.

2. Colonel Tom Parker, the legendary manager of Elvis Presley. Parker falsely claimed to have been born in the US, but it emerged that he was born in Holland, a fact which for many commentators explains why Elvis never performed in the UK – a foreign tour would have exposed Parker's true nationality.

3. *Factory Records: The Complete Graphic Album* by Matthew Robertson. Thames & Hudson, 2007. See pp.205–207 for a review of this book.

4. In The City, an annual music industry gathering in Manchester. Includes panel discussions, workshops, keynote speeches and gigs.

Design Observer playlist
2008

I've never worked in a design studio where music wasn't played pretty much constantly. Nor can I recall visiting a studio where music wasn't being broadcast, or where designers weren't wired up to headphones. What is it with graphic designers and music? Is there a symbiotic relationship between the two? Does music aid creative thinking and make us better designers? Are there studios where music is considered a hindrance?

When I launched my own studio in 1988, our first purchase – even before we bought the first drawing boards – was a CD player. With five or six people all in the same room, we had music playing all the time. I'd just come from a studio where the radio was tuned to London's main commercial radio station. British commercial radio in the 1980s was dire – it hasn't got any better, last time I checked – but somehow we lived with what the poet Simon Armitage has called the 'tinnitus' of pop radio. (Thinking back though, I can remember hearing Kraftwerk tracks amongst the wall-to-wall, whooshing synth-drum induced nausea of Billy Idol and Bananarama, so perhaps it wasn't as bad as I remember it.)

To provide a round-the-clock soundtrack for the new studio, we even had a CD budget. But it was rarely used because people preferred to bring in their own music, which resulted in a low-cholesterol diet of The Pixies and Brit indie shoegazers like Ride, Slowdive, My Bloody Valentine, and the Cocteau Twins. My own preference at the time was for David Sylvian (a taste I still have) but I could only play his lachrymose balladry when my business partner left the building. 'Boy's music,' she said, witheringly.

As the studio grew to around ten or 12 people, it became harder to get agreement on what should be played: arguments erupted and factions fought over control of the CD player. We had a leather-jacketed, bouffant-haired artworker who was obsessed with guitar wizards like Yngwie Malmsteen and Eddie Van Halen. It wasn't easy to accommodate his musical tastes, but he was a good artworker so he was given the CD remote from time to time – usually when I needed him to work all night. We had another growth spurt in personnel in the late-1990s (to around twenty people) and that meant the end of any sort of musical consensus. Not that it mattered, because this was now the era of the personal CD player and it became normal to see nearly every designer in the studio wearing headphones.

Today, the headphone-clad designer locked into his or her own audio bubble is a familiar sight. Graphic designers, or so it seems, like music and abhor silence. But is it possible to claim that music contributes more to the creative output of a studio than, say, comfortable chairs and a good coffee machine? There is no shortage of theories about the way music influences behaviour. It began with Pythagoras and his discovery of the music of the spheres, and can be found today in such disparate musicological thinking as Brian Eno's theories of ambient music, and in the way institutions are using classical music to reduce violent behaviour in public places. Music's ability to act as a sedative has long been know to medical science, as are the mesmeric effects of music as a means of inducing heightened states of emotion.

For me, I need music pretty much constantly. Having given up studio life in favour of working on my own, I gravitate towards introspective, trance-like music. This can be anything from Morton Feldman to Harold Budd. From late-period Coltrane to the latest backwoods drone rock. From Nordic electronica to exotic soundtracks. My only stipulation is that it has to be music without words: lyrics distract. Other than that, anything goes.

So, let's try a bit of blog-based research here. Let's try and find out what Design Observer readers are listening to, and build up a DO playlist.[1] I'm predicting a mixed bag, with not very much Yngwie Malmsteen. But I could be wrong.

1. This blog post produced a healthy response at the time of writing (2008). There have been 169 comments, mostly endorsing the benefits of music in studios.

Bright side of the sun
2011

Dark Side of the Moon is a pivotal record both in rock music history and in my own interior world of musical and cultural obsessions. Oddly, the position this record occupies in rock history is eerily similar to the one it holds in my personal mythology of pop: it represents the end of something and the beginning of something else.

To understand *DSoM*'s significance, you have to go back to the 1960s. If much of that tumultuous decade is now dismissed as delusional, the one thing that remains unassailable is the music. As the writer Jenny Diski noted in her brilliant memoir of the period: 'Perhaps the 60s are an idea that has had its day and lingers long after its time. Except, of course, for the music.'

Music was the sacramental vessel that contained the true faith of 60s utopianism, and if you were a believer, few albums were more important than a trio of pre-1970s Pink Floyd albums: *Piper at the Gates of Dawn*, *Saucerful of Secrets* and *Ummagumma* [see p.361]. I first heard the band's second album – *Saucerful of Secrets* – as a pop-mad schoolboy, and it felt like a door opening. It was a moment of revelation; confirmation that music could transport the listener in a way that only hallucinogenic drugs and sexual ecstasy could match (an easy assumption to make at the time, since drugs and sex were something I read about longingly rather than experienced on a regular basis.)

Saucerful of Secrets oozed Lysergic languor, space-age pastoralism, and the new electronic sound of synthesisers. This album signalled the start of the recording studio as instrument: even the Beatles noted the revolutionary vigour of the Pink Floyd's early sonic experimentation. Both bands famously recorded at Abbey Road Studios, often using the same engineers.

If you loved *Saucerful of Secrets*, and others like it, you occupied a world of epicurean good taste. You were a member of an exclusive club – one that insisted on long hair and chiffon scarves rather than blazers and ties. Rock music was the badge you wore to proclaim your allegiance to the new alternative culture.

But the 60s dream ended. It ended circa 1973 when the international oil crisis meant that the party – that had began in about 1965 – had to be paid for; it was the moment when the man came round to collect the rent; it was the moment when the music lost its virginity and the international rock business took over. And to many 60s idealists, the record that seemed to mark the end of the beautiful era and the beginning of a new darker one, was the appropriately named *Dark Side of the Moon*.

The record was Pink Floyd's eighth studio album. It was recorded in two sessions between May 1972 and January 1973, and released in March 1973. Its success was phenomenal. The facts read like the wet dream of a corporate record executive: the album remained in the US charts for 741 weeks, from 1973 to 1988, longer than any other album in history. It has sold an estimated 45 million copies. It is Pink Floyd's most commercially successful album, and in a list of best selling albums on Wikipedia, only Michael Jackson's *Thriller* (110m) and AC/DC's *Back in Black* (49m) have sold more.

When it was released, it was still possible to hear many of the qualities that made the early Floyd albums such masterpieces. But the album's huge sales and its sonic grandeur meant that, at the time, I unfairly dismissed it as 'prog rock'. I say unfair, because whatever you think about *DSoM*-era Pink Floyd, they were not noodling virtuoso prog rockers fixated with elves and magical landscapes: they wrote about madness, the loss of original band member and madcap genius Syd Barrett, and grubby stuff like ... money.

I had retained my interest in the band up to and including *Meddle*, a languorous record that seemed to combine the wayward genius of *Saucerful of Secrets* with a more accomplished rock sensibility. But by the time *DSoM* was released, I had moved onto harder stuff; jazz, krautrock, David Bowie, Lou Reed and eventually the buzz-saw whine of punk.

For the punks, Pink Floyd was the enemy – one of a handful of bands snottily dismissed as 'dinosaurs'. In punk mythology, the antagonism towards Pink Floyd was cemented when Malcolm McLaren allegedly spotted John Lydon wearing a Pink Floyd T-shirt with 'I hate' scrawled above the band's name. And although my infatuation with punk was brief, I still couldn't find a place in my heart for *DSoM*.

And yet, over the years, my opinion has mellowed. Time and the dissolving of old prejudices have revealed moments of beauty and power: the gurgling, techno-like electronics of *On the Run*; the anarchic sound effects and spoken word interjections scattered throughout the album; the plangent piano that runs through *The Great Gig in the Sky*; the strutting funky riff that propels *Money*; the monastic grace of *Us and Them* – a track that wouldn't have been out of place on *Saucerful of Secrets*.

DSoM's reinvention by postmodern experimentalists The Flaming Lips (they released their own version of the album in 2009),[1] and its continuing popularity amongst new generations of music fans with unfettered, promiscuous musical tastes, has resulted in the album's enduring relevance: whatever *DSoM* is, it is not a relic whose time has passed. When this longevity is combined with its role as one of the records that both technically and creatively changed pop music, and of course its oft-parodied and iconic cover art, *DSoM*'s permanent place in the pop canon is secure. For me, it's no *Saucerful of Secrets*, but then few records are.

1. *The Flaming Lips and Stardeath and White Dwarfs with Henry Rollins and Peaches Doing The Dark Side of the Moon* by The Flaming Lips. Warner Bros., 2009.

It's Nice That – ten records
2010

Choosing only ten records is a kind of torture. If I could choose 500, I might begin to get close to expressing my musical taste. So, I've decided to select individual records that represent a strand – or genre – of music that I go back to repeatedly. But ask me tomorrow, and I'll give you a completely different ten.

United States of America – *United States of America*

Dreamy surrealistic pop from the 1960s. Curiously undated and featuring the sort of collagist approach to music making that we take for granted today. It's full of psychedelic guitars, wan vocals and gurgling electronics. Leader Joseph Byrd was a pioneer of electronics in pop. If you like bands such as Broadcast and Stereolab – well, this is what they've been listening to.

Biosphere – *Cirque*

I listen to lots of non-vocal electronic music. There are a few dozen CDs I could have chosen from this genre, but I've gone for the chilly poetics of Geir Jenssen (aka Biosphere). It's electronic music that doesn't rely on beats for its impact. If you travelled north of the Arctic Circle and lay down with your ear next to the ice, this is what you'd hear.

Neu – *Neu 2*

This is the opposite of the Biosphere record. It is monotonous, industrial pop, propelled by nail-gun beats and intoxicating drones. It sounds like the soundtrack to a long drive on an autobahn in a fast car. I could have chosen Kraftwerk, but there's something about the monotony of Neu that makes them darker and more dangerously addictive.

Joni Mitchell – *The Hissing of Summer Lawns*

Most people love her early singer/songwriter work, but I can't get too excited about that era. Something happened to her in the 1970s, though, and *The Hissing of Summer Lawns* is a near-perfect blend of sophisticated jazz pop with visionary lyrics about being alive – but detached – in 70s LA. Prince's famously cited this as one of his favourite records.

Jandek – *Manhattan Tuesday*

You can clear a room with the Texan dronist's off-kilter music. Personally, I can't get enough of his out-of-tune voice and spectral drones. Listening to him is like stumbling into a ghostly Pentecostal church in the Texas badlands in a film by Terrence Mallick. This is music from the outer reaches. Jandek has made dozens of records, but this is one I play often. Especially if I want to be alone!

David Sylvian – *Manafon*

Any record that mentions the austere Welsh poet RS Thomas is OK with me. I've liked Sylvian since his first solo albums, and here he pushes deeper into atonal territory, working with improvising musicians and Eraserhead-type electronic scrapings. Music that gets down to the bone.

Miles Davis – *Get Up With It*

I love Miles from all eras and in all his incarnations, but I've chosen this less well known record from 1974. He is one of the great artists of the 20th century, and a shining example of a creative genius who never stopped moving, evolving and kicking down barricades.

Throbbing Gristle –
The Second Annual Report of Throbbing Gristle

As I get older I appreciate TG more and more. This is music from the realms of psychological pain, but I always find it cathartic and life-affirming. And with titles such as *Slug Bait*, *Maggot Death* and *Zyclon B Zombie*, I don't think we are supposed to find it life-affirming. As the album cover says – industrial music for industrial people.

Brother Ah – *Move Ever Onward*

Radical black music from the 70s is an obsession of mine. I toyed with choosing a Sun Ra record, but plumped instead for Brother Ah from 1975. He fuses jazz, Indian music, Oriental temple chimes, flutes and African percussion with recitations of spiritual poetry extolling black consciousness and political transcendence.

Flying Lotus – *Cosmogramma*

This is a sparkling mash-up of fragments of musical language that emerges as something entirely modern and cohesive. I can hear references to soul, funk, Hollywood movies and arcade games – all within a few bars. Mutant music for a mutant world.

Are JPEGs the new album covers?
2007

Over the past few months I've been researching a book about current record cover art. Besides hunting down examples of stimulating music graphics, I've also been looking for digital alternatives to the traditional album cover. As downloading threatens to become the main distribution method for recorded music, it is widely believed that the album cover will be replaced by some new online format – perhaps animated – that will make CD packaging redundant. Well, I might be missing something, but I've found nothing in the digital arena that offers a viable alternative to a well-designed CD or vinyl album cover. Instead, I've discovered a grim-faced resistance movement amongst dozens of tiny record labels determined to hang onto physical packaging and expressive cover art, no matter what.

This resistance movement is found mainly amongst independent labels – micro labels – often run by a single individual, and often existing on budgets that would embarrass a shoestring. And what distinguishes so many of them is a deep-rooted commitment to selling physically packaged music with resonant cover art.

It's not worth discussing what the major labels are up to: they haven't got a clue. There used to be five major record labels; when Sony and BMG merged this became four, and now it is hotly predicted that another merger will reduce the number to three. These lumbering conglomerates are doing what they have always done: waiting for someone else to show them the way forward. In the meantime, as they dither and prevaricate, their domain is encircled by Apple, Starbucks, Amazon, WalMart and various corporate entities with the wherewithal to offer digital downloads to an eager public. For anyone who cares about music, this is hardly a heart-warming prospect.

And yet, is the determination of the micro labels to continue producing CD and vinyl packaging anything other than the remnants of a fanboy obsession with recorded music common amongst people who grew up in the pre-digital era? Most of the label owners I've interviewed for my book (*Cover Art By: New Music Graphics*, 2007) have talked about the usual teenage interest in band logos, enduring love affairs with New Order album covers, and fixations with the 'smell of records.' But are we talking about something deeper here? Does music need some sort of physicality to maintain its intrinsic value? If our favourite music merely exists as a sliver of invisible code on a computer, do we lose something?

In a recent *Guardian* article ('It's a Steal'), the novelist John Lanchester wrote about literary copyright. He detailed Google's ambitious attempts to digitize the world's literature. Lanchester has some sharp things to say about the way copyright and intellectual property rights are being eroded in the digital age, but he gives a cautious welcome to Google's plans, and does not foresee the end of books: 'Personally, I think that books are going to be OK, for one main reason: books are not only, or not primarily, the information they contain. A book is also an object, and a piece of technology; in fact, a book is an extraordinarily effective piece of technology, portable, durable, expensive to pirate but easy to use, not prone to losing all its data in crashes, and capable of taking an amazing variety of beautiful forms.'

Lanchester's phrase, 'an amazing variety of beautiful forms', applies to the best music packaging as much as it does to books. There is an undeniable sense of completeness when music comes with handsome packaging and engaging graphical material.

I download music, and while I have gripes with the poor audio quality of most downloads, I do it happily enough, relishing its instantaneousness and convenience. I tell myself that there's no good reason to need music to be packaged since one of its greatest assets is its lack of materiality – if you really want to enjoy music, listen to it with your eyes closed in a darkened room. And yet, when I analyze my feelings towards the digital files that sit on my laptop, or on my iPod, or on neglected backup discs, I find that I care less about them than I care about the CDs and vinyl discs I own.

An audio file with a thumbnail JPEG of the album cover will never have the resonance – not to mention the commercial value – of a well-made piece of packaging. But if the corporate providers of downloadable music have their way, this is the future of recorded music. Who ever had a love affair with a JPEG?

Can by Can
2006

Brian Eno's famous remark about the Velvet Underground can be reformulated for Can: not many people bought Can albums at the time, but everyone who did came to the realisation that pop could be art. We can quibble about calling Can's music pop – we can call it rock, or krautrock, or avant rock – but we can't quibble about it being art.

Why do we tend to talk about Can in the past tense? We do this with some justification: only solo albums have been released since 1989's *Rite Time*; original member Michael Karoli died of cancer in 2001; Holger Czukay has been semi-detached since 1977; no new group recordings are scheduled. And yet there's an anomaly here. Listening to the majestic sequence of albums that began in 1969, is to listen to music in the present tense.

Can is present tense music. Almost uniquely, their music – especially the records from the 70s – is uncorroded by time and fashion, and free from the rust of stylistic embarrassment. Can records that were cool in 1976 are still cool today, in 2006. How many bands can we say that about?

But then other bands don't have Jaki Liebezeit playing drums. It's always the drums that make records sound dated and otiose. It's always the drums that betray the passing of time. We cringe when we listen to the leaden tub-thumpers of prog rock; we recoil from the tinny drum machines of 80s pop rock. But in Jaki, Can have a drummer who always sounds like you're hearing him for the first time. He's a present tense drummer.

This 'nowness' also comes from the alchemical mix of the Can sound. Every note is right here, right now. Listen to 'Oh Yeah' on *Tago Mago*, or 'One More Night' on *Ege Bamyasi*; what distinguishes these visionary moments of Can-ness is the subjectless nature of the recordings. They are like photographs without a subject – everything is equal. There's no virtuosic posturing. As Holger says: 'None of us was obsessed with soloing, going it alone. Jaki never wanted to play a solo, not even for money ... we thought of ourselves as a chamber orchestra in which each had his own voice. The guitarists who always have to show what they can do, don't do themselves any favour in the end, although of course there are exceptions.'

Can's unified, all-at-once sound presages techno, ambient and the sleek modern digital rush of post-rock by two decades. And they did this in the era of two track studios, and at a time when rock was about showmanship and strut and ostentation.

This sonic oneness extends to the band's fiscal life, too. As Irmin Schmidt explains: '"She Brings the Rain", on which neither Jaki nor I play: it's still a Can song and we both receive the same amount of money as the others. Each person always got the same amount of money as the others. Can was always the author. And we have never, not once, fought over that.' Considering the rancourous and disputatious nature of the life of bands, this is a remarkable statement. Yet it is only what we expect from our heroes.

Can falls outside the sacred realm of perfect Can albums. It is affectionately dismissed by Can-heads as an irrelevant curio, and it's easy to see why. When it was recorded it 1978, Holger was a shadowy presence (a credit on the sleeve reads: 'Edited By Holger Czukay'); Rosko Gee and Reebop were now established as group members (an addition that briefly disrupted the group's collectivist structure); and the Can audience had been distracted and fragmented by the appearance of punk.

In the view of Irmin, *Can* is 'actually quite a reasonable album'. And reasonable seems a reasonable word to use. Listening to *Can* today, it worms its way into our affections. It is an engaging record with enough high points to make us forgive the low moments.

The album begins with three tracks of juddery funk. 'All Gates Open', 'Safe' and 'Sunday Jam' were made in the jetsteam of disco. There's a lingering afterscent of Giorgio Moroder as Rosko Gee and Reebop ramp up the rhythmic temperature; and the fact that the record was mixed at Hansa, in Berlin, the year after Bowie had emerged with *Low*, his masterwork of dark neo-funk, tells its own story.

'Sodom' contains a long guitar work-out by Michael. Using lashings of sustain and reverb, he wails like one of the guitar heroes that Holger warns us about. Only the formal-sounding pianistics of Irmin prevent the track from turning into a guitar player's wet dream.

'Aspectacle' begins as an excursion into Weather Report territory. Written as the theme music for a German

TV programme called 'Aspekte', it features a Morricone-esque 'harmonica', but soon settles into an extended soulful groove that Curtis Mayfield would have been proud of.

The album's nadir is the jocular 'E.F.S. No. 99 Can Can'. Based on Offenbach, it begins with punk-like raucousness (in Irmin's words, 'dumb-punk') and ends like you might imagine an Emerson Lake and Palmer encore might have sounded like.

Can is a record by a group coming to the end of its natural life. It would be ten years before they released another group record (the even more neglected *Rite Time*.) And while *Can* might lack the wonderment and the coating of angel dust that characterised the first five or six Can albums, like everything released under the Can imprint, it is worthy of our attention and respect. We owe them this much.

Think of your ears as eyes
1995

ECM (Editions of Contemporary Music), a small independent label based in Munich, has been in existence for 25 years and under the guidance of founder Manfred Eicher has consistently produced sleeve designs of enigmatic and austere beauty. The label's packaging exhibits the finest characteristics of the European modernist tradition: minimalist sans serif typography fused with dreamlike black and white photography. Ignoring design trends, the label has maintained a visual identity and stylistic voice that perfectly articulates the distinctive European aesthetic of the music.

ECM is run with visionary zeal by 48-year-old Eicher from a small office above a discount hi-fi store in suburban Munich. A throwback to the days when record companies were owned by record producers, Eicher has himself produced nearly all the 500 recordings in the ECM catalogue. He defies all the rules that supposedly ensure success in the music industry, which he regards as a sort of environmental pollution. Many ECM releases lose money, only a few make a profit: 'It was never my intention to record artists who had commercial potential, it was simply music that touched me deeply,' Eicher claims.

Among the musicians who have released recordings on ECM are Keith Jarrett, Pat Metheny, Jan Garbarek and contemporary composers Arvo Pärt and Steve Reich. Most are artists ignored by the mainstream who are inspired by the integrity and independence at ECM's core. Pat Metheny, now signed to major US label Geffen, has said that the only criticism he received from Eicher was that he was being 'too commercial'.

Eicher has worked with designer Barbara Wojirsch since ECM's inception. Photographer and designer Dieter Rehm joined them in 1978, and both pay tribute to Eicher's role in the design process. Enjoying a rare freedom unencumbered by commercial restraints, Eicher, Wojirsch and Rehm have created a body of work which, paradoxically, adheres to the rules of corporate identity and brand management, but is generated by artistic conviction and personal vision rather than commercial priorities.

Eicher denies any conscious effort to create an ECM look. 'I have never thought of a visual identity for ECM. What I try to express with the people I work with, and what I have tried to express since I was very young, whether in music or visually, is a reflection of my inner state of being. This is very often in a stark and sparse way; a landscape without people ... a landscape that is to do with the enigmatic'.

As a producer, Eicher's recordings have great clarity and lucidity, almost as if the Nordic climate (he records mainly in Oslo) had entered the process. And the packaging too has a clarity, which Eicher defines as 'a certain kind of personality in our work ... something that speaks to you in the image, usually things that are enigmatic, or dry, or weird, dark or cold, images that go well with the music. What I try to achieve is to get people who don't know the name of the musician to want to find out what the music is like. If this happens then I'm lucky.'

The sympathetic rapport between Eicher and his musicians means that they rarely interfere in the packaging of their recordings. Their views are not ignored, but most are content to let Wojirsch and Rehm work unhindered. There are exceptions: bassist Eberhard Weber insists on using his wife's neo-primitive paintings on his covers, while Estonian liturgical composer Arvo Pärt persuaded Wojirsch, against her wishes, to create a calligraphic title for his seminal *Miserere* (1991). But such demands are rare and on the whole Eicher and his team are able to pursue their vision without restriction.

Eicher lists the masters of European cinema – Godard, Bresson, Tarkovsky and Bergman – as having a profound influence on him, and powerful undercurrents of their work can be seen in ECM sleeve designs. He has recently directed his first film, *Holozan*, based on the novel *Man in the Holocene* (1979) by Max Frisch, with a poster designed by Wojirsch. Many of the photographs used on ECM covers – images of solitude, the sea, desolate landscapes – have a cinematic quality [see p.378] and they are often used sequentially in the manner of movie stills, as in Pat Metheny's *Travels* (1983) and Gavin Bryars' *After the Requiem* (1991). The symbiotic relationship between film and music is elegantly demonstrated in the packaging for the double CD of Greek composer Eleni Karaindrou's elegiac music for the films of Theo Angelopoulos, *The Weeping Meadow* (1991), and the extensive accompanying booklet with its many stills.

The influence of artists Jasper Johns and Cy Twombly is also detectable in several ECM sleeves. Garbarek's *Aftenland* (1980) uses Johns' stencil lettering techniques, as does Lester Bowie's *All the Magic* (1983). Twombly's densely textured crayon scribblings provide the inspiration for several of Wojirsch's covers, including Metheny's *Rejoicing* (1983) and the Hilliard Ensemble's recording of the music of *Walter Frye* (1993).

Wojirsch trained as a painter but gave it up when she realised that the world was full of good painters. She turned to advertising, but soon became disillusioned: 'I can't tell people things that aren't true.' When Eicher launched ECM, she found a congenial creative environment, though unlike Rehm, she remains freelance. Her work is characterised by exquisitely stark, minimalist typography based on a small repertoire of sans serif typefaces – what she unpretentiously calls her 'careful use of lettering'. She positions photographs with the confidence of a designer not striving for effect through fashionable part-bleeds or random groupings of images: 'It's a picture, we choose the picture to show it, not because we want to work with it.' Occasionally she abandons her formal type for a more painterly approach, as in her watercolour lettering for the Dave Holland Quartet album *Extensions* (1990), [see p.378]. A third strand to her work is her use of hieroglyphic and runic symbols – primitive, scratchy images that impart an atavistic quality, as in Garbarek's *I Took up the Runes* (1990), Jarrett's *The Cure* (1991) and Anouar Brahem's *Conte de l'incroyable amour* (1992).

Wojirsch relishes the freedom the record cover allows; supermarket packaging and annual reports hold no attraction for her. She has little interest in computers, eschewing new digital fonts, and restricts her use of technology to the fax machine. Like many sleeve designers, she is saddened by the disappearance of the vinyl LP cover, a format that allowed her to exploit the tactile properties of board, ink and varnish at workable dimensions.

In fact, ECM sleeves have made the transition to the CD format more successfully than most: what Rehm describes as 'the reduced visual language' of the company's packaging translates well into the smaller size. In the 1980s, when record companies converted their back catalogues to CD, it was rarely done satisfactorily. Labels such as Blue Note and Impulse suffered as sleeves printed on thick card with vivid ink and varnish were crudely reduced and badly printed on cheap art paper. For Eicher, the disappearance of the 12" sleeve has implications beyond design: 'LP covers sent a better signal and there was a sensual side to them – holding a record cover in your hand was like holding a book. Now, with the absence of interesting materials, of dust, the mystery has gone. So too with the music – digital recording has made the sound more neutral. It means there is a mainstream of rather good sounds but we don't hear things at the edges.'

Today, ECM no longer issues recordings on vinyl and some of Wojirsch's best work is found in CD booklets, where she creates drama and tension by the dynamic use of white space and blocks of asymmetrical type, as in her designs for the recent recordings of Jan Garbarek. She readily acknowledges the influence of Jan Tschichold and strives for what she describes as 'purity' in her typography.

Dieter Rehm joined ECM straight from art school, where he trained as a photographer. His first contact with the company was when he showed Wojirsch a photograph of a blue sky marked only with a distant aircraft vapour trail (an archetypal ECM image, subsequently used on a 1978 Azimuth recording), and has been part of the family ever since. Like Eicher and Wojirsch, he derives inspiration from painting; otherwise he confesses to a brief infatuation during the 1970s with the work of Hipgnosis. He recognises that record sleeves offer a freedom other areas of design would deny him and sees the process as threefold: 'You have a picture, which is a cut-out piece of the world, then you have a title which may have many associations, and thirdly you have the music.'

Rehm uses the Macintosh to help with typography, but without any great enthusiasm; his main interest is photography. He works with a small group of photographers who assist in his search for images that express the recurring ECM themes of solitude and beauty: the Hungarian Gabor Attalai and the Swiss Christian Vogt are ECM regulars; Eicher praises the black and white work of Jim Bengston. In recent years a more naturalistic tone has entered the photography, with less use of the cinematic drama exemplified by the Gary Peacock album *Guamba* (1987).

ECM packaging has its critics: the champions of the new brutalism in music and graphics claim to find it anodyne, a flight from reality. Others praise the fundamental honesty of expression and independence of vision that ECM has pursued for 25 years. The best ECM covers have a presence that justifies their claim to greatness. Through images that lead to introspection and what Eicher calls 'the inner landscape', they bypass the lingua franca of hype, and speak in the language of psychological archetypes. There are also many ECM imitators, but like fake Rolex watches sold on street corners, they are easy to spot.

Sources

Tony Wilson –
the postmodern
mythmaker.
Design Observer,
14 August 2007.
See pp.178–180.

Design Observer
playlist.
Design Observer,
18 April 2008.
See pp.181–182.

Bright side of the
sun. Publication
unknown, 2011.
See pp.183–185.

It's Nice That –
ten records. *It's
Nice That*, Issue 4,
October 2010.
See pp.186–187.

Are JPEGs the new
album covers?
Design Observer,
11 April 2007.
See pp.188–189.

Can by Can.
Sleeve note for
remastered reissue
of *Can*, Spoon/Mute
Records, 2006.
See pp.190–192.

Think of your ears
as eyes. *Eye* 16,
Winter 1995.
See pp.193–197.

Reviews

Logorama – the film[1]
2010

We learn to live with the encroachment of branding into daily life; like the weather, most of us just accept it as part of everyday living. But the more we become inured to the bludgeoning intrusiveness of commercial lapel-grabbing, the less likely we are to take notice of it: the inevitable consequence of this lack of attentiveness, is that the brand owners – and the designers who work for them – ramp up their efforts to engage our interest.

I caught a glimpse of the increasing intensity of these exertions when, just before Christmas, I went to the O2 Arena in London. I hadn't been to this national landmark before. Previously called the Millennium Dome it was built with public money to celebrate the start of the new millennium in 2000. It quickly became a subject of national ridicule. The writer Iain Sinclair called it a 'yellow-spiked Teflon tent like a genetically modified mollusc'. In 2001 the Dome was bought by the American billionaire Philip Anschutz, and in 2005 the naming rights were sold to O2, a British mobile phone company. Since then it has become an entertainment centre with a vast indoor arena and bars and restaurants.

The interior is undeniably impressive; its sheer scale is inspiring. Yet what struck me most was the staggering amount of corporate intervention. Giant BMW logos greet the visitor; brand messages fizz around the arena on electronic screens; every square inch is colonised by the brand hieroglyphics of banks, car makers, sportswear manufacturers, food companies and TV networks. It felt like a semi-hysterical display of infantile attention seeking: like being locked in a room with a thousand babies demanding to be fed.

A world entirely colonized by brand owners is the theme of a new film by French designers and filmmakers H5. *Logorama* is a slick 17-minute-long animated movie that appears to lampoon both the Hollywood blockbuster – violent, crude and adrenalised – and the world of branding, a world where logos festoon every surface and where it is normal to be exposed to brand activity at every turn [see p.379]. I say appears to lampoon, because the intention of the filmmakers is unclear.

The film is beautifully made. It is set, presumably, in a fictive Los Angeles – a CGI city that lives up to Reyner Banham's description of LA as 'Autopia' and a city of the 'immediate future'. The screen emits a supernatural brightness; colours pop with chromatic intensity; everything is hygienically pure; it's *Die Hard* with the product placements taking centre stage; it's a disaster movie set in Brand Utopia. It's what will happen when brands make movies (as if they don't already).

The movie tells the story of two cops (styled as rotund Michelin men) chasing a gun-toting, child-kidnapping, bad guy (Ronald MacDonald – who else?) through – in the words of the filmmakers – 'an over-marketed world built only from logos and real trademarks'. As the writer on motion graphics Mark Webster has noted, the film contains numerous subtleties and in-jokes: 'The Quicktime wall clock; the Energizer street lamps; the 007 guns and homage to Maurice Binder's barrel shot; KFC getting flattened by the beef jerky store, Slim Jim; and Ronald McDonald being taken out by Weight Watchers.' *Logorama* climaxes in a series of cataclysmic natural disasters engulfing this pixel-built city of a million brands.

But instead of turning us against brand ubiquity – something the O2 succeeded in doing to me – H5 leave the viewer with the suspicion that perhaps they think this logo-dominated, freeway-gridded world is really something to admire. It's almost as if they relish this homogenised world of brand ubiquity. Their famous music video for Röyksopp shows a similar fondness for the world of corporate infographics and PowerPoint pie-chart aesthetics.

So while I struggled to find the message in H5's film, I couldn't help being seduced by it. I was reminded that many of the logos on show are rather wonderful – fine examples of the art and craft of graphic design. And it's here perhaps, in the age-old conundrum that all designers face, that *Logorama*'s true worth might be lurking.

Logorama reminds us that our job, as designers, is to create seduction and allure for our clients, which like a lawyer defending a criminal, we mostly do with professional detachment. But as commentators have been telling us for decades, there are consequences – moral, political and cultural – attached to our desire to create this 'beautiful' world.

One of those consequences might just be a branded world like the one depicted in *Logorama*. Scary thought.

1. *Logorama*, written and directed by H5 (François Alaux, Hervé de Crécy & Ludovic Houplain), 2009. Production: Autour de Minuit.

Factory Records
The complete graphic album[1]
2007

A few years ago, I was asked to design a printed document to help promote the film *24 Hour Party People*, the spunky and hyperbolic retelling of the Factory Records' story. At the time, the movie was uncompleted, and something was needed to ignite the interest of foreign film buyers at one of the big international film markets.

I presented our work to the film's director Michael Winterbottom. We had created a spread of ideas that paid affectionate homage to Peter Saville's great Factory legacy [see p.380]. Winterbottom dismissed all our proposals. For him, Saville's disciplined aesthetic was only a small part of Factory's chaotic and tumultuous legacy. This view perhaps explains why Saville only appears fleetingly in Winterbottom's film, and why Central Station Design – and not Saville – created the movie's campaign graphics.

But it's different for designers: Saville's contribution to Factory is monumental. It looms large in the modern designer's imagination. It is one of the great tales of design mythology. It's that rare occurrence: the designer as hero; the designer as bona fide star.

I concede to no one in my admiration for Saville as a master of graphic styling. But he had help. In Factory's founder Tony Wilson, he had his own personal mythmaker. Wilson is the master spinner of pop myths, and Factory is the story of his ability to read the code of pop and relay it back to an audience hungry to buy into the great pop myths of outsiderdom, hedonism and death. Wilson, a loquacious, Cambridge-educated, Mancunian ('a 40-year-old hipster in baggy Comme Des Garçons' to use his own description), is probably the only boss of a record label capable of making references to Herman's Hermits, Anthony Burgess and the Marxist literary critic Terry Eagleton in the space of a few sentences. Yet despite Wilson's idealistic desire to create a genuinely enlightened record label (Factory famously had no contracts and bands were allowed to own their own music) there was another side to him: in his book *From Joy Division to New Order: The Factory Story* (1996),

Mick Middles describes Wilson as 'veering from Machiavellian cynical entrepreneur to artistically guided business buffoon'.

Looking back on Factory from the cool detachment of Matthew Robertson's new book, we see a utopian fusion of art, pop culture, design, style, business and inspirational pop music. But as Winterbottom's film makes clear – it wasn't really like that. Factory was a seething, hubristic, pharmaceutically-challenged mess. Death, guns, drugs, debauchery, bankruptcy were all active ingredients in the Factory story, and there were many tragic causalities along the way.

But regardless of the psychic and fiscal car wreck that Factory became, its graphic legacy stands proud, and in Matthew Robertson, Factory has found its archivist. He plots the story with dogged, genealogical thoroughness. I thought I knew the entire Factory catalogue, but Robertson has unearthed a few surprises. For anyone who thinks Factory is only Joy Division, New Order and Happy Mondays, this book will be an eye-opener.

Peter Saville didn't have a monopoly on Factory sleeves. A number of early covers were done by Martyn Atkins – sometimes on his own, and sometimes with Saville. Atkins went on to become an important music industry designer in the 1980s and his studio, Town and Country Planning, was responsible for sleeves for Depeche Mode and Echo and the Bunnymen. We also encounter Mark Farrow, whose early 80s Factory sleeves hint at the refined aesthetic he would later bring to his work for, amongst others, the Pet Shop Boys.

We also encounter Trevor Johnson who individually and as part of Johnson/Panas, carried on the typographically sophisticated tradition established by Saville and later by 8vo. 8vo's contribution, although smaller than Saville's, is almost as substantial: their cerebral cover art for Durutti Column and their majestic posters for The Haçienda, stand out as being amongst the most articulate graphic statements made in music design. Other designers who took the Factory shilling included Alan David-Tu, Julian Morey, Brett Wickens, Bill Smith, and even Neville Brody. And it wasn't only graphic designers who designed Factory sleeves; so too did the conceptual artist Lawrence Wiener, the music writer Jon Savage, and Tony Wilson himself.

Yet as Wilson notes in his introduction, 'the second half of the Factory story is best summed up by the painterly eccentricity of Central Station [Design].' It is Central Station Design (functioning like the Toulouse-Lautrec of Madchester) who chronicled the untidy demise of Factory. Their anarchic work – the antithesis of Saville and 8vo's controlled and formal expression – captured the hallucinatory implosion of the label, and as Winterbottom realised, created the most accurate picture of Factory.

Matthew Robertson has designed his book in a lucid if slightly pedestrian style. He also contributes an introduction, and as an ardent Factory admirer he sees only Factory's virtues; his tone is respectful and uncritical. These two small carpings aside, Robertson has created a rigorous and painstakingly assembled documentation of the Factory design story, and for this all Factory and graphic design fans should be grateful.

1. *Factory Records: The Complete Graphic Album (FAC 461)* by Matthew Robertson. Thames & Hudson, 2006.

Design disasters[1]
2009

The title of Steven Heller's book *Design Disasters* is a bit of Helleresque sensationalism. Perhaps the great man has been spending too much time casting his connoisseur's gaze over lurid pulp fiction book covers. The two 'D' words are cannily pitched to make us think about those hellish moments every designer has when work comes back from the printer on the wrong paper stock; or when the binding option we chose causes a brochure's spine to crack; or when the client's name is misspelt. Yet this is not a book about workplace mishaps or technical glitches. It's a book about the F word: failure, and the designer's psychological and practical relationship to it.

Failure stalks the designer's every move. Who has ever designed anything that was perfect? Who has ever – other than the terminally smug – held up a piece of work and said: 'I'm thrilled with every aspect of this'? We are far more likely to hear designers say: 'This is ok, but there's a widow on page 203 and it kills me.'

Perpetual dissatisfaction is the designer's natural state, and it's a refrain that runs through the twenty or so essays in this book. In an eloquent hymn to creative self-doubt the writer David Barringer defines the creative condition: 'It always helps to know that it's normal to regard one's work as both worthless and worthwhile. I have to reassure myself that it's worthwhile enough to have done it and yet not good enough to prevent me from continuing to improve and experiment.'

Barringer is just one of a group of able commentators assembled by Heller to muse on the subject of failure. All of them eschew the macho posturing of the dominant success culture that has been with us since the 1980s, in favour of embracing the rich possibilities afforded by failure, mistakes, wrong turnings and misjudgements of all kinds.

Richard Saul Wurman extols the heuristic benefits of failure. For him, failing is 'the moment of learning – the moment of jeopardy that is both interesting and enlightening. The fundamental means of teaching a course in structural engineering is to show the moment when a piece of wood breaks.'

More prosaically, Ralph Caplan points out the link between failure and embarrassment: 'Failure, which small children encounter at every turn, frustrates them, but it does not embarrass them ... As they grow older they develop what Adam and Eve got as a gift from God – a sense of shame that impedes learning for life.' Many of us will recognise this fear of embarrassment as the reason why we don't take risks, plumping instead for safety.

Since design is often seen as a quest for perfection, failure is regarded as something that has to be vanquished. Yet as writer after writer notes in the pages of this book, failure and mistakes can be the designer's guardian angel. There's even an argument to say that within the creative process, there is no such thing as failure. In her essay 'When Things Go Wrong', the designer Amanda Bowers quotes Aristotle: 'the accident reveals the substance of a thing'. And she reminds us that the 'Freudian slip' is often more revealing than the bald statement of fact.

There is even a place for deliberate error within creative endeavours of all kinds. The illustrator Dan Fern told me that he often left a cardboard frame on top of plies of images stored in the drawers of his plan chest. Every time he opened a drawer he found a new framing – sometimes one that he could use.

This splendid little book has a strong flavour of the zeitgeist about it. It barely merits its publisher's categorisation as a 'graphic design' title. In fact, it's a treatise for those who reject the now-discredited cult of success and winning. Who would have thought that this cult would ever be questioned, far less challenged. But thanks to one of the great 'failures' of the modern era – the cataclysmic collapse of banks and financial institutions around the world – we are being forced to re-examine notions of success and failure. The idea of the 'loser' – the idea of failure itself – is being reassessed before our eyes.

1. *Design Disasters: Great Designers, Fabulous Failures, and Lessons Learned* by Steven Heller [Ed.]. Allworth Press, 2008.

Obsessive branding disorder[1]
2008

Lucas Conley describes in vivid detail the extent to which branding has permeated modern culture, and the lengths to which brand owners will go to promote their products. This will not be news to graphic designers – especially those doing brand-related work. Designers will not be surprised to read about branded urinals; branded golf holes; branded beach sand; Proctor & Gamble sponsored mobile toilets; product placement in movies; fake bloggers eulogising products; 'customer evangelists' who use clandestine word-of-mouth strategies to sell toothpaste and deodorant to unsuspecting friends and neighbours.

What might come as a surprise, however, is to have the branding phenomenon forensically examined not by an anti-corporate, No Logo-advocate, but by a contributing writer to *Fast Company* magazine. Lucas Conley is a business writer. His measured and controlled indignation over the excesses of branding is not caused by moral or ethical considerations (although it's clear that he is personally affronted by much of what is going on); instead his indignation is based on far more pragmatic concerns.

In Conley's view, corporate America is in thrall to the cult of branding and this has led to the abandonment of the 'trusty, dusty principles of business – innovative products, good service, solid management' in favour of the 'idealism of branding ...' He berates executives for becoming 'so focused on the strength of the all-encompassing idea – the brand – that they ignore the physical properties that compose it.' In other words, branding has become the quick fix that promises instant success: why bother with expensive improvements to products and services when it is widely believed that a new logo, a ritzy strap line, and an online brand guidelines manual can do the job just as well and at a fraction of the cost?

Conley's book reads like a ripping yarn. He finds countless examples, from the mundane to the more sinister forms of invasive branding that threaten our sense of self. He believes that branding has led to the cult of 'instant behavioural transformations' and asks: 'What does it mean when our "sense of meaning" and our "sense of identity" are shaped by someone trying to sell us something?'

It might seem as if the culprits in all this are the ad agencies, but Conley sees branding as having 'superseded the advertising industry, either claiming advertising outright or dictating the message that advertisers are allowed to deliver. Increasingly, marketing has also become a division of branding.' And he does a good job at naming the professional culprits. Cincinnati is full of them, apparently. 'What Los Angeles is to plastic surgery,' Conley tells us, 'Cincinatti, Ohio, is to the branding business.'

And it's here, amongst the latter day equivalents of turn-of-the-century frontier snake-oil vendors, that Conley delivers one of his most damning indictments of modern branding. After an encounter with a branding fundamentalist, he notes: 'The more he describes branding, the more it appears to consist entirely of vague idealism and seemingly vain efforts to create something meaningful and permanent of what is often superfluous and transient. The simpler the product, the more Byzantine the branding seems.'

What does this mean for designers? If we put to one side the ethical and moral questions of being foot soldiers in the consumerist engulfment of modern life (in my view, a matter for individuals to decide for themselves), designers nevertheless have to question the practical wisdom of allowing graphic design to be subsumed into branding.

On the one hand it's a sensible way of maintaining demand for design services. Clients 'get' branding in a way they don't always 'get' design, so why not woo them with talk of 'brand promise' and 'brand essence'? On the other hand, it may not be such a smart business manoeuvre; by aligning itself with branding, design risks being sucked down with it when, as with most business credos, branding falls out of fashion or becomes discredited – and don't think it can't happen. Look at what happened to Wall Street's Masters of the Universe. Who would have guessed a year ago (six months ago!) that their financial wizardry would be exposed as not much better than banditry, and that they'd have to go begging to the government for a bail-out?

Yet perhaps graphic design's biggest mistake is the same mistake made by those businesses that are turning to branding for instant salvation. Conley nails the problem: '... branding, when it's consistent, provides us with clarity and simplicity in a progressively hectic world. But branding has become unhinged from its initial principles, and its aims have become increasingly exaggerated and warped.' Seems to me, we can say the same thing about graphic design. By allowing graphic design to jump the species barrier and become branding, designers acquire a new set of dubious guiding principles, and divorce themselves from the tradition of being an honest conduit for communicating simple truths. Sure, graphic design has always been used to wallpaper over cracks and create bogus impressions, but now that reduction and deception (to use two charges that Conley levels against branding) have become its raison d'être, graphic design is changed forever.

1. *Obsessive Branding Disorder: The Illusion of Business and the Business of Illusion* by Lucas Conley. PublicAffairs, 2008.

'Alan Fletcher Fifty years of graphic work (and play)'[1] 2007

There isn't a British graphic designer working today who doesn't owe the late Alan Fletcher a debt of gratitude. Fletcher did as much as anyone to create the model of a modern graphic designer. The undisputed monarch of British graphics, he oozed talent, wit, intelligence and the glamour of professional eminence. For the past four decades, graphic designers have craved his gruff approbation and taken delight in being admitted to his charmed circle.

Fletcher's ascent to the throne of British design began in the 1950s with a trip to the USA where he studied at Yale and met and worked with Paul Rand and Saul Bass. Returning to England in 1959 he later formed Fletcher/Forbes/Gill, where he combined his dry Anglo wit with US ad man Bob Gill's mercantile swagger and Colin Forbes' business nous.

When Gill left in 1965, Fletcher and Forbes formed Pentagram, an institution that has remained the benchmark for cultured independent design groups. Latterly, after retiring from Pentagram due to the intolerable demands of recessional early-1990s Britain, he retreated to his Notting Hill studio where he worked solely on projects of his own choosing including producing his magnum opus, *The Art of Looking Sideways* (2001) – a book of almost overpowering artistic and physical heft. But more importantly, Fletcher's final years offered a generation of younger designers a dignified lesson in growing older yet staying sharply relevant, a remarkable feat in a business obsessed with youth, the silicon wizardry of new technology and perpetual innovation.

And yet, unlike just about every other graphic designer I know, I never became a fully paid-up member of the Alan Fletcher fan club. Although he was universally worshipped, I stuck by my rather churlish opinion that anyone as widely revered as he was can't be that good. My guilt over this lack of enthusiasm for the great man was partly assuaged by his view that design solutions should derive from subject matter with no preconceived graphic style. Here was something I could hold against him. All my favourite designers had a 'preconceived style' – they were people with strong signatures. Fletcher's journeyman ethos, although professionally irreproachable, gave me a reason to resists his allure.

'Alan Fletcher – Fifty years of graphic work (and play)' at the Design Museum is unquestionably seductive. The man was a powerhouse of image generation. Ideas poured out of him and curator Emily King has done an inspired job of showing the breadth and range of his work. The show gets off to a dazzling start with his *Fortune* magazine covers from 1958–59. These are followed by beguiling Penguin jackets from the early 1960s; Pirelli ads from a slightly later period; and mountains of sketchbooks, posters and printed ephemera. Visitors will be charmed to see that one of his most famous works – the book jacket for Ernst Gombrich's *The Story of Art* (1995) – is an actual stone carved panel and not a graphic representation, as I'd always assumed it to be.

My personal favourite from the show is his 1965 identity for Reuters. This is a stunning piece of marketplace graphic communications – and showed that Fletcher could hack it with the best in the world when he tackled big, business-world projects.

Graphic Thought Facility's exhibition design neatly catches the pre-digital plan chest and Caran d'Ache aesthetics of Fletcher's work; letterheads are stuck inside Rymans see-through wallets and pinned to the wall; other exhibits are laid out in vitrines; others are suspended on modular frames. The effect is of casual informality and the freewheeling, undogmatic nature of Fletcher's work is allowed unfettered expression.

After an hour's close scrutiny I was nearly converted to the Fletcher faith. But not totally. For my brutish taste there are too many 'smile in the mind' moments: a self-initiated poster called 'Love is a Hole in the Heart' has a heart shaped hole in it; it looks better than a shop bought greetings card, but not much better. Yet despite the graphic puns and occasional moments of corniness, this is an exhibition that shows a master at work. Non-graphic designers can be encouraged to see it, safe in the knowledge that it will be enjoyed avidly. How many graphic design exhibitions can you say that about?

1. 'Alan Fletcher – Fifty years of work (and play)' exhibition at Design Museum, London, 2007.

Contemporary graphic design[1]
AGI (Alliance Graphique Internationale): graphic design since 1950[2]
2007

The Internet has changed graphic design book publishing. Publishers say that monographs, even of famous designers, don't sell anymore. The days are gone when David Carson could shift 200,000 copies of one of his books. But this is hardly surprising. Most designers have a website where their work can be viewed, so why would we spend money on a book when we can see the contents free online?

If you are prepared to hunt for it, nearly everything in Charlotte and Peter Fiell's blockbuster *Contemporary Graphic Design* (2007) is available to view online. But design books aren't finished yet. Designers still love books. Print reproduction is superior to on-screen reproduction, and the web simply can't match the tactile permanence of books, or the commentary and critique found in the best printed collections of graphic design.

Contemporary Graphic Design, however, is noticeably lacking in this regard. Apart from a thin introductory essay and a few words from each of the 117 contributors, it is 560 pages of commentary-free graphic imagery. The book is a sequel to the couple's equally gargantuan *Graphic Design in the 21st Century* (2003). The new volume uses the same format: each designer – or studio – gets four (sometimes six) pages to show sparsely captioned work. Biographical details, awards and clients are listed, and each entrant supplies a short statement about themselves – most of which sound numbingly similar.

The editors have rounded up a formidable list of contributors. Any book that includes work by Philippe Apeloig, Irma Boom, M/M (Paris) and Jan van Toorn can't be all bad. And although it's a pleasurable enough experience trawling through what is undoubtedly some of the sharpest contemporary graphic design around, certain large questions raise their heads. Why is much of what the authors class as graphic design in fact illustration? Why is there hardly any web design? What is the criteria for inclusion? I suspect that these and other questions will be considered otiose by many of the book's eager purchasers, excited by the prospect of gorging themselves on such an abundance of visual delights.

At 720 pages, *AGI (Alliance Graphique Internationale): Graphic Design Since 1950* (2007) is an even bigger book. But it is a bigger book in more than size; it has more commentary, and a much greater range of work on display. For many designers, AGI is a mysterious, Masonic-like organisation. Mention it to young designers and most of them look blank. Membership is confined to 300 or so individuals, and you can't apply to join, you have to be invited, and then you have your application vetted by sharp-eyed gatekeepers.

AGI's website describes it as uniting 'the world's leading graphics designers and artists in a professional club of common interest and achievement. It is an elite club. Its members have been collectively responsible for the identity design of most of the world's top corporations and institutions as well as for countless examples of globally known packaging, publications, illustration and posters.'

It's that word 'elite' that sits uncomfortably with the reality of modern graphic design, surely the most demotic of the visual arts? But reviewing the work in this book, it's clear that AGI comes close to encompassing the best that graphic design has had to offer over the past half century.

The book features the work of every member, living or dead, admitted to AGI since its inception in 1951. Amongst the stellar names you'll find Saul Bass, Wim Crouwel, FHK Henrion, Herbert Matter, Josef Müller-Brockmann, Bruno Munari and Paul Rand. And although its membership is predominantly American and European, AGI is admirably international in its ethos, and includes Brazilian, Iranian, Turkish and Venezuelan designers.

Each AGI member gets two pages in which to show images of work and provide a short biography. There is also over 200 pages of essays by, amongst others, Pierre Bernard, Bruno Monguzzi and Wolfgang Weingart. It's likely that the AGI book will appeal most strongly to AGI members, yet it's worthy of the attention of non-members. Even the most assiduous of design fans are likely to discover a few names that are unfamiliar, and the Bos' deft control of the editorial rudder makes it an enjoyable and informative tome to get lost in.

Inevitably, however, non-AGI members will be drawn back to the question, what is AGI for? In the interest of impartiality, I should declare that I was once 'put up' for AGI membership, and turned down.[3] I have no sour grapes about this. Groucho Marx's view on club membership is close to my own. But after spending a few enjoyable sessions with this book, I'm on the side of the argument that says it's better to have AGI than not to have it. And this massive authoritative volume is the evidence for the defence of that claim.

1. *Contemporary Graphic Design* by Charlotte and Peter Fiell [Eds.]. Taschen, 2007.

2. *AGI (Alliance Graphique Internationale): Graphic Design Since 1950* by Ben and Elly Bos. Thames & Hudson, 2007.

3. Later, in 2010, I was invited to put myself forward for a second time. On this occasion I was accepted.

Summer of love
Art of the psychedelic era[1]
2005

By chance, I read this book immediately after finishing the music critic Simon Reynolds' *Energy Flash* (1998). The book is an engaging survey of 'rave music and dance culture', and one of the few serious attempts to describe the hedonistic, 'second summer of love' of 1988. The current exhibition of psychedelic art at the Tate Liverpool (27 May–25 September 2005), for which the book under review is the show's catalogue, is an examination of the 'first summer of love' of 1967.

Reading both books in quick succession prompted the speculation that now that the art world, or at least Tate Liverpool, has deigned to recognise 1960s psychedelic art, we might soon see some publicly funded art institution staging an exhibition of the art of 'rave music and dance culture'. The notion of a show devoted to smiley-face nightclub flyers, drug education literature and Sven Väth album covers, seems less implausible than it might have done a year or two ago.

The art world's traditional resistance to 1960s psychedelic art is met head-on by Christoph Grunenberg, director of Tate Liverpool, and the catalogue's editor. He quotes art critic Dave Hickey's blunt assertion that psychedelic art is 'anti-academic' (Hickey contributes an essay to the catalogue, as does Reynolds). In a scholarly introduction, Grunenberg expands on this line of thought: 'We are dealing with an aesthetic which has generally been relegated to the realm of applied art, bad taste and stylistic aberration, obscured by an art historically and institutionally sanctioned view of the period which has positioned the aesthetically and conceptually purified statements of pop, minimal and conceptual art at the centre. There seems to be deep-seated suspicion towards psychedelic art's formal exuberance and its suspicious proximity to popular culture, suggesting the continued domination of high-modernist and formalist principles.'

If the Tate show is the first step towards dispelling the 'deep-seated suspicion', and allowing psychedelic art, with its grubby pop culture and pop music associations, to enter the sacred palace of art (a palace guarded zealously by curators, art historians and academics), then the art world should be aware that it is admitting another even less desirable alien: graphic design. Faced with the dizzying array of work in this exhibition – much of it beautifully reproduced in the catalogue – it's hard to avoid the conclusion that the best psychedelic art is, in fact, graphic design.

Grunenberg makes a strong case for the existence of 'pure' psychedelic art – paintings, films, sculptures and light-based installations. He writes: 'psychedelic art takes many stylistic forms, though most works share a bias towards a maximalist representation of cosmological visions through formally complex, obsessively detailed, self-involved abstract designs.' He offers work by artists Isaac Abrams, Lynda Benglis and Abdul Mati Klarwein, the latter famous for his album covers for Miles Davis and Santana, and cites the influence of psychedelic culture on Andy Warhol, Richard Hamilton and Robert Indiana.

Yet much of the psychedelic 'art' Grunenberg champions is barely recognisable as 'psychedelic'. When placed alongside the posters, the album covers, the clothes and the light shows (what another contributor to the catalogue calls 'the psychedelic vernacular'), it is abundantly clear that psychedelic art has its most pure and recognisable expression in graphic design – a fact that may delay the moment when psychedelic visual expression can claim full 'institutionally sanctioned' art world acceptance.

The sober and lucid design of this catalogue [see p.380], by London-based designers A2/SW/AK, raises the interesting question perennially faced by designers when designing art and design books: does the designer design the book in the style of the book's subject, or in a neutral style that allows the subject matter to stand in stylistic isolation? A2 wisely avoids designing in the psychedelic style. Instead, they lay the book out with rigour and elegance. As is customary in their work, A2 have designed a typeface especially for the project. The font they've created is a conventional typewriter-like font with just enough quirkiness to hint at mild psychedelic derangement.

1. *Summer of Love: Art of the Psychedelic Era* by Christoph Grunenberg [Ed.]. Tate Publishing, 2005.

Fanzines[1] 2011

This book is a densely illustrated and sharply argued history of the humble fanzine. Written by Teal Triggs, a graphic design academic, it is a switchback ride through the outlaw terrain of samizdat zine publishing. Triggs shows how fanzines offer a maverick history of pop culture; how they have acted as pathfinders for stylistic and editorial developments in mainstream media; and how they presaged the DIY publishing revolution made possible by the Internet.

Triggs is a surefooted guide: she maintains a cool analytical detachment and avoids tipping over into fanish obsession, or for that matter, academic turgidity. Her book begins by delving into the antecedents of zines. The term 'fanzine', she observes, was coined by the American sci-fi enthusiast and zine producer Louis Russell Chauvenet in 1940 'when he declared his preference for the term "fanzine" rather than "fanmag".' By 1949 the word had entered the cultural lexicon and appeared as an entry in the Oxford English Dictionary.

The author somewhat fancifully connects contemporary fanzines with publishing activity at the time of the French Revolution, Thomas Paine's pamphlet *Common Sense* (1776), and the engravings of William Blake (1778). She is, however, on more measurable ground when she links zines to the pamphleteering of Dada, Fluxus and the Situationists. From the publications of these avant-garde groups we can follow a lineage that travels through sci-fi 'fan' mags of 1940s America, on through the underground press of the 1960s, and finally arrives in the Xeroxed and stapled fanzines of the 70s and 80s.

If the punk eruption of the mid-70s ushered in an era of DIY music and labels, then a generation of writers, designers and editors also seized the moment to bypass the publishing establishment and speak directly to like-minded audiences. Triggs stresses the importance of Jamie Reid's *Suburban Press* (1970–75) – 'a Situationist-inspired publication that, along with *Sub* magazine and King Mob, provided a bridge between the hippie press and punk fanzines', and the appearance in 1976 of Mark Perry's *Sniffin' Glue*. She points out, however, that Perry rejected the 'first fanzine' tag and cited Greg Shaw's

Who Put the Bomp (1970–79) and Brian Hogg's *Bam Balam* (1974–c.1980s) as precursors.

It wasn't only music that fanned the fanzine revolution: oppositional political movements of all colours – anarcho-punks, skinheads and sexual revolutionaries – adopted the fanzine format to advance contrarian cultural and political agendas. Triggs devotes a chapter to the riot grrrl movement and its smart use of the fanzine format. She notes the radical subversion of feminine iconography – lipstick lettering, romance fiction, 50s housewives with aprons – to sanction the ethos that 'riot grrrls were both empowered to be feminists and had the choice to be feminine'.

Triggs makes the point that not all fanzines were oppositional, and that the scene has always been big enough to accommodate football zines, comic zines and 'a housewife from Virginia or from Hertfordshire producing a zine about collecting Pez dispensers'. She also notes the existence of a burgeoning meta zine culture involving fanzines about fanzines, academic symposia and zine festivals.

Fanzine producers were early adopters of the Internet. E-zines flourished around bulletin boards and the hacking and phreaking movements of the early 80s. But as vast swathes of the fanzine audience moved online, fanzine producers retained their stubborn fondness for paper and printed formats. Triggs quotes one zine theorist who noted that the Internet has made 'communication too easy and that the deviant socialization process of the underground might be lost as a consequence.' In the final chapter she identifies 'craft' and 'making by hand' as prime – if underrecognised – drivers in fanzine culture.

As a graphic designer in the 80s and 90s I was so bound up in learning the formal aspects of my craft – grids, the laws of typography and sophisticated production techniques – that I rarely felt much empathy with the seemingly chaotic and anti-formalist fanzine scene. Yet today, I look at the covers and spreads from early zines and I see a lost Eden: a graphic arcadia that has been submerged in a tidal wave of uniformity, visual conservatism, and the homogenizing effect of rampant commercialism.

1. *Fanzines* by Teal Triggs.
Thames & Hudson, 2010.

This ain't no disco[1]
2005

It's hard to imagine why this book exists. It mostly contains material which anyone with even a passing interest in record sleeve design will be abundantly familiar with, and it adds nothing to our understanding of a rich and fertile period in graphic design history – and record sleeve design history in particular.

The problems begin with the book's subtitle: 'New Wave Album Covers'. Since when were Roxy Music, Kid Creole, Peter Gabriel and Kraftwerk – to choose only four names – categorised as 'new wave'? Pop music categories are famously elastic and notoriously resistant to scholarly analysis (what is 'pop', for a start?), but in the late 1970s and early 1980s, there was an identifiable type of music called 'new wave.' At a stretch you can call most of the bands and musicians whose covers are featured in this book 'new wave', but it involves a very slack reading of the term. A more rigorous reading would demand that you dump dozens of the entries as ineligible.

The term was used to describe a strand of music that emerged from the infamous CBGBs club in New York in the late-1970s. It was applied to artists like Television, Patti Smith and Blondie in America; and in the UK to bands like The Jam, Elvis Costello and the Attractions and Joe Jackson. It's true that it became a term that was lazily applied to anything from the late-1970s to the mid-1980s that wasn't processed pop or disco; author Jennifer McKnight-Trontz (she's also the book's designer) takes full advantage of the elasticity and catch-all qualities of the name, but as a result her book is conceptually flawed.

In her introductory essay (which is as slim as Paul Weller's tie on the cover of The Jam's *In The City*), she acknowledges that 'new wave' encompassed many styles. She notes: '(It) comprised Post-Punk, Synth-Pop, Neo-Psychedelia, Neo-Mod, Power Pop, New Romantic, 2-Tone, and Goth ...' But this is almost the extent of her attempt to define the term. Sporadically, throughout the book, McKnight-Trontz adds tiny editorial footnotes. These scraps of usually banal information do little to increase our understanding of what we are looking at, and read as if they've been added by an external 'editorial' hand trying to give the book extra heft. (They also contain typos – *Rolling Stone* magazine is called 'Rollingstone' – and there is some dire hyphenation).

Typical of the sketchy inadequacy of the footnotes is an entry accompanying an unremarkable Eurythmics sleeve designed by Rocking Russian: 'Al McDowell formed the British design firm Rocking Russian. In 1980, McDowell along with ex-art director of *Vogue*, Terry Jones, started *i-D* magazine.' But the author appears to think that it is it not worth adding that McDowell is now one of Hollywood's foremost production designers whose credits include *The Terminal*, *Minority Report* and *Fight Club*? And while on the subject of McDowell, isn't the fact that he was the first employer of the young Neville Brody worth a mention?

In her introduction, McKnight-Trontz touches fleetingly on the most interesting aspect of the sleeves collected here. 'This was the last significant genre of music,' she writes, 'before the death of the LP, and therefore the last to exploit the glorious potential of the 12" square canvas.' You might quibble with her assertion that 'new wave' was the last genre of music to exploit the 12" square canvas; surely that was dance music, which championed the 12" vinyl disc into the 1990s and up to the present day? But her comment does draw attention to the fact that these covers are significant as the last hurrah of sleeve design before the marketing people moved in and brought with them the reduced canvas of the CD, the music video and the constraints of marketing-led music campaigns.

There are some great covers in this squat little book, and some complete stinkers, too. After salivating over covers by Barney Bubbles, Peter Saville, the great American art director Roy Kohara, and Keith Breeden, the forgotten genius of British sleeve design, you can guffaw at the sleeves of The Romantics who look as if they are having trouble breathing in their skin-tight magenta and pink leather suits. The lack of any real editorial stance means that superlative design is placed alongside kitsch to no apparent pattern. The result is that this is a book for nostalgia junkies rather than design enthusiasts.

1. *This Ain't No Disco: New Wave Album Covers* by Jennifer McKnight-Trontz. Chronicle, 2005.

'Cold war modern'[1]
2008

Prior to the global economy being chucked into the deep fat fryer, it was commonplace to read in the glossy interiors and architectural magazines about £250,000 kitchens. Readers were treated to beautifully art directed picture spreads showing sleek metropolitan types cooing over marble work surfaces and industrial-sized hobs. But as a dazzling exhibition at the Victoria and Albert Museum reminds us, the fetishisation of the kitchen isn't new.

There's an image in the 'Cold War Modern: Design 1945–1970' exhibition at the V&A that shows it wasn't just the space race and the arms race that were the battlefields of the Cold War. The 1950s kitchen, with its Formica surfaces, washing machines and labour-saving appliances, was one of the more unlikely staging grounds for the ideological battle that raged between East and West. In an unforgettable photograph taken at the American National Exhibition in Moscow in 1959, Nikita Khrushchev and Richard Nixon are seen shoulder to shoulder, gazing at a modern fitted kitchen. They have such serious-browed expressions that they might be surveying the arsenals of weapons that both superpowers were amassing.

It's tempting to think that as the world shivered under the threat of nuclear Armageddon, the humble kitchen with its utopian promise of the end of drudgery was really what the Cold War was all about. It's just one of hundreds of images and artefacts on show at this most engaging exhibition. 'Cold War Modern' is a bravura melding of political history and design history, and provides a ringside seat to that white-hot moment when the world changed faster than it had ever changed before.

The exhibition celebrates the transformation of the developed world from the machine era into the era of space travel, scientific discovery and mass produced technological goods. And it tells us that it is the design of buildings, products and clothes, as well as the art of the time, that defines this era best. This was the first time that design was the defining characteristic of the age. If we think back to the Victorian era, design was something that only the rich could enjoy. Later, with the modernists, it was for the avant-garde. But here was design that had freed itself from the yoke of formalism and the aping of natural forms. Here was design that could be enjoyed – and used – by everyone. Here was design that offered a utopian sense of universal enfranchisement. And it is astonishing to think that this design revolution was made possible by the same technological and scientific revolution that produced the atomic bomb. Annihilation and salvation in the same package.

What 'Cold War Modern' shows is that artists, designers and engineers working under the tension of the nuclear threat produced work of visionary daringness. It suggests that the creative spirit, to perform at its best, needs a dizzying mixture of opportunity and fear. Perhaps, as we face our own equivalent of the postwar nuclear nightmare – ecological disaster – a new design vision will emerge to get us through it. 'Cold War Modern' is brilliantly curated (by Jane Pavitt and David Crowley) and brilliantly designed (by Universal Design Studio with graphics by Bibliothèque). It made me nostalgic for the future. It made me want to go back to the future. It looks like a much better place.

1. 'Cold War Modern: Design 1945–70' exhibition at the V&A, London, 2008.

Volume: writings on graphic design, music, art and culture[1]
2011

It's an odd experience to review a book in which you find yourself to be the recipient of a hearty kicking by the author. It's even odder to find that you are nevertheless full of admiration for the writer's calm-eyed analysis of the design world. I don't deserve the kicking, but more of this later.

Kenneth FitzGerald's *Volume: Writings on Graphic Design, Music, Art and Culture* (2010) is an important addition to the library of graphic design writing. Many followers of the discourse surrounding design over the past two decades will be familiar with FitzGerald's texts, principally for *Emigré*, but also *Eye*, *Voice: AIGA Journal of Design* and occasionally for this site [Design Observer]. He is currently Associate Professor of Art at Old Dominion University in Norfolk, Virginia.

FitzGerald is a fine writer with a gift for potent phrases ('As no military plan survives contact with the enemy, no design concept survives contact with the client.') His prose is agile, unmannered, and always at the service of strong ideas born out of wide reading and deep engagement with contemporary culture, of both high and low varieties (look out for references to Thomas Pynchon *and* Garth Brooks). In other words, he's highly readable. This is important. Design critics bemoan the lack of interest in design writing (it's a near constant theme in FitzGerald's book). But shouldn't writers bear some responsibility for this? When designers say they don't read, the onus is – at least partly – on writers to make their writing more engaging. It can't all be down to language-averse designers – can it?

Volume brings together a batch of FitzGerald's essays and corrals them into four sections. In fact, the book reads as one longish mediation around a few recurring themes: a stubborn refusal to accept received wisdom (Lester Bangs is a hero); regret over the disinclination of professional designers to engage in critical self-investigation; the difference between art and design; design education; and the idea that the design world is as much stratified by class as any other world.

Volume opens with an essay in which FitzGerald questions his fitness to teach: 'I warranted suspicion as a recent MFA graduate with "little or no professional practice or teaching experience" ... I was teaching some undergraduates with more professional experience than I had.' But his self-doubt is unfounded. In a later chapter he describes some of his classroom exercises. These make him sound like an inspirational instructor, and my guess is that the classroom is his natural habitat.

FitzGerald is at his incisive best when he brings his forensic gaze to bear on the class system that is built into design. In his view, the naked bones of design's class structure can be seen in the work of elite designers employed by 'celebrity-oriented, moneyed cultures (fashion, architecture, entertainment, and the arts)'. His willingness to expose design's stratification extends into his teaching strategies: 'I urge students to adopt awkward methods, and embrace the unfamiliar. Often, these are no more exotic than working at a dramatically different speed. This is different from the standard academic tactic of introducing them to "new ideas".' He goes on to note dismissively that 'new ideas' usually means exposure to the works of established designers: 'Emulating an admired artist is the standard method of directing students toward a sophisticated model of creativity ... [students] are called upon to simultaneously regard and ignore the work, as we don't want them copying it.'

It's not only his students FitzGerald wants to refrain from gazing admiringly at the great and the good of the design world. His own combative approach to criticism means that he doesn't shy away from roughing up representatives of design's elite: Alan Fletcher ('*The Art of Looking Sideways* ... a formless data-dump of quotations, aphorisms, diagrams, reproductions, commentaries, and folderol'); John Maeda ('sterile, programmed ornamentation'); Paul Rand ('... students will become even more marginalized and disenchanted with their work and status if they attempt to define themselves by Rand's fallacies'); and Stefan Sagmeister ('*Made You Look* ... a fatiguing compendium of almost every optical, production, and advertising-creative artifice devised since Gutenberg').

In the final group of essays ('Inference and Resonance'), FitzGerald moves away from what we might call the politics of design to the philosophy of design. Here he meditates on the big questions that stalk the design jungle such as graphic design's relationship with art. He is not in the least starry-eyed about art, and he's quick to point out art world hypocrisy and double-dealing: 'It is a delusion that the activity of fine artists is divorced from commercial considerations. It isn't even a matter of degree. All that separates art and design is the kind of marketplace one chooses to operate in.'

This willingness to attack sacred cows makes FitzGerald an entertaining commentator. But it also raises the question – what does he really believe in? Occasionally I have the suspicion that he is a sharp-brained polemicist who can muster an argument in favour – or against – any known view. This is relevant to the kicking I receive from him.

FitzGerald takes me to task for a short review I wrote of *Emigré* No.64: *Rant* for *Eye* magazine ('Back on the old battleground', *Eye* 48, Summer 2003). In retrospect, I admit to a bit of over-heated rhetoric, and feel chastened by the swish of FitzGerald's corrective rod. But I stand by the gist of what I wrote. I criticized the writers in *Rant* for their preoccupation with a 'wished for' design world where designers were free to make the sort of work that restored graphic design to its avant-garde roots, yet simultaneously failed to recognise the mundanities of working life in the 'trenches' – FitzGerald's word, not mine.

The reason I stand by what I wrote is helpfully provided by FitzGerald himself: in his essay 'Trenchancy', he writes: 'Consideration of the spectrum of design activity from Massimo to MacTemp usually focuses on the upscale.' My point exactly: if critics focus only on the Massimo component of design, critical writing will remain irrelevant to most designers.

And besides, not all designers need to engage with critical thinking, design theory and the higher discourse. Those of us who are perpetually examining ourselves and our craft – and doing the same to others – are often riven with doubt, fear and loathing. Sometimes it's enough just to be good at your job. Sometimes it's OK not to want to open the box and look inside. But after reading Kenneth FitzGerald, you'd probably want to have at least a peek.

1. *Volume: Writings on Graphics Design, Music, Art and Culture* by Kenneth FitzGerald. Princeton Architectural Press, 2010.

'Communicate' at the Barbican[1]
2004

'Communicate', the 40-year retrospective of graphic design currently showing at the Barbican in London, affords a rare opportunity for the general public to view graphic design in a gallery space. Of course, there are those who say that graphic design has no business hanging on gallery walls; the place for graphic design, these pragmatists will argue, is in the marketplace solving the problems of commerce.

But you only have to look around to see that graphic design has become a cultural force that – occasionally – transcends the mundane requirements of business, branding and messaging. It's part of the culture now. We seem to have reached a point where we can enjoy graphic design as graphic design. In 'Communicate', curator Rick Poynor has assembled a potent collection of exhibits that can be enjoyed purely for their aesthetic worth.

Yet 'Communicate' has been shamefully ignored by art and cultural critics. *The Times* and *Guardian* unimaginatively turned to Poynor to write about his own show. (*The Times* also invited Peter Saville to produce a companion piece to Poynor's article: and in the interest of full disclosure, I should mention that I 'previewed' the show for *The Sunday Times*' CD Rom, 'The Month'.) But why didn't Jonathan Glancey, Stephen Bailey, or even Will Self, wander down to the Barbican with a sharp pencil and an even sharper critical eye?

The only blip on the otherwise flatline of critical interest was a whimsical think-piece by former *Melody Maker* journalist Caitlin Moran. In her column in *The Times Weekend Review* ('Wallowing in the Shallow', 18 September 2004), she delivered a dismissive and sniggering rebuke to graphic design in general, and the 'Communicate' show in particular. Now, I admit we designers can't have it both ways: if we want our craft to be taken seriously, we have to be prepared, as designers, to take criticism, and as a rule designers are not very good at taking criticism. Design doesn't have much tradition of criticism: boy bands, computer games, stand-up comedians, architecture, interiors and furniture get written about critically, but no one thinks it's worth reviewing graphic design.

So personally, I welcome Moran's views. However, she should be careful about allowing the word 'shallow' to appear above any article she writes. This word aptly describes her attempt at a critical appraisal of graphic design. She kicks off by declaring 'Let's face it – the primary purpose of graphic design is so that people who wear too many trainers to buy proper art have something to put in their front room'. She goes on: '"Communicate" ... is a slightly classier version of walking around the bit in Ikea where they have all those framed pictures of giant peonies for £12.'

There's more in this critical-lite vein. In Moran's view, graphic design is something you hang in the front room, and she fails signally to take seriously either design's professional manifestations as a modern business tool, or its more cultured role as a way of defining the zeitgeist in a world dominated by the visual. She reveals her hand when she writes: 'As amazing and iconic as the cover to *Sgt Pepper* is, it's dwarfed by the record that sits inside it. No one's had their life changed by the cover of *Sgt Pepper*. No one's fallen in love to it. No one's described it to someone in a coma. Michael Jackson didn't want to buy the rights. It doesn't make you cry.'

It's possible to challenge almost every daffy assertion made by Moran here. Take her shallow-as-a-puddle opinion that graphic design isn't life-changing. She clearly hasn't met many graphic designers, or bothered to ask the ones she has met what made them become graphic designers in the first place. If I had a fiver for every designer who decided to take up the craft because of an epiphany-like exposure to a Peter Saville Factory record cover, or seeing the mid-80s work of Neville Brody, I'd be enjoying a well-upholstered retirement in the Caribbean. You might not chose to 'describe' graphic design to someone in a coma (you're right there, Caitlin), but an encounter with a piece of graphic design might well set someone off on a satisfying and fulfilling career that lasts a lifetime.

It's hard to get cross with Moran, though; it is refreshing to find graphic design discussed in a serious newspaper, even if her tone rarely rises above the level of a *Hello!* editorial (I presume *Hello!* has editorials?). And Moran's response is at least preferable to that of the art critic who Patrick Burgoyne, editor of *Creative Review,* invited to write about the show: after visiting the exhibition, the critic declined his invitation. Perhaps it doesn't matter that the critical elite have avoided writing about 'Communicate'; according to the Barbican press office: 'Daily attendances are more than double that anticipated, and in the first five weeks the figures are over half our budgeted income.'

1. 'Communicate' exhibition at the Barbican, London, 2004.

Robert Brownjohn: sex and typography
2006

There's an essay on Liberace by art critic Dave Hickey in his book *Air Guitar* (1997). It's an essay so full of vivid insight that it persuaded me, on a recent trip to the US, to visit the Liberace Museum in Las Vegas. Amongst other things, Hickey describes the great entertainer's visit to drab postwar Britain in 1956. Liberace's arrival in Britain caused a furore. He was the Lady Gaga of his era, and as a consequence, he was subjected to indignant abuse by the reactionary popular press. *The Daily Mirror* wrote: 'Without doubt he is the biggest sentimental vomit of all time. Slobbering over his mother, winking at his brother, and counting the cash at every second, this superb piece of calculating candy floss has an answer for every situation ... [a] slag heap of lilac-coloured hokum.' Liberace sued and won substantial damages.

Hickey uses Liberace's castigation by the British press for some typically sharp-brained conjecture. He writes: 'But what intrigues me about (the) invective is the possibility that it might just mark the official beginning of the "Sixties", as we call them. Because Liberace had this great idea. He had touched a jangling nerve, and I like to imagine young John and Paul up in Liverpool, young Mick and Keith down in London, little David Bowie, and the soon-to-be Elton John, in their cloth caps, all full of ambition and working class anger, looking up from their *Daily Mirrors* with blinking lightbulbs in talk balloons above their heads.'

Liberace's taboo-busting outrageousness may well have marked the beginning of the 60s (the historian Arthur Marwick, in his book *The Sixties*, 1998, defines the era as running from 1958 to 1974), but for us Brits, Hickey is describing something else as well. He is describing the beginnings of a mass adoption of American popular culture by a British populace emerging from its feudal past into the electronic media age.

Brits growing up in the second half of the 20th century grew up in thrall to America pop culture. It was unavoidable, and for most of us (there were of course some dissenters) it was a thrilling encounter. American pop culture seemed utopian and offered a striking alternative to the staid life of the average Briton. And even if you despised the hegemony of American political culture, which many left-inclined people did, you could still embrace US music, movies and art without demur: Mick Jagger famously turned up at the Grosvenor Square anti-Vietnam demonstration at the same time as he was making records that sounded as if he'd been born in Memphis.

The influence of American pop music (especially black music genres) on British pop music, and the way it was subsequently re-imported to the US, is well documented. But the current exhibition at London's Design Museum devoted to Robert Brownjohn, and the publication of *Sex and Typography* (2006), Emily King's examination of Brownjohn's life and work, neatly illustrates British graphic design's epiphany-like encounter with American graphic design in the early 1960s.

Brownjohn wasn't the only American designer to arrive in Britain at this time. There were others – most notably Bob Gill and Lou Klein – and they shook up the moribund British advertising and design scene with a splash of US graphic swagger. The British designer Alan Fletcher was typical of a British sensibility that looked to America for inspiration. In *Sex and Typography*, Fletcher eulogises the American mini-invasion: 'What impressed me was there was a group of them, about eight or ten of them, all the same age, trying to do the same thing. There were designers like that in London, but there were fewer of them and they were less – how can I put this? – well, I found them less interesting.'

British graphic design, during the early and middle part of the 20th century, wasn't often able to match the fizz of American design, or the studied introspection of European design. Britain, having famously resisted European Modernism between the wars, preferred instead to cling to its Victorian past – a past where Britannia had ruled a vast global empire and where it was imagined that if you were British you'd won first prize in the lottery of life. Why give all that up for concrete, rectilinear architecture and asymmetrical typography?

But many British graphic designers (Ken Garland, for example) were attracted to the refracted modernism of the American designers. They liked the mercantile strut of American graphics. They liked the fact that here was graphic design at the heart of mass advertising and big business. But most of all they liked the fact that American graphic design was about 'ideas'.

British graphic design throughout the 60s and 70s was fixated with the notion that all graphic design statements had to be underpinned by an 'idea'. This normally meant puns and allusive jokes. Design annuals from the period are full of visual gags. Training in a studio in the mid-1970s I was always asked what my 'idea' was? I didn't always have an 'idea'. I liked design that gave aesthetic pleasure and so chose colours and typefaces that I liked or that suited the task rather than underpinning everything with an idea. This was usually met with scowls and disapproving chin stroking. I blame Robert Brownjohn for this. Like Liberace, he's got a lot to answer for.

1. *Robert Brownjohn: Sex and Typography* by Emily King. Laurence King Publishing, 2005.

'Slightly off the ground'
Vaughan Oliver and v23 poster designs[1]
2007

Music industry fly posters, put up in British cities in the middle of the night by illegal street teams, used to form a vast urban tableaux of what Vaughan Oliver calls 'free art'. Advertising the latest albums and singles, many of these posters were examples of graphic art at its most expressive and unrestrained.

But the music industry poster is a thing of the past. Fly posters have been successfully outlawed by city councils who claim to be reducing visual pollution, but who are in fact preserving the urban terrain for big buck advertisers. Record labels no longer even bother with 'legal' shop posters either, and as a consequence, music posters have joined vinyl album covers as cherishable artifacts from a nostalgia-soaked and increasingly distant past.

Viewing 'Slightly Off the Ground', a collection of Vaughan Oliver and v23's posters, mostly for the label 4AD, is to realize that in Oliver's hands the large format poster is an even better setting for his vivid displays of theatrical typography and dramatically charged imagery than the 12" album cover. Most of the posters are derived from Oliver's celebrated 4AD sleeves. In fact, he describes his posters as 'reconfigured album covers'. Many are encased in elegant black frames, but the show is greatly enhanced by large partitions made out of corrugated zinc fencing on which real fly posters have been stuck. These installations effectively replicate the experience of encountering banks of multiple posters in the street.

By chance, on the day that I visited the gallery – a moodily lit modern space on the campus of Kingston University in southwest London – Oliver was present. He showed me round, telling stories about the genesis of many of the works on display. Many of his best known images have their inspiration in childhood incidents or remote and highly personal observations.

Oliver is a likeable man. People who meet him expect a darkling prince from a Tarkovsky movie, or a man riven with poetic tumult and occult imaginings. Not so; he's big, burly and cheerful, with a sly sense of humour and speaks in a softly musical County Durham accent. He talks about his work like a benign football manager describing the merits of his affectionately regarded team. It was hard to keep in mind that this was the same man who can be seen on one of his most famous album covers – The Breeders' *Pod* – dancing naked except for large, flapping eels strapped to his waste [see p.381].

Oliver has joined that small group of graphic design immortals. Like all great designers, his work is instantly recognizable and seems above the humdrum preoccupations of mere graphic communication. Nevertheless, Oliver is a man without a clear direction. Ever since he was ejected from the enchanted garden of 4AD (while at the label, Oliver was given a studio, a handsome retainer and enough creative freedom to satisfy a regiment of designers), he has struggled to replicate the creative fecundity of this golden era. 'Slightly Off the Ground' reminds us of Oliver's greatness, but begs the question, what's next?

1. 'Slightly Off the Ground' exhibition at Kingston University, London, 2007.

Instant light
Tarkovsky Polaroids[1]
2006

Film directors who began their careers as stills photographers are not as common as might be expected. Stanley Kubrick is perhaps the most celebrated example. Larry Clark is another. Considering the epic stillness found in the films of Andrei Tarkovsky (1932–86), and considering his grand obsession with the filmic suspension of time, it is not surprising to discover that the visionary Russian (actually born in Belarus) director was also a gifted snapper.

Tarkovsky is one of the great aesthetic filmmakers. His films are cinematic poetry, suffused with a lambent intensity rarely found in contemporary cinema. He is the antithesis of modern Hollywood filmmakers. Tarkovsky is about introspection and, above all else, slowness, while modern cinema, with its motorised editing and attention-grabbing micro-narratives, is about extroversion and frenetic speed. As Maximilian Le Cain has written: '... he (Tarkovsky) proposed a cinema based on the rapt observation of the present moment as opposed to a plot-driven preoccupation with what will happen next.'

The famed Tarkovskian themes of memory, decay, melancholy, nostalgia and the effects of light, can be seen in the sixty Polaroids assembled in this handsome little book. Once you get past the initial shock of finding his distinctive imagery crammed into the square, white-bordered format of the Polaroid – and not the more generous ratios of the cinema screen – you realise that Tarkovsky's oeuvre is well suited to the static medium of the still photograph.

The Polaroids are reproduced at actual size and form a dreamlike mapping of Tarkovsky's elegiac sensibility. The images were taken between 1979 and 1984, and document time spent in Russia and in Italy, where, exiled from his native land, the director spent his last years. They show tender scenes of family life, mist-festooned landscapes and Vermeer-like domestic interiors.

In the age of digital photography, Polaroids are a neglected medium. They have their own aesthetic flavour: a sort of nostalgic, almost vulnerable quality that makes them closer to paintings than to photographs. Since paintings cannot be 'recreated' by going back to a negative, they share with Polaroids the distinction of being 'originals' – a state that makes them vulnerable to both damage and the passing of time, which in turn imparts a quality of preciousness.

For Tarkovsky, as a master of slowness and stillness (he wrote a book of film theory called *Sculpting Time*, 1989), the difference between his photography and his filmmaking is slight. Screen ratios apart, it is almost as if the images in this book are frames from his movies. Yet these poignant glimpses of Tarkovsky's life away from filmmaking throw up the difference between shooting photographs and shooting film: in film, every image is part of a sequence of images; the director and cinematographer have to concern themselves with the next image and the one after that, as well as the frames that have gone before. With stills photography, there is only the single moment.

1. *Instant Light: Tarkovsky Polaroids* by Giovanni Chiaramonte and Andrei A Tarkovsky [Eds.]. Thames & Hudson, 2004.

Bossa Nova and the rise of Brazilian music in the 1960s: original cover art[1]
2011

Like pewter beer mugs and horse brasses on the walls of English pubs, album covers are now part of the nostalgia industry. There is already a generation whose idea of sleeve art is circumscribed by the postage stamp-sized JPEG covers on iTunes. In the digital domain, the album cover has been dragged into the trash icon of history. If not quite dead yet, cover art is beginning to smell funny.

So why do we still have a stream of books devoted to the subject? Well, it seems that amongst certain types of musico-cultural anthropologists the appetite for cover art remains as strong as ever. For image-hungry cool hunters, graphic designers, illustrators and, of course, music nostalgiaists, the album cover retains its emblematic allure: LP sleeves have become the Ordnance Survey maps of musical psychogeography.

This collection of Bossa Nova cover art, mainly from the 1960s, is the second such offering from compilers Gilles Peterson and Stuart Baker. Previously they strip-mined the depths of revolutionary black jazz, resulting in *Freedom, Rhythm and Sound* (2009). Now comes a similar act of reclamation, this time of the album covers of the music widely known as the putative soundtrack to the early 1960s jet-set and cocktails lifestyle.

In an informative essay, Baker delineates the history of Bossa Nova. He describes how the music grew out of the indigenous samba rhythms of Brazil, and how it was shaped by the nation's 'search for a national cultural modernism'. He charts the growth of the music beginning with the young João Gilberto performing in apartments, displaying his new style of singing and guitar playing – 'a "conversational" voice distilled to a whisper without an ounce of tremolo, accompanied by a unique guitar beat derived from emulating the rhythmical pattern of the pandeiro (a type of tambourine) played in samba groups.' He concludes with the phenomenal success of the Bossa Nova sound on the international stage in the 1960s.

Most of the album covers featured here combine a dash of sans serif modernist rigour (many are in black and white) with the free expressionism of Reid Miles's famous Blue Note covers and the sleeve art of American exotica and easy-listening jazz recordings. If Bossa Nova sleeve designs are not as original or as uniquely Brazilian as the music they enwrap, most of the covers have an airy magic that is hard to resist. They are well suited to the vapour-light, warm-breeze propelled music. And like all the best album covers, they make you itch to hear the music.

Soul Jazz should put a bit more effort into the design and production of their books. The design of Bossa Nova is rudimentary and the production is basic. At a time when all printed matter is under threat from electronic downloads, books need a powerful reason to exist – and one of those reasons is high quality presentation. I know designers who would like this book but will be put off by the quotidian layout.

1. *Bossa Nova and the Rise of Brazilian Music in the 1960s: Original Cover Art* by Gilles Peterson and Stuart Baker [Eds.]. Soul Jazz Records, 2010.

The Blank Tape Spillage Fete
2006

Cecil Sharp House – home of the English Folk Dance and Song Society – sits incongruously between the grimy street theatre of Camden Town and the celebrity-clogged enclave of Primrose Hill. It has the musty ambience of a village hall, and like a well-tended war memorial it seems impervious to the modern world. I can't think of a better location for an exhibition devoted to that quaint artefact of recent audio folklore – the cassette tape.

Cassettes, like corn dollies and hand-made clogs, are relics from a pre-digital world. I hadn't spotted it before but the plastic casing of an audiocassette, with its two spooling holes, closely resembles the human face. In the era of recorded music as an invisible data-stream, there is an endearingly humanistic quality to cassettes, with their warm enveloping bath of tape hiss and their propensity to snag and break.

The organisers of The Blank Tape Spillage Fete, Mat Fowler and Matt Hunt, invited 21 artists to each fill a cassette with music and create artwork to go with it. The result is a delightful outpouring of outsider audiovisual art: like an episode of *Vision On* presented by Joseph Beuys, with a soundtrack lifted from a 1960s John Wyndham TV dramatisation.

Beat-up portable tape players, many smeared with dirt and disfigured with hand-writing, are laid out on the sort of trestle tables more commonly used to display jars of home made jam, and visitors are invited to listen to the music on headphones. Bunting and paper doilies add to the notion of a fete in the Village of the Damned. In an hour's worth of listening, I didn't find a single piece of music without merit; it was a mix of nu-folk, lo-fi camp-fire rumbling and electronic drones. Was this an early sighting of a New Weird Albion school of outsider folk and crumbly electro? Contributors who stood out were Russell Warwicker, MMC, Phil Gardner, Erotic Dog, My Dark Aunt, Marcus Oakley, Woodworms (featuring the sounds of Giffle) and the organisers' own band, Bontakt. But I could name a dozen others.

Mayo Bucher: open sign [1]
2002

For the past thirty years, ECM founder Manfred Eicher has run his famous record label with visionary zeal, oblivious to the conventions and diktats of the modern music industry [see pp.193–197]. ECM is almost as famous for its cover art as it is for Eicher's towering musical achievement as a producer and label owner. But fans of the label's idiosyncratic sleeves regret the retirement of the legendary Barbara Wojirsch. Her design credit on an ECM cover was a guarantee of stylistic diversity and typographic purity. A devotee of Tschichold, she pioneered the austere, sans serif modernist look that remains the label's hallmark to this day.

Since Wojirsch's departure, Eicher has developed an over-reliance on monochrome photography, usually wintry landscapes and numinous phenomena from the natural world. These photographs are undeniably beautiful, but after a while they pall, and you find yourself yearning for the range, depth and aesthetic quirkiness that Wojirsch brought to ECM covers. But hidden amongst the many desolate landscapes and mournful shorelines, you'll find the work of artist Mayo Bucher. The Swiss-born artist offers a painterly alternative to the visionary photographic landscapes.

Bucher's paintings combine two fundamentals of visual expression: abstraction and geometry. You might say the spiritual and the pragmatic; reality and unreality; silence and noise. It's therefore hardly surprising that Eicher should find a resonance in Bucher's work, as these are the themes that define Eicher's aesthetic endeavours as a music producer. Bucher's canvasses are rich, textural exercises in colour and mood; occasionally dark and brooding, sometimes light and transcendent. Into his Rothko-like surfaces, Bucher occasionally gouges wire-thin lines. Sometimes only a single line of Klee-like purity is dragged across a canvas. Sometimes he makes more complex diagrammatic constructions that remind you of the sad beauty of dimly remembered school geometry textbooks.

Bucher trained in Switzerland as a graphic designer. It shows in his confident use of brutal letterforms (he favours a robust Brody-esque Compacta) enlarged to nudge the extremities of his canvasses. The book *Open Sign* is the usual superb Lars Müller production.

1. *Open Sign* by Mayo Bucher
and Bernhard Bruckmann.
Lars Müller Publishers, 2006.

Scott King: art works[1]
2011

Can design be art? This question remains a persistent favourite amongst graphic designers. But increasingly it feels like an old and tired debate – especially when you consider the astonishing levels of interest amongst the current generation of design students in using design skills to tackle social issues. And yet, because I keep meeting designers who think, speak and behave like artists, I can't quite forget about this old chestnut. Like a throbbing boil on the end of my nose, I just can't help noticing it.

I blame it on the tutors in design schools. There is a generation of tutors who were radicalized in the 90s and who now hold senior positions within design schools. These teachers – mostly in their 40s – were inspired by the notion of the designer-as-author. They threw out the 1980s fixation with designing wine labels and logos for pasta restaurants, and replaced it with self-initiated briefs and the cult of self-expression.

The result of this is an education system – in the UK, at least – that produces large numbers of graphic designers who view their work with the inward-looking subjectivity of fine artists; designers who produce work laden with autobiographical intent and self-expression; a generation who yearn to see their work on gallery walls (or their contemporary equivalent – design books) and whose ambition is to produce design solely to be admired by other designers.

None of this bothers me. From the time I started my first studio in 1988 I've agonised over the role of design education and the suitability of graduates for the workplace. But not anymore. I've stopped fretting: people go to art school to study a subject they love, and until the fees climb to a level that only the children of Russian oligarchs can afford, idealistic people will want to go to art school to have their molecules shaken up. And they should be allowed to do so.

Yet I still come back to the question: are those designers who are currently making design to hang on gallery walls, and for use in books and blogs intended for other designers, doing art or design? One place to look for an answer is in the work of Scott King. Conveniently, he has recently produced a monograph – *Scott King: Art Works* (2010).

This is not – repeat not – a standard graphic design monograph. It is full of witty and acerbic commentaries on the contemporary scene. It contains unfussy, often brutal work, and is not in the least self-congratulatory. King's mode is oppositional, contrarian, occasionally offensive, but always self-doubting. And self-doubt is not a good quality for a graphic designer: graphic design is about upbeat optimism, and the fiercely held conviction that designers are always right, and that the message is always worth broadcasting. Graphic designers are like puppies – endlessly exuding good feeling and happiness. Imagine an ad for washing-up powder that said – 'well, we think this powder will get your clothes clean, but maybe not always. There might be times when it, you know, doesn't work too well.' Unthinkable, of course, but that's what happens when you have self-doubt: you start telling the truth.

Does King's self-doubt – his truthfulness – make him an artist? His early career places him firmly in the graphic design camp. He was born in 1969, and studied graphic design at Hull. He worked as art director of *i-D* and was creative director of *Sleazenation* (his famous Cher Guevara cover for *Sleazenation* has become a globally recognized image, see p.382). He has designed record sleeves for the Pet Shop Boys, Morrissey and Earl Brutus, memorably described in this book's introduction by writer Jon Savage as a 'scabrous glam/hooligan group.'

So – Scott King graphic designer: case closed. Well, not quite. Nothing is straightforward in King's world of restless interrogation and critique. In parallel with his commercial commissions, King has created an equally impressive body of personal work – none more so that the 'art magazine' *Crash!* which he produced with cultural historian Matt Worley.

The Ballardian title hints at *Crash!*'s agenda of subversion and eagerness to confront things we find objectionable or banal ('... I always like the crapness in things, the sadness and the plain amateur haphazardness ...'). In *Crash!* text and image collide at high speed: sledgehammer graphics, agit-prop typography and the dull conventions of business graphics mash together to make statements of subversive power. The 1999 Prada Meinhof cover is unrivalled in its bone crunching critique of fashion as a sort of neo-liberal terrorism.

King himself isn't much help in the matter of deciding whether he is art or design. He appears undecided, tentative, typically doubtful. In a long interview with Lionel Bovier in this book, King says: 'When it's a solo gallery show (I have no problem with group shows) when it is solely MY work, something else happens – I don't know what it is, but I become a jibbering wreck, all my confidence disappears. It could be something as simple as "audience expectation", it could be something as simple as I don't yet truly believe myself to be "an artist", it could be that I don't understand the art gallery system or have a valid critique of that system (if indeed I need one). I don't know. But this is why I've put myself in this position – this is why I do it, I want to work it out. It would have been much easier for me to stay solely in the world of graphic design, but I prefer it this way.'

Yet, despite his hesitancy in putting himself forward as a bona fide artist, King also confesses to strong doubts at the outset of his career about his fitness to be a graphic designer: 'At college, though I was studying graphic design, about halfway through the course, I stopped doing any of the college projects – I made a conscious decision only to work on self-set projects ... what they call in graphic design circles "personal work". It's a long time ago of course, but I remember clearly thinking – "If I design wine bottle labels, there's a good chance I will become a wine bottle label designer" – which I didn't want to be. This wasn't just petulance, I struggled initially with graphic design because I just didn't "get it". I didn't understand how people made aesthetic decisions, or why they copied work from design annuals or why they bothered to try and think of new ways to repackage baked beans etc.'

What King describes as his 'initial struggle with graphic design' led him to ask how he could use design to say something more than 'just rebranding or repackaging', or doing what was 'current'. To achieve this, King reached the conclusion that he would have to write his own text: 'I realized that I was less interested in typographic design than I was in what the type actually said and where it appeared – you know: first the words THEN the design. First the idea, then the context, then the design.'

It's this fusion of text and form that makes King's work so visceral. Sometimes the text is his, and sometimes it comes from one of his collaborators, but it gives his work a fuck you immediacy that, like a car wreck on the motorway, you can't help but slow down to look.

But is it art?

Within the art world the notion that anything can be art, as expounded by pretty much everyone since Duchamp, is held to be a truism. Well, yes, but only so long as you don't include graphic design in your definition of anything: no graphic designer, regardless of how radical or how boundary smashing, is accorded hundredth of the status granted to even a minor artist by the art world.

Philosophers have struggled with this question for centuries. The philosophical definition of art has varied over time to an astonishing degree. Most of us would not recognise the definitions that have prevailed in past eras, but today we seem to have reached a point where our definition is governed by what is known as 'the institutional theory of art.' This theory states that an object can be called art when it is connected to the institution known as 'the art world'. In other words, its status as art is conferred by its association with galleries, curators, critics, art education, the art market, etc. Or to put it yet another way, we are willing to allow a work to be designated as art – even if it doesn't chime with our own view of what is and isn't art – because it is in a gallery or in a book or magazine presented by a knowledgeable authority.

Since design has nearly always kept a clear separation between itself and the art world, the 'institutional' definition of art automatically excludes most forms of design. There is also, of course, a well-developed institutional theory of design. It is based around certain principles that are anathema to the art world: design's dependency on commercial commissioners; its reliance on mass production rather than unique 'one-off' creations; and its lack of authorial content – designer's communicate other people's messages, not their own.

But as discussed above, graphic designers now routinely bypass the institutional straightjacket of design. They make their own work which they publish in a demi-art world of pop-up galleries, blogs and publications that do not follow the commissioned-by-client model. And in Scott King, we have someone who has at least one foot – even if tentatively placed –

in the 'real' art world. King is reviewed in serious journals and has exhibitions in Berlin and other art world capitals. He has even received the contemporary art world's ultimate bestowal of approval – his work has been acquired by the king (no pun intended) of contemporary art – Charles Saatchi.

So that really is case closed: Scott King is a bona fide artist, and graphic design can be art. Well, not quite. It's a debate that can never end because there is no answer to the question: 'What is art?' In the end, our relationship with art is a deeply personal association between us and the objects or works we choose to engage with. If we can shed the tribal and cultural conditioning that determines so much of what we think and do (especially about art), we realize that in art we are free to find aesthetic pleasure wherever we choose. In the realm of art we have total freedom to find it anywhere we choose and make it in anyway we please.

It certainly seems to be a view that Scott King inclines towards: 'It's an on-going dilemma,' he notes, referring to the art vs. design debate, 'but I'm slowly beginning to reach the conclusion that if I'm doing it, then it's all art ... or at least it's all my art.'

1. *Scott King: Art Works* by Jon Savage. JRP|Ringier, 2010.

Eats, shoots & leaves[1]
2004

Like thousands of others this Christmas, I was given a copy of *Eats, Shoots & Leaves* (2003) by Lynne Truss. I wasn't given the book by Lynne Truss, you understand. What I mean is, it was written by Lynne Truss. I thought about writing 'Lynne Truss's *Eats, Shoots & Leaves*', but you can't be too careful with Ms. Truss. Her book is subtitled 'The Zero Tolerance Approach to Punctuation'. And she means it.

The book is a publishing phenomenon: a bona fide bestseller. But of course, the really astonishing thing about its success is its subject matter. Who'd have thought it: a hit book about punctuation. Well, it made a change from the usual Christmas presents of Old Spice gift-boxes and string-backed driving gloves.

My first instinct was to dislike *Eats, Shoots & Leaves*. I assumed it was a reactionary, back-to-the-1950s tract for *Daily Telegraph* readers. There is always the suspicion with literary pedants – 'sticklers' as Lynne Truss calls them – that they are showing off, flaunting their superiority over the less well-educated. And anyway, getting hoity-toity about punctuation in the era of texting and global electronic communications is a bit like calling for the return of saluting policemen and TV newsreaders in dinner jackets.

But I was unexpectedly seduced by this witty book. It is not in the least snooty, and Truss is endearingly quick to poke fun at her obsession with the correct use of commas, dashes, question marks, capital letters, etc. Her passion appears to be one-part personal foible ('While other girls were out with boyfriends getting their necks disfigured by love bites, I was at home with the wireless listening to [a] quiz called *Many a Slip*, in which erudite and amusing contestants spotted grammatical errors in pieces of prose'), and one-part altruistic crusade (without correct punctuation, she states, 'there is no reliable way of communicating meaning'). She failed, however, to convert me to her dotty notion of forming vigilante groups to go around with magic markers correcting greengrocer's signs.

But I was struck by something else in this book: a curious omission. Truss asserts that we are witnessing the collapse of national punctuation standards, but she makes no direct reference to the role of graphic designers in this. She deals out sharp whacks to sub-editors, takes hefty swipes at global entertainment corporations and puts the boot into greengrocers. But graphic designers escape scott-free.

I suppose we should be glad about this. Designers don't need any more bad press. When graphic designers are mentioned outside of professional circles it is usually to be abused for charging too much for tweaking a much-loved logo, or for giving a daft name to a new conglomerate. Yet it's odd that Truss spares graphic designers, because many of the examples she gives of atrocious punctuation are undoubtedly the work of designers sitting at Apple Macs using industry-standard software.

She is especially indignant about a 'printed banner' she saw on the concourse of a petrol station. '"Come inside," it says, "for CD's, VIDEO's, DVD's and BOOK's."' In a typically sharp phrase, she condemns the poster for its 'satanic sprinkling of redundant apostrophes'. She is equally enraged by the title of the film *Two Weeks Notice*: 'Guaranteed to give sticklers a very nasty turn,' she seethes, 'its posters slung along the sides of buses in letters four feet tall, with no apostrophe in sight.'

I asked Sean Perkins of highly regarded design company North if he thought graphic designers were contributing to the poor standards of punctuation. 'They are major culprits,' notes Perkins. 'In my view there is no excuse for grammatical and punctuation errors. It's down to laziness, carelessness, ignorance and lack of concern. Our job is about using the English language to communicate, so it has to be correct. We occasionally hire copywriters to correct and oversee our work. We'd do this more often, but time and budgets prevent it.' Perkins readily admits to his own uncertainty about the finer details of punctuation, and points out, rightly I think, that this is common amongst designers.

Lynne Truss comes close to outing designers when she turns her wrath on the unnecessary apostrophe in the name of poor, short-lived Hear'Say.[2] The errant tadpole in the band's name excites an explosion of venom: 'Idiotic showbiz promoters stick apostrophes in names for purely decorative purposes,' she thunders. But perhaps it wasn't an idiotic showbiz promoter who was responsible. In fact, the Hear'Say logo was designed by music industry design company Form.

I asked partner Paul West about the contentious logo. 'It's not something we really want to be remembered for,' he laughs. 'But basically the band thought of the name, and the name conjured up the idea of using speech marks. The H and Y are fashioned on single inverted commas, and as the name is two words I wanted to have a device that separated the words but linked them graphically while also harking back to the original inverted comma of the H. I could go on, but it was never meant to be rocket science.'

Truss acknowledges that 'institutions, towns, colleges, families, companies and brands have authority over their own spelling and punctuation (which is often historic), and there is absolutely nothing we can do except raise an eyebrow and make a mental note.' She strays even deeper into the world of graphic design when she bemoans the 'inexorable rise of lower case into book titles, television captions, company names and (of course) everything on the non-case-sensitive Internet ...'

But this is where I part company with her. I think there's a critical difference between grammatical howlers and what she disparagingly calls 'graphic frivolity'. Let's preserve meaning and clarity at all times, but our perception of meaning and clarity changes; moreover, what was correct a hundred years ago is laughable today. She mentions a sign which reads 'No Dogs Please'; she calls this 'an indefensible generalisation, since many dogs do please'. But find me someone who doesn't understand this sign? It seems to be a perfectly acceptable and understandable formulation.

Yet it's hard to resist the conclusion that if Lynne Truss and her vigilantes have their way, graphic designers will have less scope for novelty and innovation, at a time when increased visual literacy means that individuals can cope with graphic inventiveness that plays fast and loose with the traditions of punctuation. I say this as someone who was, until recently, creative director of a design company that left the vowels out of Primal Scream's name and album title on the cover of one of their recent records (Primal Scream became Prml Scrm; Exterminator became *Xtrmntr*). We were told it wouldn't work. No one would be able to read it, said a nervous record company. But we went ahead, the album was successful, the design won a few awards and no one died.

Sean Perkins concurs: 'I am a big fan of taking creative licence and substituting dashes, slashes, plusses, points and colons for graphical effect. However, this should only be used to enhance the message and create an improved visual solution, and has to be done with great skill and concern as the message should always be grammatically correct.' And despite escaping Lynne Truss's wrath, it's clear that designers have a duty and a professional responsibility to ensure that they don't contribute to an accelerated decline in punctuation standards.

Many designers are, of course, fastidious and hyper-attentive to typographic and punctuational detail. But when graphic designers moved from reliance on trained typesetters to near-total reliance on personal computers to generate typesetting, they assumed a huge responsibility. In the view of Perkins, this removed the 'last line of defence between designers and their lack of punctuation skills': and few would argue that there hasn't been, overall, a drop in standards. You see a lot of bad typography and a lot of dodgy punctuation. Let's just hope Lynne Truss doesn't spot that designers are often to blame. She might turn up at your studio with a magic marker. She's deadly serious.

1. *Eats, Shoots & Leaves: The Zero Tolerance Approach to Punctuation* by Lynne Truss. Profile Books, 2003.

2. Hear'Say were a short-lived British manufactured pop group in 2001.

Yellow submarine
2004

John Lennon's interest in the 1960s avant-garde is well-documented, but it is less well-known that Paul McCartney – the man who gave us 'The Frog Chorus' and 'Mull of Kintyre' – was also a staunch supporter of the avant-garde. He famously attended a lecture in 1965 by the experimental Italian composer Luciano Berio which was invaded, to Berio's consternation, by scuffling paparazzi looking for the mop-topped star. This interest in 1960s experimentalism partly explains why The Beatles granted permission for the making of the full-length animated film, *Yellow Submarine*. However, it is also rumoured that they agreed to the making of *Yellow Submarine* to avoid the contractual obligation of appearing in a third Beatles live-action movie. As George Harrison explained: 'The thing I liked most about the movie was that we didn't really have anything to do with it. They just took our music, we met them, and then Heinz Edelmann, who was fantastic, went off and created all these characters, showed them to us and that was basically it.'

Heinz Edelmann is *Yellow Submarine*'s presiding genius. It is his design and art direction that makes the film a classic and a work of enduring visual invention. Born in Czechoslovakia in 1934, Edelmann's style was a quintessentially 60s melding of pop art, MC Escher and the American cult illustrator Peter Max. *Yellow Submarine* is justly revered in animation circles, and its influence can be seen today in *The Simpsons*, where the vivid flat colours echo Edelmann's film.

Yellow Submarine is a work of high-psychedelia. Yet Edelmann was no hippy acid-head: 'I had never taken any drugs,' he noted in an interview. 'I'm a conservative working-class person who sticks to booze ... so I just knew about the psychedelic experience ... I guessed what it was.' Paul McCartney had no doubts about the film's psychedelic credentials: 'To me it kind of seemed surprisingly modern. It's quite trippy, it's a bit of a "head" film really, although apparently kids do like it,' he said. Well, a new generation of 'kids' can 'get into' *Yellow Submarine* via a book published by Apple[1] and children's book imprint Walker Books.[2]

Unfortunately, the book isn't a patch on the movie. The famous luminosity of the film can't be captured in four colour printing, and what appeared mercurial and vivid on the screen is static and one-dimensional on the printed page. *Yellow Submarine*'s tripped-out surrealism (viz the famous 'sea of holes' sequence), its courageous combining of numerous animation techniques, its wonkily brilliant script (voiced by Beatles sound-a-likes), and its admittedly somewhat dated 60s charm simply doesn't translate into the book format. There have been *Yellow Submarine* books and magazines before (you can see them on eBay), but other than to cash in on the lucrative Beatles' collectors market, it's hard to see who is going to buy this slim 40-page book. My advice is buy the DVD instead, and then go and score a tab of ... oh, never mind: just watch the film. It's a trip.

1. *The Beatles' Yellow Submarine* by The Beatles. Subafilms Ltd., 2011.

2. *Yellow Submarine: Mini Edition* by Heinz Edelmann. Walker Books, 2011.

Blink: the power of thinking without thinking[1]
2005

Malcolm Gladwell's bestseller *The Tipping Point* (2000, subtitled 'How Little Things Can Make a Big Difference') became a must-read for marketing people who sensed that it contained a new blueprint for promoting brands and flogging consumer goods. Gladwell is credited with promoting the use of 'viral' marketing techniques, and he now enjoys Zeus-like status amongst US business people.

Gladwell's new book is called *Blink* (2005), and although intended for the general reader, it contains much that will be of interest to designers. Gladwell says his book is about 'rapid cognition ... the kind of thinking that happens in the "blink of an eye".' A staff writer for *The New Yorker*, Gladwell introduces his readers to the notion of 'thin-slicing', which he defines as the ability to make snap decisions that are surprisingly accurate. At its most simplistic, 'thin-slicing' is the ability to get out of the way of a lorry bearing down on you at speed; at its most complex, it is the ability to make an accurate character assessment, in a matter of seconds, of someone you've just met for the first time.

Gladwell gives numerous examples of 'thin-slicing'. He cites the individual who could tell whether a doctor was likely to be sued for malpractice simply by listening to a few short excerpts from the doctor's conversations with patients. He discusses the tennis coach who could predict a double-fault by the body shape of a player about to serve. He describes the near-instant recognition by art experts of an elaborate and cleverly executed fake statue.

Gladwell asserts that we are traditionally encouraged to dismiss fast thinking in favour of prolonged contemplation, a supposition he challenges. He even hints that by reading his book we will learn how to 'thin-slice' more effectively and thus improve our lives. Clearly designers will benefit from learning how to 'thin-slice'. We often need to make rapid decisions. For instance, when we meet clients it is important to decide quickly what they want from a relationship. If we can read their intentions correctly, then we can adjust our approach accordingly. Often we are required to have ideas on the spot. If we can do this, it's going to be to our advantage. It demonstrates nimbleness of mind, and helps cement relationships at an early stage; we always tell our clients we want time to cultivate ideas, but to survive we know we've got to move fast.

However there's a problem with 'thin-slicing': it seems that if 'thin-slicing' is to work effectively then it usually needs to be accompanied by 'specialist knowledge' (the examples given above are all by 'experts'); and for 'thin-slicing' to be effective, it has to be free from manipulation by others.

Gladwell has some illuminating and original things to say about the way market research is conducted. Focus groups are an increasingly popular way for clients to evaluate new design: after all, as he states, the best way to find out how consumers feel about something is to ask them directly. Well, true up to a point. But as demonstrated by the numerous examples Gladwell provides, to get an answer that has some value, how and what you ask is the most important part of the equation.

Gladwell devotes much space to the 'New Coke' debacle. This notorious marketing disaster was caused by Pepsi's invitation to drinkers to 'take the Pepsi Challenge'. In fact, they invited drinkers to take a 'sip test', with the result that the instant sugar rush of Pepsi did better than Coke. In tests where the entire drink was consumed, the opposite result was achieved, and Coke was preferred. But the outcome of the Pepsi 'sip test' was that Coke was panicked into launching the ill-judged 'New Coke'. It's hard to care too much about the clumsy machinations of fizzy drinks corporations, but there's a lesson here; asking the public what they think about something doesn't always get you the right answer.

So, when a piece of design is shown to a focus group for comment, what value is the response? Gladwell writes illuminatingly about the Herman Miller Aeron chair. The chair's revolutionary design tested appallingly in research. It was called 'ugly'. Yet the company stuck with it, 'trusted their instincts', and ended up with the best selling chair in their history. Herman Miller triumphed because they dismissed the results obtained from short exposure times, and relied on prolonged exposure to deliver a more accurate response.

Blink is a book about perception. But it's not about the way we see with our eyes, it's about the way we see with our minds. Gladwell has some interesting – and disconcerting – things to say about the manipulation of perception, which he treats in an oddly amoral manner. For designers there is much to contemplate in this readable book.

1. *Blink: The Power of Thinking Without Thinking* by Malcolm Gladwell. Little, Brown and Company, 2005.

Sources

Logorama – the film. Design Observer, 13 January 2010. See pp. 202–204.

Factory Records – the complete graphic album. Publication unknown, 2007. See pp. 205–207.

Design disasters. *Eye* 71, Spring 2009. See pp. 208–209.

Obsessive branding disorder. Design Observer, 17 November 2008. See pp. 210–212.

'Alan Fletcher – fifty years of graphic work (and play)'. *Blueprint*, 2007. See pp. 213–214.

Contemporary graphic design – AGI (Alliance Graphique Internationale): Graphic design since 1950. *Blueprint*, 2007. See pp. 215–217.

Summer of love: art of the psychedelic era. *Eye* 57, Autumn 2005. See pp. 218–219.

Fanzines. *The Wire #324*, February 2011. See pp. 220–221.

This ain't no disco. Publication unknown, 2005. See pp. 222–223.

'Cold war modern'. *Design Week*, 4 December 2008. See pp. 224–225.

Volume: writings on graphic design, music, art and culture. Design Observer, 25 January 2011. See pp. 226–228.

'Communicate' at the Barbican. *Design Week*, 4 November 2004. See pp. 229–231.

Robert Brownjohn: sex and typography. Design Observer, 19 Janaury 2006. See pp. 232–234.

'Slightly off the ground' – Vaughan Oliver and v23 poster designs. *Eye* 63, Spring 2007. See pp. 235–236.

Instant light – Tarkovsky Polaroids. *Eye* 60, Summer 2006. See pp. 237–238.

Bossa Nova and the rise of Brazilian music in the 1960s: original cover art. *The Wire*, #325, March 2011. See pp. 239–240.

The Blank Tape Spillage Fete. *The Wire*, #272, October 2006. See p. 241.

Mayo Bucher: open sign. *Eye* 45, Autumn 2002. See pp.242–243.

Scott King: art works. *It's Nice That*, Issue 5, March 2011. See pp.244–248.

Eats, shoots & leaves. *Design Week*, 4 March 2004. See pp.249–252.

Yellow submarine. *Design Week*, 26 August 2004. See pp.253–254.

Blink: the power of thinking without thinking. *Design Week*, 3 March 2005. See pp.255–257.

Essays

Education

The unreal world
2010

Whenever I talk to design students I always avoid using the phrase 'the real world'. Yet it is a term I often hear used by both students and tutors: they talk about 'joining the real world' or looking forward to tackling 'real world projects.' They do this in a way that suggests they think that the world of university and of college projects is somehow not real.

In fact, it is students who live in the 'real world' and it is professional designers who live in an unreal world of irrational clients, impossible deadlines, and the lunacy of using design skills solely to add spin, hype and gloss to third-rate products and services. The professional design world is a world of camouflage and – sometimes – deception. It is a world where designers have to learn to dissemble, compromise and become masters of dozens of skills that have nothing to do with design.

A good design education, on the other hand, provides a period of learning, self-discovery and engagement with design in its purest sense. Nor is a design education without its own demands and complexities: students have project deadlines; they are set demanding briefs; they have grades to achieve; and as if all this wasn't enough, they have eye-watering fees to pay.

So – never let anyone tell you that, as a student, you are somehow not in the real world: you are. But you are about to leave it for the unreal world of professional life, and this means that you have to ask yourself if you are ready for the transition from the real to the sometimes unreal: from the pure to the sometimes impure; from the meaningful to the sometimes meaningless.

OK, so I'm not painting an attractive picture of professional life, and in truth, the professional world is mostly well-intentioned, honest and productive. And just as I make a habit of never talking about the 'real world' when discussing post-university life with students, I would never criticise anyone for the way they earn a living. We live in an unforgiving world, and just so long as we are not working for a weapons manufacturer, or an oppressive regime, it is nearly always better to be employed than to be unemployed. I'd go one step further and say that – landmine companies and oppressive regimes apart – there is no such a thing as a bad job in your first few years of professional life.

But how do you preserve the idealism of student life in the face of commercial pressures? And how, when you are told from every angle that the only thing that matters is commercial success, do you preserve a vision of design as something more than an aerosol spray that gets squirted on dubious activities? Well, there are a few simple steps you can take to avoid the more paralysing effects of professional life. Most of them are common sense; they are reflexes that come naturally to smart-thinking designers anyway, and they all helpfully begin with the letter 'e'.

Enthusiasm: I'm not talking about the puppyish enthusiasm that most designers intuitively feel for their subject – the enthusiasm that flares up every time we find a book, magazine or blog full of cool work. What I'm talking about here is the enthusiasm that makes us fight for good design in the face of opposition and indifference. It is not easy to maintain enthusiasm when you are confronted with the inevitable knock-backs that all graphic designers experience. And there's a paradox here: without enthusiasm we can't summon up the energy to win our battles, and if we don't win our battles, our enthusiasm drains way. So we must not take enthusiasm for granted: we have to fight to retain it when everything conspires against it. And that's easier to say than do.

Experimentation: One of the best things about student life is you get a period during which you can experiment. Opportunities for experimenting become far less plentiful after graduation. Yet if you want to build a body of work that you can be proud of, you have to find the time to push yourself into new, sometimes uncomfortable situations. It is a common failing amongst designers that they reach a period of comfort and then, like a vehicle in deep sand, become stuck. The only way out of this is to experiment, and by doing so, to risk failure. Now, you might have to restrict your experimentation to your own time, and for that you will need the third quality I want to talk about.

Energy: All designers think they need inspiration – they do. But more than inspiration, they need energy. You might think that since design is a passive activity – passive in the sense that we mostly do it sitting down – you don't need energy. But you do. You need doggedness and determination – and to acquire these two attributes, you need energy. Lots of energy. Here's what I mean by energy: by the end of most projects we are tired – perhaps even exhausted. Yet this is when we are at our most vulnerable. Because we are running on empty, our judgment is weakened and we have a fatal tendency to accept the mediocre. It is only by summoning up additional energy when our mind and body tells us to quit that we will produce our best work. Energy always counts for more than inspiration.

Conclusion: Looking at the work of the great designers, we often feel that it looks effortless and friction-free; yet we can be sure it wasn't. Nothing good emerges without enthusiasm, experimentation and energy. All the best designers I have ever known have these 'real world' qualities in abundance. But you knew this anyway: after all, you are living in the real world already.

The student sensibility
2011

Something is stirring in the basement of British public life. Rioting students; politicians called to account for broken election promises; near-universal disgust with tax-avoiding corporations and greedy bankers; even the heir to the throne attacked on his way to the theatre (as an arch traditionalist, Prince Charles should be pleased about this. There is a noble tradition of mob attacks on royalty; it really is part of the job description).

What are the implications for design in all this? We can be sure of one thing: the world of professional design will never be the same again. For a start we've witnessed the emergence of a new student radicalism. And although I've seen it dismissed as 'a middle class revolt', and as a 'misguided manifestation of youthful political immaturity', it seems to me to be something more deep-rooted than either of these descriptions.

Over recent decades the young have been regarded as non-ideological, overtly passive and unengaged with the political process. I've never been entirely convinced by this categorisation: it has always seemed an oversimplification. But now it's plain to see that there really is a generation which takes politics seriously and has a view of the world that is idealistic and political, yet uncoloured by the dreary machinations of Westminster (so effectively exposed by the MP's expenses scandal).

This is not an overnight phenomenon. For some time now I've been watching the emergence of a new type of design student. I've seen it repeatedly in the numerous visits I've made to design schools over the past five or six years. Where once I encountered students designing CD covers and indulging in the cult of the 'designer as author', I now see students working on projects with a social or ethical focus. In other words, using design skills to help others: or to use that slightly goofy sounding phrase – 'trying to make the world a better place.'

This shift in the student psychological ecosystem raises many questions for the mainstream design world. Will the colleges of the future produce enough graduates to keep the design production-line flowing? Will there be enough designers to produce the branding, packaging and messaging demanded by design's corporate paymasters? Will students emerging onto the job scene in the next few years have the market-oriented sensibilities to be of any use to the conventional design world?

There may even be a more urgent threat to the supply of oven-ready graduates for the design industry. The Browne report[1] has recommended that the government should be free to withdraw public funding from all but 'priority' subjects. And guess what? The arts and humanities are not regarded as priorities. So if, as seems likely, the government withdraws all funding for arts and humanities higher education, the effect on the UK design industry is likely to be far reaching. We may begin to see clients routinely sending design briefs to China, India and Brazil.

My own view is that a head-to-toe reassessment of the role of design is the best thing that could happen to design and designers. The more design is placed at the forefront of the radical new thinking that is going on around finance, urban living and social change, the more likely it is to prosper in an increasingly global and automated world where knowledge is the most valuable commodity. We may be in for a painful period of readjustment as old calculations of design's value and its role in the market place is reassessed. (We've already seen what is happening to design budgets: they are falling.) But as new ways of using design and new priorities for designers emerge, the future will begin to look warmer. Well, warmish.

1. The Browne Review (Independent Review of Higher Education Funding and Student Finance) was a review into higher education funding in England. Chaired by Lord Browne, the former chief executive of BP; it was published in 2010. It recommended sweeping changes to the way universities were funded, including removing the cap on the level of fees that universities can charge, and increasing the income level at which graduates start to pay back their loans to £21,000.

Too many design students?
2009

The education of designers is a perennially hot topic. Amongst design's chatterati it's an issue guaranteed to raise blood pressure as well as hackles. Two unlikely bedfellows have recently chucked petrol onto the debate. In this publication [*Design Week*] Ian Cochrane has advised students to 'get out of this business. It is inundated with graduates and there aren't the jobs, especially at this time.' And in his recent D&AD President's Lecture, Peter Saville questioned the point of colleges producing '50,000 design graduates a year'.

Cochrane and Saville are riffing on a familiar theme. Warnings against the intensive farming of design graduates have been issued with deadening frequency in recent years. But is it a problem? Perhaps Cochrane knows something no one else knows – namely that the current financial situation is going to last forever. I'd have thought that studying design over the next few years will allow graduates to avoid the worst of the aftershocks thrown up by the current implosion. It could even see them emerging into a saner world where, after a decade of financial greed, fraud and ineptitude, design is valued as a force for social good rather than merely a lubricant of consumer indebtedness. I know of one university that has had a marked rise in applications for next year – a spike they attribute to a desire amongst students to avoid the worst of the recession.

Peter Saville's lack of enthusiasm for the overproduction of design graduates is easier to fathom. Since he is responsible for many of them choosing a career in design in the first place, he is perhaps experiencing a twinge of culpability.

But I think both are just plain wrong. A design education – even a fairly rudimentary one – equips individuals with many of the skills that will prove invaluable in an information-based, digitally-rooted global culture. Just as Britain produced engineers to force the industrial revolution, and scientists to push the technological revolution, the information revolution is being – at least partly – driven by designers. I can't think of many skills that will be more useful in the coming years than a mastery of digital tools and the ability to present information in a variety of media.

When I first started employing designers in the late-80s, I found them mostly to have been soured by their educations. Most of them were in retreat from an education that had encouraged them to think of themselves as service sector fodder. Towards the end of the 90s, a new breed of tutors, radicalised by theoretical developments within design, started to produce graduates with a disdain for the old notion of design as only a problem-solving process, and saw it as a means for self-expression and creative experimentation. The notion of design as art took hold in design schools – or at least in the imagination of students – and it's been hard to dislodge.

But after recently spending time in two universities, I think the balance has been redressed. Both schools knocked me out with the standard of teaching on offer, and the imaginative level-headedness of the students. I think we've reached a point where a design education is a bit like a history degree. History graduates don't necessarily become historians. Instead they use their analytically trained brains to work in business, research and education. Today, we can say the same about a good design education. Design graduates are equipped for life in the modern world. Let's have more of them.

Dan Fern and his RCA legacy
2010

You can spot them. They're different. They have a steely self-belief that is almost Jesuitical. Who am I talking about? Old Etonians? Graduates from the madrassas of northern Pakistan? No, I'm talking about former students from the RCA's Communication Art & Design course, which for the past decade or so has been run by Dan Fern.

Fern is retiring and the search is on to find his replacement.[1] Whoever gets the job will have to contend with their predecessor's considerable legacy. But opinion is divided over that legacy. Some say that he has presided over the creation of an elite corps of smart thinkers and super designers, while others point out that he has produced unworldly dreamers who live in a playground between art and design, not quite making it in either.

I'm a long-time fan of Fern's postgraduate course. When I used to run a studio, the RCA degree show was the only one I never missed – and the only one where I hired a graduate on the spot. On occasions I tried to hire other designers from the course, but snaring them was difficult because under Fern's regime, with its emphasis on self-reliance and autonomy, many of the best students went straight into self-employment after graduation.

Henrik Kubel of A2/SW/HK is a typical Fern/RCA graduate – independent, talented and resourceful, and it's hard to imagine him working for anyone other than himself. Kubel is fulsome in his praise of Fern: 'He saw my qualities and gently pushed my development by asking questions and listening, which to me is the essence of a great teacher.' Fern's roots in illustration did not prevent him from recognising and nurturing Kubel's ability as a typographer: 'I was at all times greatly encouraged by Dan and my other tutors to explore and indulge in the qualities of the hand-made – I spent almost a year in the letterpress department away from the computers – great memories.'

I've always believed that Fern's sophisticated fusion of graphic design craft and pragmatism with the fluid expressiveness of illustration is the main reason why his course has produced so many remarkable practitioners. It's a factor recognised by Andy Altmann of Why Not Associates, a graduate of the RCA in the pre-merged era. While at St Martins, Fern set Altmann a project: 'He brought in lots of stencils, rubber stamps, etc.,' recalls Altman, 'to show how you could create type instantly without reverting to specifying to a typesetter (no Macs in those days). He was very enthusiastic and made me look at typography in a new fresh light.'

James Jarvis, illustrator and toymaker, is at first glance not a typical Fern/RCA product. He confesses to some reservations about his time on the course. 'If I had a criticism,' he says, 'it would be that I felt that the kind of vernacular art that I make was not really understood nor greatly valued. I think that perhaps Dan had an agenda to expand the remit of what illustration could be, and I felt that in embracing new and different forms, my particular graphic vision felt a bit swept under the carpet. That said, I found one-to-one tutorials with Dan very rewarding.'

Yet with the benefit of a glance in the rear-view mirror of a successful post-RCA career, Jarvis has come to place a higher value on his time at the college: 'Given the direction my career has taken, finding less traditional ways of working as a graphic artist, I think that the RCA might have been more influential than I perhaps realised at the time. For me, the most important thing I took away from Dan and the illustration course was an academic approach to and awareness of image making, something that has informed everything I have done since.'

The artist Sara Fanelli is, on the other hand, the archetypal RCA graduate. She has a distinctive, non-formulaic style. She is a published author, and occupies the terrain between art and commercial illustration. She is unequivocal in her praise for Fern. 'Dan has been a special person for me ever since I met him during my interview for the course,' she says. 'I admire the way he has led the course with such dedication and integrity. We all can imagine how hard it must be to please everyone in such a position, so I really respect him for making decisions, staying faithful to his beliefs, and not taking compromising paths which might have sometimes been easier.'

Fern's critics hope that his successor will push the course towards creating graduates with 'real world' skills in branding and digital communication. That's the safe option. I'd prefer to see someone who could update Fern's vision of a course which produces creative people capable of exploring new ways of thinking from a perspective of craft informed by artistic vision, for a world where commercial imperatives are no longer the only benchmarks for success. It will be a brave person who can pull that one off.

1. At the time of writing, Dan Fern's successor had not been appointed. Shortly after, Neville Brody was chosen as his replacement. Later Brody invited me to join the teaching staff in the newly titled Visual Communication course at RCA.

Ten things you should know about design students 2011

In my roles as an external examiner at a number of universities, and as an occasional lecturer and part-time teacher, I've spent most of the past two months in design schools in the UK and Ireland. I've witnessed at first hand the attitudes, fears, tastes, prejudices and creative output of the current generation of graduating design students. Here are ten things you should know about today's visual design students.

1. The good ones are as good as the best from any year you care to choose. In fact, I'd say the standard of top performing UK educated design students is so high that it is hard to distinguish their work from some of the best professional work. Or to put it another way – they're bloody good.

2. Most design students have abandoned the design fetishism of the past two decades. There is far less emphasis on the stylistic beautification of graphic expression and in its place there is a renewed emphasis on content and returning graphic design to its modernist roots of form following function.

3. Many of the current generation of students seem to be motivated by social concerns. Where once their energies might have gone into designing CD covers and identities for cultural institutions, it is now commonplace to find students investigating ways in which design can drive social change. This seems to me the biggest single difference between today's graduates and those from past years.

4. Student graphic designers are increasingly functioning like journalists: this is more noticeable at postgraduate level, but I've been struck by the number of undergraduate designers operating like self-publishing reporters. In recent years, an obsession with research for research's sake has led to dry outcomes, but now there is evidence of designer's producing original research and then presenting it in a graphically coherent way. As print journalists search for new ways of functioning, perhaps the journalist/designer is a blueprint for the future.

5. It is getting harder to tell the difference between the work of students studying illustration and those studying graphic design.

6. In one school I went to recently, the tiny handful of failures and thirds would have been top students 15–20 years ago.

7. Few students seem interested in web design. Most admit to being print fixated. This is a worry.

8. Many top students in UK schools are from abroad and many of them are exceptionally talented. What does this mean for UK design? Will they all go home to China, Korea, India and Brazil and join – or set up – world-beating studios? Will they go back and teach in schools thus reducing the need for foreign students to come to the UK for an education? Will they stay in UK and enrich the design gene pool?

9. I still hear complaints from professional designers and studio bosses that students are unfit for purpose, i.e. they are not oven-ready graphic designers. This is often true. Some students have no concept of – or interest in – the professional realm. But it is also true that many others are more advanced, forward-thinking and future-proofed than the studios demanding graduates with 'real world skills'.

10. A final thought for anyone who scoffs at student experimentation and perceived immaturity: students are told constantly by their tutors to be 'original, different and don't copy'. If their attempts to do this sometimes fail, it should not be assumed that they are a lost generation. They are merely doing what generations of students have always done – trying to find what is new, fresh and vibrant. Why else would anyone want to study design?

Hyper Island
Learning by doing
2011

A recent visit to Hyper Island, the digital media school in Stockholm, gave me an insight into an important question that is prevalent in contemporary design: what is being done to train the digital designers of the future?

It's a pressing question. I know studio heads who are tearing out the hairs in their goatees with frustration because they can't find designers fluent in the new digital disciplines; or more accurately, can't find designers capable of working in the digital domain with the sort of creative panache that they find in 'old media' designers.

I'm also continuously surprised by the number of students I meet with zero interest in the digital arena. I'd go as far as to say that the most common response I encounter is mild hostility towards subjects such as web design and app development. There's boundless enthusiasm for poster design, logo creation and book making – but not much interest in catering for the biggest technological change to hit communication since Gutenberg.

How many top UK design schools are offering digital media design as a discrete subject? Not many, I'd guess. There's certainly nothing to rival Hyper Island with its exclusive emphasis on the digital. Formed in 1995 by Jonathan Briggs, David Erixon and Lars Lundh, its motto is *learning by doing*.

Hyper Island runs courses in Digital Media, Interactive Art Direction, Motion Graphics, eCommerce and Mobile Applications. Over 260 students study full-time at the school each year – most are required to have worked for at least two years before becoming eligible for entry.

But what makes Hyper Island different is that it functions without teaching staff. The students learn by doing projects brought in by commercial companies, or by working on tasks set by interested groups and individuals. Importantly, students are encouraged to work in teams. This seems essential preparation for working in digital media where teamwork is obligatory. But you can also see how it flies in the face of the dominant view in design schools which seeks to encourage the individual in the Alan Fletcher/Paul Rand/Stefan Sagmeister model of the heroic and solitary solo performer.

By offering on-the-job learning, Hyper Island encourages its students to acquire that elusive quality most frequently demanded by studio bosses – 'real world' experience. I was mightily impressed with the students I met in Stockholm. They came from every corner of the globe. They were super bright. And in their modern open-plan studio (more Silicon Valley start-up than trad design school) they exuded commitment and enthusiasm.

I saw some student work while I was there. It was mainly characterized by business and communication savvy. It felt closer to advertising than design, and although there was plenty of evidence of digital competence in their thinking, it didn't feel tech-led – it felt ideas-led.

But there was one area where I detected a weakness: the good thinking and the business savvy couldn't disguise a lack of design verve. It wasn't bad design – far from it, but it was routine, unexceptional, conventional. Which takes us back to my friends trying to recruit digital designers: are they right to despair, or is it possible to combine design flair with digital nous? I'm beginning to wonder.

Education in the age of rising fees and speed learning 2012

For centuries, design was taught via the apprentice system. The master/pupil formula lasted well into the 19th century before being superseded in the first decades of the 20th century by the Bauhaus. Here was a pedagogical philosophy based on the doctrine of modernism and machine age progress that set out to codify a system of mastering basic design principles through studying abstraction and universal truths. Its influence was profound and is still detectable today in the curricula of design schools around the world.

But does it have a place in the new, networked, technologically advanced and globalized world? In a controversial essay published on the Core 77 website in 2010 ('Why Design Education Must Change'), the author and design commentator Don Norman wrote: 'New skills are required, especially for such areas as interaction, experience, and service design. Classical industrial design is a form of applied art, requiring deep knowledge of forms and materials and skills in sketching, drawing, and rendering. The new areas are more like applied social and behavioral sciences and require understanding of human cognition and emotion, sensory and motor systems, and sufficient knowledge of the scientific method, statistics and experimental design so that designers can perform valid, legitimate tests of their ideas before deploying them.'[1]

Norman's post drew a heated response. There was plenty of support for his view that designers need to be trained in more rigorous modes of practice. But he was also attacked for denying the benefits that an imaginative designer, free from the need to 'prove everything', can bring to the problems of modern life.

These two positions result in the tension at the heart of modern design education. Is design a discipline that must be taught with the rigour of science, engineering and computing, or is it an intuitive craft that is learned by 'doing', and encouraging and stimulating the visual awareness and critical mentality (the 'what if' gene) that most designers possess?

If this was the only question that design educators faced, we might have some hope of coming up with a solution. But it's not. The elephant in the academy is the rising cost of study. Thanks to a government that wants to reduce public spending regardless of social and cultural impact, design education – like all other forms of education – has become hugely expensive.

One of the many side effects of this is that it is prompting the rise of cheaper alternatives to universities and other established places of academic learning. The other day I was sent an email by Amazon Local offering me an 'online web design training package with 23 courses including Dreamweaver, SEO and Photoshop for £79 (regular price £959.98).' Or consider Shillington College, an Australian-based operation, now in London and New York, offering three month and one-year courses in graphic design. They don't list fees on their website, but they state their aims: '... to create a positive and inspirational learning environment where students are taught relevant industry skills, ensuring they have the best possible chance of employment as a graphic designer or to further the careers of those already in the industry.'

It's easy to see why these industry-focused, fast-track approaches would appeal to students daunted by the cost of three or four years of study with no guarantee of work at the end of it. Seen as retrogressive by many, cheap skills-based education systems receive tacit encouragement from employers who demand technical skills above conceptual skills.

Faced with this sort of competition, and the need to raise fees, universities need to concentrate on what matters most in a world of change. Three considerations predominate. The first is the need for collaboration: rather than teach designers engineering and science, as Don Norman advocates, teach the art of collaboration. The second is the need to promote critical thinking: passive acceptance of the status quo produces nothing of value. And thirdly, teach the art of learning. The only thing we can be sure about when we contemplate an uncertain future is that most of us will have to learn new skills and abilities. If we have learned how to learn, we stand a better chance of surviving.

1. www.core77.com (December 2012).

Sources

The unreal world. Winchester School of Art student publication *Out of dust; Power and Light*, 2010. See pp.262–624.

The student sensibility. *Design Week*, 6 January 2010. See pp.265–266.

Too many design students? *Design Week*, 2 April 2009. See pp.267–268.

Dan Fern and his RCA legacy. *Design Week*, 4 March 2010. See pp.269–271.

Ten things you should know about design students. *Design Week*, 28 July 2011. See pp.272–273.

Hyper Island – learning by doing. *Design Week*, 3 March 2011. See pp.274–275.

Education in the age of rising fees and speed learning. *Design Week*, 22 November 2012. See pp.276–277.

Miscellaneous

New York – still the greatest city in the world 2009

A recent trip to New York confirmed, for me at least, that the Big Apple is still the capital city of the world. It continues to exude an overwhelming power that is frankly unmatchable. And yet, there are signs that the great metropolis is coming to the end of its reign as the pre-eminent global supercity. Beijing, Mumbai, Bangkok and Rio are breathing down its neck in the race to take the title, and despite the gleaming steel and glass towers – unexpectedly radiant in some freakishly sunny November weather – it occurred to me that many aspects of New York's infrastructure look ramshackle. The old-fashioned bridges and the crumbly subway are signs of a city with its ancestry in the 19th century.

But I'm biased. I refuse to see New York as diminished. Its culture is in my bloodstream. The jazz age hip-hop of Duke Ellington; the surgical precision of F Scott Fitzgerald's prose (I defy anyone to read the descriptions of New York in *The Beautiful and Damned* (1922) and not feel a burning urge to walk down 5th Avenue); 1940s film noir; abstract expressionism; the saturnine cool of Miles; the Beats; Andy Warhol; the Velvet Underground; the sleazy glam of Studio 54; Don DeLillo; the graphic design of Lubalin, Dorfsman, Scher and Sagmeister. All these, and countless other aspects of NYC, have combined to form the way I see the world and to make me the person I am.

To that list I would have to add the photographs of Robert Frank. My visit coincided with a dazzling show of Frank's pictures at the Metropolitan Museum of Art. The show is a reappraisal of his most famous work, *The Americans* (1958) – the book that catapulted him to fame and which caused postwar America, then at the height of its imperial power, to look at its dark side and to reluctantly acknowledge that not everyone shared in the greatest economic miracle the world had ever seen [see p.382].

Like so many of New York's greatest figures, Robert Frank is an immigrant. Born in Zurich, he received a traditional Swiss photographic apprenticeship where he learned the mixing of chemicals, printing techniques, retouching and photo- and typographical montage (something that can be seen in his use of lettering, often gouged out of the emulsion of prints, in his later more self-expressive work).

Frank left Switzerland for the USA in 1947. He worked at *Harper's Bazaar* doing fashion shoots, but in 1955, with a grant from the John Simon Guggenheim Memorial Foundation, he went on an epic journey round America. Yet instead of photographing the nation's grandeur, he chose to shoot its poor, its rejects and its dark places.

He shot lunch counters, jukeboxes and lonely faces at windows. He shot everything with a revolutionary and egoless disregard for the conventions of framing, composition and subject matter. Few of Franks' subjects ever seem to be aware of his presence. His pictures are often out of focus. They appear 'found' rather than composed.

It was the vision of an outsider – a Jewish European man with a foreign accent – in a nation of outsiders, and it changed the way every photographer who followed Frank has seen the world. Now aged 95 – he might just be one of America's greatest living artists. And as a long-time resident of Bleecker Street (although he has also lived in Nova Scotia since the 1970s) he is yet another compelling reason to love New York.

Apprentice advertisers
2010

I've long since given up watching *The Apprentice*. It has gone from being a mildly amusing TV show to a serious blight on the cultural and business landscape. The idea that Lord Shoogha (an upgrade from the basic Siralun version) is representative of modern business is laughable.

Lord Sugar's 19th century mill-owner antics are only slightly less laughable than the ludicrous notion that he might actually want to employ any of the show-offs and airheads who cavort in front of him each week. Quite how any of these people have merited full-time employment contracts in the past is beyond belief. It says something about corporate Britain that makes my blood congeal.

It's time this ghastly piece of sham nonsense was pensioned off. It's not much better than that section of the 1970s TV game show *The Generation Game* where contestants were invited to try pottery, juggling or circus tricks with the sole intention of failing miserably and thus causing mirth in the homes of pre-Thatcher Britain. Younger readers should check YouTube to see what I mean.

But when I noticed that the customary episode devoted to launching, marketing and advertising a product was to be aired, I couldn't resist watching. In this episode, two teams of wannabe apprentices were invited to 'brand and advertise' a cleaning product. The fact that they made a dismal mess of the task is hardly worth mentioning. What really rankled though was the session in a 'top advertising agency' (can't recall which agency, but they had nice glass partitions in their offices).

The contestants were invited to make their pitches to a panel of agency people and a solitary client from an FMCG company. The agency people smirked, rolled their eyes and shook their heads as if they were witnessing a tipsy vicar conducting a wedding service.

After watching the predictably awful TV commercials made by the Apprentices, the agency bigwigs made sententious pronouncements. I think they thought they were on the panel of the Man Booker Prize. The client approached the task of commenting with all the seriousness and solemnity of a high court judge adjudicating on a case of national importance. These people should look at the state of current TV advertising before turning their noses up at the efforts of amateurs. I could name dozens of woeful ads that are no better than the amateur attempts on display here.

Supermarkets, big retailers, insurance companies and banks have dragged advertisings back to a sort of 1950s brutalism. But it's an odd time to be producing duff advertising: consumers are voting with their fingers and clicking off into new digital zones where they can't be easily reached or dictated to. Technology means we can escape into a new space where ads can be avoided. If agencies and clients want to reach us they are going to have to be much smarter and more engaging with their advertising.

Yet what is adland's response to this new challenge? Advertising that is deprived of wit and style; advertising that seems to assume that consumers are all morons; in fact, advertising that looks as if it has been produced by people from *The Apprentice*. Agencies in glass-partitioned offices should not be throwing stones.

Celluloid, laptops and digital magic
2008

Until the arrival of video cassettes, it wasn't easy to own movies. You could own books and records, but it was virtually impossible to own a film. In cinema's golden era, film was a public medium – a once-only medium. Movies needed special premises and special equipment in order to be viewed, and the viewer was required to turn up at an appointed time. Only the rich – and hardcore movie buffs – had private screening rooms; for everyone else, films were unpossessable.

But this only added to the allure and mystique of the cinematic experience: the essential unattainability of film was one of its great attractions. This attraction increased when you factored in the atavistic power of the great movie stars, and increased still further when you added the fact that to make a film – any sort of film, live action, animation, documentary – required vast resources. You needed a crew, equipment, actors, locations and money – lots of money. But most of all, you needed film craft, and it was in the interest of those who made films to shroud that craft in Masonic-like privacy.

Film is an art form, but it isn't an especially democratic art form. Despite its mass popularity, film has always been an elitist medium. Participation, on either side of the camera, was for the few; movies could only be enjoyed on terms dictated by studios and distributors. When films started to appear on TV, a slow process of erosion began, but it took the arrival of the home video recorder – followed by laser disc and now DVD[1] – to finally dent cinema's elitism. Film now entered the domestic realm and became, for the first time, a private medium; and as it migrated to a small-screen equivalency with television, it shed some of its mystique. Yet although video undoubtedly changed the way we watch films, and the way we make them, films still retained their essential aloofness and their own syntax – a syntax as distinctive as that of literature or painting. It took the arrival of digital film to offer a viable alternative to the traditional grammar of film.

Yet it can be argued that in Hollywood, nothing has changed. In Hollywood, 'digital' means 'special effects'. It means digital post-production, and the opportunity to make 'epic' cinema in the air-conditioned hush of the editing suite. It certainly doesn't mean better films. Compare Martin Scorsese's *Mean Streets* (1973) with his more recent *The Aviator* (2005). Which is the better film? *The Aviator* contains trace elements of Scorsese's cinematic genius, but it is ultimately a showy spectacle over-dependent on digital post-production technology. *Mean Streets*, on the other hand, was made using traditional film skills and with meagre resources. Pauline Kael famously called it 'a triumph of personal filmmaking', and it stands at the pinnacle of independent visionary movie making.

Martin Scorsese's films may not be improved by digital technology, but other, younger directors are using digital filmmaking techniques to create a continuum between *Mean Streets* and contemporary cinematic expression. Directors like Michael Winterbottom, Peter Greenaway and Mike Figgis (Steven Soderbergh is rumoured to making a series of digital films) are all making movies with digital cameras and digital editing equipment that can be compared with the best analogue tradition of cinema. However, not everyone agrees with this. The Master of the Cinematic Universe – Jean-Luc Godard – is unconvinced. In a recent *Guardian* interview to coincide with the release of his latest film *Notre Musique* (2005), the writer Geoffrey Macnab noted: 'In one of the most poignant scenes in *Notre Musique*, we hear a voice asking him [Godard] if small digital cameras can save cinema. There is a close-up of Godard's face: he scowls and says nothing at all. The inference is clear: the battle is already lost. As our meeting ends, I put the question to him again. There is still no answer.')

Godard's scepticism aside, the arrival of digital film has undoubtedly wrought changes to the aesthetics of film. Yet attempts to reinvigorate film syntax (Mike Figgis' *Hotel* is a courageous example) are few, and it's hard to justify a claim that digital filmmakers are offering a genuinely new cinematic experience. Most digital filmmakers – or at least digital filmmakers concerned with the narrative tradition of filmmaking – are content to work within the existing syntax of contemporary film. What we see when we look at new digital filmmaking is a return to lo-fi Cassavetes-like speed and realism, but more importantly, we see filmmakers claiming the freedom to make compelling films that bypass the suffocating power of Hollywood and other media owners. Ironically, the new digital production companies have been likened to Hollywood studios in the 1930s rather than to futuristic models for new filmmaking. These companies own their own cameras and editing facilities as a means of owning and controlling the production process, but it appears that their aim is to replicate what has gone before rather than creating a new blueprint.

If we want to see a new film syntax evolving we have to look to the digital filmmakers working outside of mainstream – or independent – cinema. We must look to advertising, music video, experimental animation and increasingly, computer gaming. Crucially, this is rarely the work of traditional film-makers. It is more likely to be the work of graphic designers, architects, computer games designers, maverick animators, music video directors and web designers. Today, only a tiny handful of students emerge from art school without the ability to produce some sort of moving image. Inexpensive software such as Flash, After Effects, Final Cut Pro, and cheap computers with hefty processing power, enable the visually astute to produce time-based programming that exhibits aesthetic and technical qualities as engaging as that of traditional film and animation. We live in the age of 'the garage Kubrick' – to use William Gibson's memorable phrase.

As Peter Lunenfeld notes in the introduction to his book *The Digital Dialectic* (1999): 'no matter how much digital systems resemble film or television, they are fundamentally different. The computer, when linked to a network, is unique in the history of technological media: it is the first widely disseminated system that offers the user the opportunity to create, distribute, receive and consume audiovisual content with the same box.'

In this new frontier, the camera has been replaced by the computer as the principal tool of the digital image maker. The processing power of the microchip has replaced light as the primary component in moving images. But most critically, digital technology has put the ability to make time-based media into the hands of individuals unversed in traditional film craft. It is now possible to make visually compelling moving image sequences in your bedroom. And what does that remind you of? The bedroom apocalypse of punk, perhaps?

You wouldn't want to push the comparisons between digital filmmaking and the mid-70s punk movement too far, but parallels exist. Punk was a grassroots eruption of musical expression that grew partly out of the political and social climate of the time, and partly out of technological advances that resulted in cheap musical equipment becoming widely available. But it also grew out of a sense of monumental frustration with the controlling power of the major record labels. And here a comparison can be made with guerrilla filmmakers and their exclusion from mainstream media. In Jon Savage's masterly account of punk, *England's Dreaming* (2005), he notes the suffocating dominance of the record industry: 'In the autumn of 1975, the mainstream music industry was not sympathetic to new groups that wanted to make an abrasive socio-cultural noise. As Dave Laing notes in *One Chord Wonders*, the music industry had reacted to the huge market that opened up in the 1960s by organising itself globally: over 60% of the English market was dominated by six multi-national companies. Their "gigantism" dominated pop music, in the market approach of flinging mud against a wall and in the favoured musical style, progressive rock, which was expensive to record, package and promote.'

This same 'gigantism' exists today. Cinema screens and TV screens are owned by a handful of media owners who are dependent on advertising revenue, and this means that there is not much room for radical and experimental filmmaking. Today, only the Internet (and one or two remote corners of the broadcast landscape) offers an outlet for the radical and the experimental.

Amongst print-based graphic designers there is much talk about authorship. Yet, for print designers, there's a problem here: graphic designers are conditioned to respond to briefs. It is part of the psychology of being a graphic designer: it's in the DNA. Secondly, graphic designers require 'content' – and whoever supplies content, controls the outcome. Content can be pictorial or textual, it can be narrative or abstract, but it is not something that designers are particularly good at providing. To the individual moving image designer, the notion of 'being the author' is entirely natural. Using the easy-to-learn, cheap-to-buy tools of digital image makers, a new generation of film makers are offering a viable aesthetic alternative to both mainstream and indie filmmaking, and this self-reliance has lead to an explosion of maverick expression.

The notion of filmless films – of movies made in computers – is intoxicating. This new sort of filmmaking opens up numerous avenues of exploration, and offers a set of intriguing possibilities not open to the conventional filmmaker. The all-digital realm is different. Take for example the notion of a work of art being 'finished': this is an alien concept to the digital filmmaker. Unlike 'film-based' film, when a print is made, that's it. The film can't be changed – well, not easily, and not without huge expense. But a digital film can be changed easily. If a sequence is constructed from binary information, it can be endlessly remixed. In the digital world the notion of a 'finished' work becomes redundant: think of digital music – tracks are reconfigured endlessly by remixers to the point that the notion of an 'original' is irrelevant, and music can now be said to exist in a state constant flux. Of course, this new fluid meta-universe of change doesn't always guarantee better 'art' – but it gives us a new syntax for moving image (and music) that the great artists of the past could not have envisaged.

In his book *Techgnosis* (1999), the writer Erik Davis coined the phrase 'silicon wizard world'. Like his fellow traveller in cyberspace, William Gibson, Davis is fascinated by the numberless possibilities opened up by digital technology. For Davis and Gibson (and you suspect for many of the people engaged in experimental filmmaking) the digital domain is a magical realm, but one that contains echoes of a much older pre-rational world. As Davis writes: 'Powerful new technologies are magical because they function as magic, opening up novel and protean spaces of possibility within social reality. They allow humans to impress their dreaming wills upon the stuff of the world, reshaping it, at least in part, according to the designs of the imagination.'

The idea of equating the digital with the magical is persuasive. Looking at the sort of work that has emerged over the past ten years (almost the same period that onedotzero has been collating the outpourings of this subterranean world), it is clear that we need new terminology to define this new sphere. The strange hybrid creations emerging from the digital underground are barely categorisable as 'films'. Can the men and women who make these fabrications be described as filmmakers or film directors? The language feels wrong. Perhaps 'magic' is the only word that captures the miraculous improbability of the best experimental digital work. And yet magical was how people described early cinema – the 'magical' flickering of light on a white screen – so perhaps not much has changed after all.

1. Written, of course, before the era of films downloaded from the Internet.

We're all stellar design gurus, now
2006

In her book *The Substance of Style* (2003), the writer Virginia Postrel notes that 'Worldwide, at least fifty graphic design magazines publish regularly.' Since Postrel wrote this in 2003, it seems likely that the number will have risen since then. There's an interesting study to be written about the current state of the various graphic design journals from around the world. But this is not it. Instead, I want to write about advertising in design magazines: or to be more specific, advertising aimed at designers.

Pick up any design magazine – highbrow or lowbrow – and the ads strike an oddly discordant note. They seem to be addressing a slightly different world from the one addressed by the magazines they appear in. Ads in the design press tend to be anodyne and patronising, especially in the way they speak about 'creativity', a concept bandied about as if it was a new wonder-ingredient in breakfast cereal.

Why is this? Surely a visually literate target audience might be expected to attract visually literate advertising? You'd have thought that the picture libraries, software vendors, educational establishments, illustration agencies, font houses and business services who regularly advertise in the design press would create advertising that tapped into the spirit of contemporary graphic design. Yet this is rarely the case.

In a recent issue of *Print* there was a total of 13 adverts for picture libraries (a mixture of double page spreads and single pages). The same issue also carried ads for printing services, paper companies and hardware manufacturers. One or two of the advertisers created ads that exhibited a bit of panache and adopted a tone that seemed to acknowledge that they were talking to a sophisticated and media-savvy audience. But the majority didn't.

A stock library called Inmagine treated us to a full-page ad featuring five immaculately styled uber-business types. Here was the award-winning sales-team from some go-go business: a band of young and spotlessly good-looking spreadsheet warriors who'd clearly just won 'sales team of the month'. We see them punching the air with choreographed delight. A headline screams 'Winning Edge!' It's a depressingly clichéd advertisement.

A few pages earlier, a company called Modern Postcard offers designers a direct mail and postcard printing service. It's easy to imagine this being an attractive proposition for small studios struggling to promote themselves. Yet the ad features a highly styled picture of a glamorous woman – a Sandra Bullock look-a-like photographed in a wind tunnel – with a bold headline announcing: 'Your ideas are fearless', while the body copy assumes an even more ingratiating tone: 'You're a stellar design guru. Able to conjure up mind-blowing ideas without breaking sweat.'

Is this the language that advertisers think will appeal to designers? Do they imagine designers will be flattered by being addressed as 'stellar design gurus'? I suspect most designers will feel patronised, rather than flattered. Of course, by saying this, I'm doing what the advertisers are doing: I'm assuming I know the audience I'm talking about. I'm assuming that because I'm patronised by this hyperbolic language, other designers will be too. How can I possibly know? Perhaps what I'm complaining about is advertising in general, and its lamentable tendency to treat great swathes of the population as if it is made up from identical individuals.

The dull and uninspiring ads that clog up the design press can at least be party explained by the smallness of the 'designer market'. It's doubtful if the combined spending power of graphic designers amounts to more than a tiny blip in the charts of hard-nosed media buyers – and as a consequence design journals attract low-grade advertising. Poor ads in the design press also make us think about the symbiotic relationship between advertising and graphic design. After all, these ads are executed by graphic designers working in ad agencies.

Advertisers – both clients and agencies – will point out that advertising can't be personal, it has to take a buckshot approach. They will say that the market decides what sort of advertising any particular sector gets. Yet advertising in the design press is surely different. To execute these ads, advertisers use the tools, tropes and attributes of graphic design. Advertisers are targeting an audience that will look at their ads with hypercritical and informed eyes. They will sniff out the half-baked, the clichéd, and the patronising.

Perhaps it's just that when advertising is targeted specifically at me, I fail to recognise the 'me' that it is being targeted. Perhaps we only recognise advertising's lack of precision when we are its intended audience. Perhaps we get the advertising we deserve.

Charles Dickens and the BBC
The case against dumbing down
2005

An alarming amount of my time as a graphic designer and art director is spent dissuading clients from taking the safe option. This doesn't come from a desire to be radical for the sake of being radical. Instead, it comes from a pragmatic conviction that success in most forms of communication (commercial and non-commercial) is best achieved by crediting audiences with intelligence, and avoiding clichés and formulaic gestures. But this is a hard argument to win. Brave clients are rare; there is security in sameness, and safety in dumbing down. Of course, dumbing down extends beyond the sheltered groves of graphic design: for countless activities, dumbing down is now the default position.

Scanning the cultural landscape for suitable examples to demonstrate that dumbing down is unnecessary is often fruitless. Good specimens are hard to find, especially for graphic designers (there are only so many times that you can wave a Dutch design book in front of a client). Yet a surprise candidate has appeared on the British scene. Who would have guessed that a prime-time BBC costume drama would provide us with Exhibit A in the defence's case.

The BBC's recent serialisation of Charles Dickens' *Bleak House* was a triumphant example of mainstream entertainment that had style and integrity, and was devoid of patronising tones. *Bleak House* is Dickens at his effervescent best – a thousand-page masterpiece of ravishing invention with enough darkness (and macabre horror) to keep James Ellroy fans transfixed yet sufficient romantic sentiment to melt all but the most stoney-hearted. With unexpected verve, the BBC took this epic novel and parsed it into 15, twice weekly, half-hour episodes. The £8m production was broadcast at 8.00pm (or 8.30pm) on Thursdays and Fridays – peak-viewing slots normally reserved for soap operas, quiz shows and other types of banal standardised entertainment.

The BBC has a long tradition of producing well-crafted costume drama. But *Bleak House* was something entirely different. The scriptwriter Andrew Davies took a forensic eye to Dickens' book and distilled it into a series of pared-down, dramatically-charged episodes. His script was brought vividly to life by two directors, and the art direction brilliantly transformed London into a kind of Victorian-era *Blade Runner* set. The acting was consistently strong, notable for some unexpected casting choices: *The X-Files*' Gillian Anderson, for example, played the female lead with impeccable aristocratic hauteur. Dazzling camera work made the series feel at once dynamic and relevant by contemporary production standards, and the editing made use of the sorts of fashionable slam cuts more commonly found in music videos and the better TV commercials. Apart from a lacklustre title sequence (surely some of the budget could have been spent on graphic design?) the production was practically flawless.

Though historically accurate, this was not a snooty, over-precious reworking of Dickens. It was vibrant and engaging, and – like Dickens himself – shamelessly populist. (Many of his novels were published in instalments and the author promoted them with frequent public readings.) It was brilliantly scheduled and cleverly promoted, and as a consequence, grabbed 29% of the UK viewing public.

To a global audience, the fact that the BBC has produced 15 episodes of high-quality costume drama will hardly raise an eyebrow. For most people around the world, the BBC is a paradigm of quality and integrity; indeed, serialisations of such classic novels are precisely what the public has come to expect. Yet for the British TV viewing audience, our sense of the BBC is different. The 'Beeb' still beats most of its commercial rivals for programming excellence and range of content, and we still turn to it instinctively at moments of national crisis. But in recent years, it has become drearily keen to serve up far too much dross for no reason other than to crow about its share of the viewing audience.

But why should the BBC chase ratings? After all, it is owned by the nation and paid for by a levy (the licence fee) charged to every UK household that owns a television set. It is a genuine public service broadcaster. Yet paradoxically, it's the BBC's public sector status that has led to its ratings-obsessed drift toward dumbed down broadcasting. So great is the fear that a free-market inclined government will revoke the Corporation's charter and cut it adrift to survive in the open market, that the BBC has felt compelled to insure against this eventuality, and it does this by ratcheting up its viewing figures by whatever means possible.

The UK government is currently reviewing the BBC's charter, and for some observers, the corporation's courageous dramatisation and daring scheduling of *Bleak House* is a calculated and cynical act of self-preservation. What better way to show the policy makers that the BBC is still committed to first-rate public service broadcasting than to stage a prime-time dramatisation of one of the classics of English literature?

This may be the case, but it doesn't negate *Bleak House*'s contribution to the dumbing down debate. A more effective rebuttal of the notion that dumbing down is a prerequisite of attracting a mass audience will be hard to find.

Register now to avoid disappointment
2010

Since voting in elections has become about as popular as summer holidays in North Korea, the Electoral Commission has decided that public money needs to be spent persuading us to re-acquire the habit of putting crosses on ballot papers.

A modest, unpretentious TV commercial is currently reminding us not to allow anything to get in the way of performing our democratic duty to appoint the person of our choice to represent us in Parliament. The experience of a young, independent, dog-owning female called Liz is offered to us as a warning.

A modern everywoman, Liz is dressed in Gap and lives on her own. We know this because why else would she take her dog to a polling booth? (Are dogs even allowed in polling booths?) We see her emerging from a grim looking block of flats. A sub-*Amélie* mandolin and piano soundtrack accompanies her as she sashays through the local park. She could be taking part in a low-key yogurt commercial rather than a publicly funded TV commercial exhorting us to vote.

Brimming with democratic intent she arrives at her nearest polling station, yet before she can fulfil her electoral duty she walks Marcel Marceau-style into an invisible glass wall and lands on her back. Poor Liz. She allowed something to get in her way; she neglected to register to vote.

On their website, the Electoral Commission announce themselves to be an independent body set up by the UK Parliament, 'Our aim is integrity and public confidence in the democratic process.' Integrity and public confidence, eh? Hardly words we currently associate with our governing class.

Of course, our reluctance to vote might be caused by any number of reasons: the fact that the insides of polling stations usually resemble sets from an episode of *Dad's Army*, for example. Or it might be because of those annoying people with rosettes who ask us for our voter's roll number as we leave the polling station. A more likely reason, however, is the massive zeitgeist-weighted feeling that all politicians are greedy 'cabs for hire'[1] without a shred of integrity between them.

Will this ad persuade people to register? Perhaps. But I think it will take more than sassy Liz and her dog to drain the abscess of public disillusionment with politics from the national consciousness.

1. Shortly before this commercial aired, a prominent former government minister was caught on film touting for lucrative consultancy work. The film was a sting by a TV journalist to highlight the ease with which former government officials could be hired by political lobbyists and others seeking to influence governments. The minister described himself as a 'cab for hire'.

Listomania
2006

About the same time that student designers confront the challenge of making typographic lists look superior to handwritten shopping lists, they also become acquainted with another graphic design staple – the reading list. The English design group Spin has just produced a publication called *50 Reading Lists*, which allows the reader the double pleasure of admiring the handsome presentation of fifty lists, as well as the chance to study the reading habits of fifty graphic designers.

Spin is run by designer Tony Brook, a collector of posters and books from the golden age of modernism. His enthusiasm for the period can be seen in his studio's work. In an introduction to *50 Reading Lists*, Brook notes that when he began his design education he was given a reading list: 'The recommended books covered many important subjects – Art, Architecture, and Photography – everything but Graphic Design, which simply didn't feature.' Today's graphic design student is unlikely to encounter such an omission. Graphic design books are only slightly less plentiful than celebrity diet books. The problem now is deciding which books are worth reading.

Brook asked his fifty contributors the same question: 'What are the top ten books that you believe designers should read? They don't necessarily have to be about Graphic Design ...' The contributors come mostly from the sharp end of the British design scene: Ian Anderson (The Designers Republic); Jonathan Ellery (Browns); Michael C Place (Build); Mark Farrow (Farrow Design); Daniel Eatock. A few Europeans make the cut: Experimental Jetset; Karl Gerstner; Wolfgang Weingart; Wim Crouwel.

Brook invited a number of US practitioners to take part, but only Bill Cahan, Allen Hori and the peripatetic Gelman responded. Cahan is also the only contributor not to submit a listing. Brook prints Cahan's explanation: 'This is going to sound awful, but I stay away from reading any journals about design. I find that I am so immersed in the design experience every day that I don't have the energy to work more by reading about what I am doing ... so for me it's a random experience picking up art books, going to museums, talking to people, quirky articles. It's just a more organic process so maybe I am just a really lazy person ... not sure but I hope this response is ok.'

Cahan's reply reminds me that until recently it was fashionable to hear designers say in interviews that they 'never look at design magazines or books'. I always found this dubious. I'm sure occasionally it was the truth, but mostly it felt like aloofness – a desire to be seen to be above the fray, a declaration about imperviousness to influences. You don't find it so often now – citing influences has become fashionable again.

Cahan aside, there is no coyness amongst Brook's contributors. The selections make interesting reading and provide a snapshot of current design thinking amongst an admittedly specific group of practitioners. The overriding bias is towards the defining texts of modernism. There is a preponderance of books by and about Josef Müller-Brockmann, Wolfgang Weingart, Wim Crouwel, Emil Ruder, Otl Aicher, Karl Gerstner and anything to do with grids.

The late Alan Fletcher includes his own book – *The Art of Looking Sideways* ('... because it contains fifty years worth of my own reading lists'). Paul Elliman chooses 'The newspaper' and 'The radio'. Ed Ruscha seems to be the modern designer's favourite artist. Books by contemporary designers such as Stefan Sagmeister, Bruce Mau and Peter Saville make only fleeting appearances, and no one mentions David Carson or Neville Brody.

Design books predominate, but there is a healthy quota of non-design titles. The works of John Berger are prevalent, as are the writings of Malcolm Gladwell. Evelyn Waugh's *Brideshead Revisited* (1945) and Thomas Hardy's *The Mayor of Casterbridge* (1886) make unexpected appearances, and there are some endearingly eccentric selections such as Michael Place's naming of *Incredible Cross-sections: The Ultimate Guide to Star Wars Vehicles and Spacecraft* (1998) and Peter Saville's inclusion of *Marquis De Sade: A Life* (1999).

There are no books on the hot design topics of the day – nothing on digital and electronic design (except a solitary entry for John Maeda); nothing on branding and hardly anything on advertising. Still less on green issues and not much that is overtly political – not even Naomi Klein shows up.

What would an educated, disinterested observer make of these lists? Would they conclude that designers are craft-obsessed introverts with not much interest in the world beyond the hidden power of grid systems and typographic nuance? Would they see a group fixated with ideas rooted in the pre-commercial era of modernist idealism? The selection of reading matter is of course mediated by Brook's choice of contributors. He hasn't strayed outside of a group of independent designers most of whom are engaged in cultural work. You can't help wondering what someone from the world of corporate or branding design might have chosen?

I should mention that I am one of the fifty designers invited to take part. Looking at my list, I see that I slot into the same readily identifiable profile as most of my co-contributors. Now that I've seen everyone else's selections, I'd like to re-do my own. Next time I'd be tempted to include one of the choices of another contributor, the creative director Brett Foraker. He chose an A5 blank cartridge notebook.

The estate we're in
2006

I suppose there must have been a time when driving was enjoyable. Today it is an almost unbearable chore; the aggression, the tailgating, the cutting up, the lane hogging – and that's just me, don't get me started on other drivers. In my admittedly jaundiced view, driving is an activity best avoided. Not only is it damaging to the environment, hideously expensive and laced with Ballardian anxiety, but as soon as I get behind the wheel, I turn into a different person – an unpleasant person.

I recently had to face up to my dislike of automobiles (and the person I become when I drive) when the family car needed replacing. I began by amassing a library of 'family' car brochures. Despite vast photography budgets, these documents are as insipid as motorway service station coffee, and mostly indistinguishable from each other. Surely not everyone fantasizes about driving at 140mph through the Atlas Mountains? And yet, despite my autophobia, I have a palely-flickering interest in the design of cars. Even I can see that there are well-designed vehicles, and vehicles that are just plain ugly. As a consequence, my purchasing decision was based mainly on 'looks' – but I also wanted a car with a low harmful emissions count, and a high miles-per-gallon score.

After consulting the brochures, I visited three dealerships. Car show rooms share a design ethos with the reception areas of provincial motels; they are designed for the Alan Partridge set. I didn't actually see any string-backed driving gloves for sale – but they had everything else the modern petrol head might want. Each of the three salesmen I saw looked mystified when I said I was concerned about emissions. 'Ah, so it's a company purchase?' they all said. Clearly this was not a question often asked by members of the public, but rather by the financial directors of big corporations looking for a tax break on their car fleets.

I ended up with an Audi. My rational, responsible citizen reason for this is that it boasted low harmful emissions and good MPG. But I will also confess to a grudging admiration for Audi's smooth Teutonic styling: if it was a typeface it would be a warm Akzidenz Grotesk rather than a chilly Helvetica.

And of course, I've now joined the Audi brand family. I've been sent a copy of a glossy magazine called *The Audi Magazine*, a slickly-designed document that oozes brand charisma. It has Jamie Callum on the cover and pictures of Pierce Brosnan and Jerry Hall on the inside. Am I supposed to be gratified by my new-found proximity to these celebs? I'm sure many people are, but in my case the effect of this crass brand engineering is to make me regret my choice of car.

And it's not just a magazine that Audi is using to woo customers with; it now has its own TV channel. According to *The Audi Magazine*: 'This ambitious initiative is a world first – the first manufacturer to launch its own TV channel and the first brand to go beyond advertiser-branded TV programmes.' It may be a 'world first', but does the world need TV channels run by brand owners? What next? The Mr Kipling TV Channel?

Branding as fibbing
2009

The giant insurance company Norwich Union is spending a lot of money telling us it wants to be called Aviva. I don't give a hoot what Norwich Union calls itself, but I care about how the communications industry conducts itself, and it looks as if it's shooting its big toe off here. Why is Norwich Union ditching its name in favour of a scrap of semantic gibberish that sounds (and looks) like a thousand other non-descript corporate names? And why is it using a misfiring TV commercial to announce its intentions? I can't help thinking that its rebranding exercises make branding into a laughing stock.

There might be good reasons for the name change. The company might be moving into foreign markets where the name Norwich is unlikely to set pulses racing; for all we know, it might be worried about the link between the fine city of Norwich and its most famous fictional son – Alan Partridge. But because we are not given a reason for the name shift, it has become a source of scepticism and derision. Newspaper articles mock the change, and to a media-savvy public it is seen as expensive and unnecessary spin.

What's more, the TV commercial presents us with a flawed proposition. It shows four celebrities who have changed their names. Yet the chosen quartet comprises people who have name-swapped for dubious reasons. When Ringo joined the Beatles it was the era of Billy Fury and Adam Faith, so he went from Richard Starkey to Ringo Starr. But if the Beatles were starting out today, he wouldn't need to do anything so corny – he could use his real name.

Alice Cooper could hardly have become a glam rock star called Vincent Furnier. But everyone knows that dear old Vince doesn't lounge about all day dressed in leather, petting his python and applying mascara; he's far more likely to be on the golf course. In reality he's no more 'Alice Cooper' than Alistair Darling is.

Most people know that Dame Edna Everidge has two names – Barry Humphries and Dame Edna – and both co-exist happily. And as for Walter Bruce Willis becoming Bruce Willis? Well, hardly even qualifies as a name change.

But there's a more serious matter here: by making an expensive fuss about its name change, Norwich Union is in danger of telling us that it cares more about its corporate image than its core business. When branding becomes the main selling point, it's time to get suspicious.

In his book *Obsessive Branding Disorder* [see pp.210–212], the business writer Lucas Conley puts forward the notion that the quasi-religious cult of branding has now, in many instances, become a substitute for good business practice. He writes: 'By abandoning the trusty, dusty principles of business – innovative products, good service, solid management – for the idealism of branding, companies reveal the true escapist appeal of their new religion.' In other words, the brand evangelists have become so effective that companies believe they can brand their way to success.

But this evangelism is in danger of backfiring. When branding is linked to failure (think US car industry and Wall Street), and when it is used to make meaningless name changes (think Aviva), it risks becoming discredited. And don't think it can't happen; business credos fall out of fashion just like haircuts and eyewear. Designers who dumped the old-fashioned term 'corporate identity' in favour of 'branding' might soon be thinking about doing a bit of name changing themselves.

The designer as buffoon
2005

I recently attended a publisher's party. In a room above a smart London restaurant I spent a pleasant couple of hours drinking lukewarm Chardonnay and chatting about books and book reviews to a bunch of literary types – publishers, editors, writers, journalists and book world movers and shakers. I'm a keen reader and try to keep up with the latest reviews and publishing-world news. During a conversation with a reasonably well-known English novelist I was asked if I 'reviewed much fiction?' I said: 'No, I'm a graphic designer.' I might just as well have tipped my drink over her. She recoiled in mild disgust, made an excuse and vanished into the canapés-guzzling throng.

What was this – simple literary snobbery or confirmation of the pariah status of designers? My guess is that it was an example of the low esteem in which designers are held by the educated – and the not-so-educated. This phenomena can be seen in two, big-budget, prime-time advertising campaigns currently showing on British television. Both Ford and Ikea are promoting their respective products by offering us pumped-up caricatures of designers and inviting us to guffaw at them.

Ford use a fictitious fashion-designer to endorse the Ford Focus, an inexpensive and surprisingly well-designed mass-market car. In a sharp bit of casting, our designer-hero is ruggedly handsome with a stubble-etched face and a shaved head. He semaphores his designerlyness by wearing flouncy shirts and exuding a faint whiff of camp. His 'otherness' is further accentuated by a bumbling, sycophantic 'straight man' – a sort of butler-cum-business manager – who fails repeatedly to meet our hero's exacting standards. In a series of unlikely vignettes the designer is revealed as a finicky fusspot obsessed with the look of everyday objects, and whose behaviour is verging on the unhinged.

Ikea offer us an even more ludicrous figure. There's no subtle casting here. Ikea's man is the designer from hell. He's some sort of European design fascist; a buffoon who appears to live in the house and garden you might imagine Elton John owns. He wears a beret and looks as if he's about to explode in a fit of designer pique. He even has a name and a manifesto:

his name is van den Puup, and he represents 'Elite Designers Against Ikea'. His role is to make Ikea look sensible, practical and democatic, a feat he achieves by espousing elitism and behaving hysterically.

What do these unflattering portraits tell us about the current status of designers? The message is ambivalent. By using designers as central motifs in their campaigns, these two global brands appear to want their cake and eat it. They want us to laugh at the designers – we can't possibly like or admire these preening monsters – yet they also want something that these two men have: they want to extract the cool quotient of design and inject it into their own products.

In a further twist, the depiction of both characters carries an undercurrent of sexual stereotyping. Both designers appear to be pandering to residual anti-gay prejudice. But yet again, there is ambivalence at work here. In Britain, over recent decades, the effeminate gay man has been a staple of TV comedy shows and sitcoms: today, however, the notion of the gay man as a paradigm of stylishness and superior taste has become embedded in popular culture. Modern sitcoms occasionally have gay characters who are allowed to behave with an enviable élan; TV makeover shows have gay men instructing clumsy heterosexual men how to dress, cook and decorate. In the popular imagination, gayness and designer fastidiousness are likely to be two sides of the same coin.

Ford and Ikea want to harness (or, as Orwellian brand-speak would have it, 'own') the undoubted coolness of both design and gayness. Yet at the same time, they want to distance themselves from the fundamental reality of both. In other words, they want a bit of design fascism, but not too much; the merest hint of design-lite will do. They achieve this by offering us ludicrous caricatures of designers, while calculating that just enough design star-dust will simultaneously adhere to their products to make the connection worthwhile. So why not use a real designer? A 'real' designer wouldn't have the dramatic impact of an overblown caricature; the audience would be turned off by the seriousness of the real thing.

You might think that to have design occupying a central position in mass-culture advertising is good for the image of design. Both advertisers might just as easily have chosen some other attribute of their products – affordability, practicality or green credentials – with which to promote themselves. And there may well be some cumulative benefit to design through its use as a component in advertising. Yet my guess is that when Ford and Ikea move onto other campaigns, and other messages, they will leave behind a global-village folk memory that depicts designers as preening ego-maniacs drowning in their own hauteur. And that wouldn't be right, would it?

Ethics and design
2007

Two examples of ethical weirdness in modern business. Example one: a female contestant on a TV show was asked to sell confectionary to children at London Zoo. She failed miserably. When Sir Alan Sugar confronted her with her lack of sales expertise, the woman confessed to having ethical scruples about selling over-priced sweets to children. 'Siralan' was apoplectic. She might as well have offered to stab him. He wasn't interested in her ethics: he was in business to sell things, he bellowed. She got fired.

Example two: every Christmas, Tracy Daly, the landlady of a pub in the north of England, offers her customers a 'Family Feast'. Ms Daly was surprised to receive a letter from a heavyweight firm of London solicitors instructing her to stop using the term 'Family Feast', as it was a registered trademark belonging to their client, KFC. When she rang to confirm that the letter was serious, she was informed that it was deadly serious. We might wonder how the lawyer who wrote the letter – a Mr Pratt – is able to sleep at night, but he doubtlessly justifies his firm's actions by citing the code that obliges lawyers to represent their clients regardless of their client's morals.

As designers, we are also faced daily with ethical questions. If a landmine company approaches us and asks us to create a friendly, smiley brand identity for them, most of us will say no. But what about the cool jeans company with sweatshops in the Far East – what should our response be to them? We can deal with it in the 'Siralan' way, and say this is business and we can't afford ethical quibbles: or we can adopt the lawyerly route and say, we think this project is dubious, but we're professionally obliged to do it to the best of our ability.

The key factor here is that as long as we don't break the law, we designers are free to do whatever we want. I've always enjoyed the freedom of working in an unregulated business. But I wonder if we've reached a point where we need to be able to turn to an ethical code to govern our activities? If estate agents can have one, why can't we?

The world is changing. The green issue alone means that we can no longer be safely left to decide what is right and what is wrong: we need help and guidance. All mature businesses and professions realise that they need ethical guidelines, yet the various design bodies only seem to be interested in making design attractive to clients. Advice on ethical conduct is conspicuously lacking. This hasn't always been the case – bodies like the SIAD once had rigorous ethical codes. My guess is that most designers would embrace a sensible, fair-minded and voluntary ethical code that provided guidance on issues like free pitching, copyright and plagiarism.

But what if this ethical code had rules on minimum rates of pay for interns and prevented studios from employing unpaid labour? What if it had rules on marking-up print and other third party services that obliged designers to reveal these figures to clients? In short, what if it curbed our ability to make money – even in a small way – in a business that is already tough and competitive? Would we be so keen to sign up? Or is any initiative that doesn't further the self-interests of designers doomed to failure?

The joy (and necessity) of collaboration 2010

Human beings are instinctively inclined to believe that there are giants among us who are the sole architects of great art, big ideas and superhuman feats of invention. This need for heroic figures is widely prevalent in design.

We love our solitary geniuses: Paul Rand, Alan Fletcher, Wim Crouwel. But according to a new book called *Where Good Ideas Come From* (2010), by the science writer Steven Johnson, the notion of the 'sole architect', and of the 'eureka moment' itself, is misguided.

Discussing his book in a recent *Guardian* interview, Johnson puts forward the notion that 'It's very, very rare to find cases where somebody on their own, working alone, in a moment of sudden clarity has a great breakthrough that changes the world. And yet there seems to be this bizarre desire to tell the story that way.'

Instead, he advances the theory of the 'adjacent possible'. The term was coined by the biologist Stuart Kauffman and describes the notion that, at any given time, only certain actions and ideas are possible. 'The history of cultural progress,' Johnson explains, 'is, almost without exception, a story of one door leading to another door, exploring the palace one room at a time.'

Johnson encourages us to acknowledge the power of networks - a force he sees at work in the collective energy of cities: in the coffee houses of 17th century Europe and today via the web. As he says, 'Chance favours the connected mind.' And the best way to have good ideas, it seems, is to resist fetishising the solitary genius of the individual and embrace the collaborative approach. Design is full of heroic figures and studios with a famous designer's name over the door, yet in reality assistants, collaborators and partners often do much of the work.

Increasingly, I tend to lean towards the view that design is a collaborative process, and rarely, if ever, a solo one. This is a problem for many designers, since most (and I include myself in this camp) are initially attracted to design by the concept of personal authorship. We mostly become designers so that we can hold up a piece of work and say, 'I did that'. I was so infatuated with this idea that when I had a studio, I actively encouraged the use of personal credits for individual designers. I wouldn't do this now, mostly for the reasons Johnson describes – namely, that creativity is almost invariably a collective activity that needs the 'adjacent possible' to exist.

But also because design has now become so complex that a networked or collaborative approach is obligatory. No single designer can master all the technical and creative disciplines needed to function as a 21st-century practitioner: we have to share the load with others to a much greater degree than ever before.

But the urge for personal authorship runs deep: it starts with the education of designers. Our entire design education system is predicated on the assessment of the individual. Collaborative working among design students is sometimes tolerated, but final assessments are based on individual performances. This creates designers who envisage themselves in the mould of a Fletcher or a Rand. Yet the reality is that most design is done in groups – and is the better for it.

Progressive design studios have long since worked out that the collective approach is the most productive. The universities are lagging behind here: a new way of assessing the individual is required. The old way is out-of-date.

Even design gets outsourced abroad
2007

I was speaking to a whip-smart adman the other day – no, seriously, he was super bright. During our conversation I told him, rather smugly, that I thought that design and the creative industries were immune from the trend towards 'outsourcing' services to the so-called emergent nations. I can understand why, I told him, that we have call centres in India, high-fashion handbags made in China, automobiles manufactured in Indonesia, but it is inconceivable, I went on, that businesses would go abroad for something as culturally sensitive as creativity.

The adman shook his head. In his opinion it was 'only a matter of time' before big corporations realised that they could turn to China or India and buy creative skills at a fraction of the cost they are currently paying. Besides, he added, it's a global marketplace and Occidentals are no better equipped to deal with the realities of the new business landscape than Orientals.

Financial power is lurching eastward, and the global economic map is being redrawn before our eyes. The former Reagan-era US treasury official Paul Craig Roberts, now a virulent critic of the Bush administration, has expressed the view that America will be a third world economy within twenty years. He notes: 'Short-run goals are reducing US corporations to brand names with sales forces marketing foreign-made goods.' He paints an unremittingly bleak picture of an America that only seems to know how to create government jobs, and which has blithely ceded much of its manufacturing capabilities to the Far East.

The more you think about it, the more my adman seems correct. It is delusional to imagine that the same corporations that are currently outsourcing manufacturing – and increasingly, services – to the Far East will be shy about commissioning Chinese, Indian or Korean agencies to produce creative work if they can save a few thousand dollars every time they do it.

A report on businessweek.com entitled 'India's Designs on Innovation' describes a newfound interest in design in India: 'So far, India has only a dozen design programs, compared with 241 in China. There are 300 design colleges in Korea, in contrast to India's ten. While China churns out 30,000 design students annually, India produces just one-third of that number.'

This emphasis on design education in Asia could be a double body blow for Britain. Anyone who spends time in the design departments of UK universities will know that the courses are full of bright Asians. The British treasury does extremely well out of the revenue generated by foreign students, and if they stop coming it will leave a painful void. Not only that, but domestically educated Asian design students will staff the agencies and studios of their native countries, who in turn will compete for Western business.

Globalization means that we in the West are free to go and bang on the doors of Asian corporations and offer our services. Some are already doing this. We can be confident that we can compete in terms of quality. But can we compete on price? On speed of delivery? On appropriateness for Asian markets? The new super nations are taking over our manufacturing base, there's no reason to think they won't make a grab for the creative skills we offer.

The 'auto-tuning' of design
2010

The discovery that singers on *X Factor* use auto-tune software gave the tabloids an excuse to indulge in faux indignation. However, not everyone was outraged. The BBC's art editor Will Gompertz defended the practice on his blog, saying, 'A singer's voice is just another instrument that has already been enhanced by the use of technology over the years. Almost nobody minds when a microphone is used to capture a singer's sound and then regurgitate it through a set of speakers, an amplification process that interferes with the purity of the natural voice.'

Complaining about the use of technology in pop music is like complaining about the use of water in showering, but Gompertz is wrong to equate amplification, which simply makes the singer's voice louder, with digital enhancement. This is a singing contest, and how anyone can judge singing ability if the singer's voice has been artificially modified is a mystery.

The use of auto-tune is symptomatic of a wider problem faced by everyone involved in communication. The need to add gloss and spin is now obligatory. For many designers, it's what we do. We transform dull, ordinary and downright boring things into exciting and sexy things. In other words, we use design as camouflage.

There's nothing wrong with this, you might say. Why shouldn't everything look and sound its best? But the mania for glossing, spinning and prettification has gone too far, and carries with it the risk that designers are only ever thought of by their clients - and the public - as part of the world of embellishment and falsity.

There's a lesson to be learned from the PR industry. PR has never been more powerful. Big PR groups have usurped ad agencies as the main custodians of corporate and, increasingly, national image. PR is now the big beast in the media jungle; it dictates the content of the press and news bulletins; it controls who appears on chat shows and magazine covers. And while few deny that in a complex, always on, media world there's a need for well-managed public relations, the PR industry has also shown that the higher it flies, the more likely it is to be exposed as pedalling bogusness and sham. In the era of blogging, tweeting and social networking, lies and half-truths always get found out.

Take the ill-judged remarks by the PR firm handling Naomi Campbell's recent court appearance. In an article for *PR Week*, they wrote that as a result of his company's hard work, the majority of the media coverage on the day after Campbell's court appearance was 'dominated by broadly neutral court reporting'. Broadly neutral? What remote galaxy is this man visiting from?

They go on to say, 'We wanted the event to be low-key, respectful and unfussy.' In fact, Campbell's performance was the opposite: she turned up late, banned photographers (despite the internal proceedings being broadcast on TV), and called her appearance an 'inconvenience'. If this had been a dispute about modelling fees it wouldn't have mattered. But it was about genocide. So it mattered very much.

For those of us who work in the communication, branding and media industries, the delusional side-effects of PR offer a timely warning. It is easy to be sucked into believing in what we are asked to use our skills and talents to support and promote. It's called being professional. But these skills and talents are too valuable to be wasted on half-truths and misinformation. If we want to stop the Max Cliffordisation of design, then the unvarnished truth is always best.

Design internships
2009

Philip Hammond is the Tory MP for that downtrodden, badlands constituency of Runnymede and Weybridge.[1] In an email replying to a question by a member of the public he wrote: 'I would regard it as an abuse of taxpayer funding to pay for something that is available for nothing and which other members are obtaining for nothing. I therefore have no intention of changing my present arrangements.'

Hammond – a senior opposition figure apparently[2] – was responding to an enquiry about his compliance with National Minimum Wage regulations in his recruitment of unpaid interns. You can read about Mr Hammond's email at Interns Anonymous, a lively blog set up by two graduates: 'We want this website to be a forum for interns to share their experiences and discuss the ethics of unpaid employment.'

The site's emergence is timely. The question of internships has become a hot potato. The debate was ignited by the recent report into social mobility in Britain called 'Unleashing Aspiration: The Final Report of the Panel on Fair Access to the Professions'. The report noted that internships in the professions – parliament, law, finance – were usually open only to the privileged classes with connections in these worlds, not to mention the cash to support graduate offspring.

But not all interns come from affluent well-connected homes and it is now standard practice for businesses and institutions of all kinds to make extensive use of unpaid interns – a fact richly confirmed by the plantation owner tones of Mr Hammond. But before we dismiss MPs, lawyers, financiers and others for exploiting unpaid labour, we need to remember that design has its own system of internships. How many of us can claim a faultless record in this area?

Interns Anonymous has a section on graphic design. It makes for sobering reading. One blogger writes: 'Some of the agencies offering me unpaid placements count Coca-Cola, Nissan, Manchester United, Sony and Nickelodeon amongst their clients. Some have over a hundred staff, and have numerous unpaid interns each week. Some are part of multinational corporations. Do they seriously expect anyone to believe they cannot afford to pay interns £5.73 for a few hours a week?' Another blogger bemoans the fact that his/her duties include having to: 'organise and book my boss' holiday, book restaurants for his friends, find tickets for shows, go to the supermarket, squeeze fruit into juice for five hours for a cocktail party etc., etc.'

We designers are quick to grumble about sharp practices amongst clients – free pitching and a cavalier approach towards intellectual property are two topics guaranteed to raise our moral indignation. But we can only claim moral superiority if our attitude to interns is beyond reproach. If we refuse to pay for their services, or if we pay them a fee but neglect to devote time or effort to advancing their knowledge, then we are no better than Philip Hammond or those unscrupulous clients who want free work.

When I had a studio, I always paid the interns. I didn't pay much but I paid something, and I always made sure that I spent time with each one. Sometimes they had to do the sandwich run or make the tea, but I never once asked anyone to pick up my dry cleaning. I'm sure there are a few designers who didn't get my full attention and left without much discernable increase in their knowledge of professional life. But I've met quite a few of them since and I haven't been punched yet. Still time, I suppose.

1. Irony alert! The parliamentary constituency of Runnymede and Weybridge is in fact an affluent area of the southeast England.

2. Philip Hammond has been an MP since 1997. He has been defence secretary since October 2011. At the time of writing he was an opposition MP.

Philosophy, graphic design, and virtue of clarity 2011

I spend a lot of time looking at the work of undergrad and postgrad visual communication students. The best work is frequently distinguished by an abundance of well-intentioned and sophisticated thinking around social issues. But I notice something else; it can be described as a reluctance to express ideas with clarity and brevity. It's as if there is a fear – a loathing even – of simplicity.

It's not hard to understand why. What bright intelligent person would want to produce the sort of facile and simplistic work that characterizes most advertising, branding and consumer-driven design? Much more exciting to dive into the murky sphere of ambiguity, mystery and gratuitous complexity.

Yet it seems as if a generation of bright young things is losing the ability to produce simple, clear and straightforward visual communication. This is not a plea for reductionism. Instead, it's a plea for complex ideas to be presented with intelligence, directness, and clarity.

I was thinking about this while cycling round my local park. It's a large tract of outer-London parkland inhabited by dog walkers, red-faced joggers and mournful-looking deer. I usually listen to music while making my circuits. Lately, however, I've been listening to philosophy podcasts.

Of all the humanities, philosophy is the one that interests me most. But here's my problem: I often read philosophical texts only to discover that the experience is like cycling into a headwind. I get to page twenty and my attention flags, with the result that a great deal of philosophical thought remains tantalisingly beyond my reach.

I realise the fault is mine. Philosophy is a subject that requires intense and prolonged study – philosophical writing can't be dipped into like we might dip into an airport block-buster. Yet it would be naive to imagine that philosophers – just like young graphic designers – are never guilty of deliberate obfuscation: if everybody understands what you're saying, perhaps you're not saying anything deep?

The podcasts issued by the website Philosophy Bites offer a refutation of the notion that philosophy has to be impenetrable. Here is an audio guide to current philosophical ideas from over a hundred thinkers on subjects such as Personal Identity, Free Will, Scepticism, Plato's views on erotic love, and Aristotle's take on happiness. The format is simple. Each podcast lasts about twenty minutes and features an interview with a philosopher on a topic that they specialize in. The interviewer – Nigel Warburton – uses plain English to ask a series of succinct questions. He is quick to pounce on any replies that are not readily comprehensible, or which fly in the face of common sense. His vigilance has the effect of compelling the interviewees to respond in language that is clear and precise.

What can designers learn from exposure to philosophy via these elegant podcasts?

Since the 1950s, advertising people have turned to psychology for guidance in how to drill messages into the human psyche. Today, however, there is widespread resistance to the hard sell, and commercial subterfuges are easily spotted. Philosophy, on the other hand, with its focus on truth and ethics, seems more in tune with the contemporary zeitgeist. When this is coupled with the newfound willingness of philosophers to deal with questions that were once considered beneath the subject's lofty aims, philosophy becomes an important aid for anyone interested in addressing 'real world' problems: multiculturalism, the commodification of the body, emotion, tolerance, and why our response to certain thing is to say 'Yuk', are all topics dealt with in Philosophy Bites podcasts.

Thanks to design's connectedness to nearly every aspect of daily life, the listener repeatedly encounters observations that relate to the practice of the craft. Exposure to current philosophizing refines our understanding of the world and inspires us to develop that most valuable of skills – critical thinking. And as exposure to these podcasts reveal, it is only by subjecting everything we come into contact with to intense interrogation that we can ever hope to understand anything.

But it is not only the philosophical content of these podcasts that will benefit designers. It is also the way in which thinkers repeatedly succeed in expressing complex ideas with clarity, directness and brevity. The almost casual elegance with which all the philosophers deliver their thoughts – no verbal tics or tortuous circumlocutions – is a revelation. Without exception the interviewees are characterized by a lack of the preening self-regard normally associated with modern punditry. Many admit to doubts and uncertainties. Variations on the phrase 'If I'm right ...' are frequently uttered as a welcome and humbling caveat. Dogma is notable for its absence. Instead, the listener is invited to eavesdrop on conversations where the human condition is treated with the inevitable uncertainty that confronts anyone attempting to find truth. To see what I mean, just sample the wonderful podcast called 'What is Philosophy?': each philosopher who is asked this seemingly facile question gives a different response.

Listening to modern philosophers it's clear that philosophy has abandoned the armchair and moved into the shopping mall and cyberspace. A modern generation of philosophers are helpfully making it possible for us to travel with them and, at the same time, providing a master class in the power of condensed and succinct expression.

Werner Herzog and the deeper truth
2006

Compared to the newer technological advances that enable us to experience, and participate in art and culture (television on cellphones, MP3 players, blogs), the DVD format appears almost antique. The first DVD players appeared in Japan in 1996, and in the USA the following year. Since then, DVD has usurped the VHS tape to become the dominant domestic format for watching movies and filmed entertainment.

Yet contained within DVDs is a technical feature that enhances our enjoyment and understanding of film to an unprecedented degree: these are the spare audio tracks that allow optional audio commentaries to be added. For hardcore cineastes – and bug-eyed amateur movie buffs like me – this is an invention of Gutenbergian proportions. Few technological advances in the realm of art and culture can equal the joy afforded by an articulate and perceptive commentary specially prepared to accompany a movie.

At its best, DVD commentary amounts to a new artform. I was alerted to this during a recent weekend spent enraptured by a DVD box set of the films of Werner Herzog. The film writer Mark Cousins, in his book *The Story of Film* (2004), said this about the maverick German director: 'After John Ford he is the most important landscape filmmaker to appear in this history of film.'

I've loved Herzog's movies since seeing *The Enigma of Kasper Hauser* in the 1970s. *Kasper Hauser* is an archetypal Herzog tale: it tells the true story of a teenage foundling in 19th century rural Germany. The real Kasper Hauser was locked in a dungeon at birth and deprived of all human contact until late adolescence, when he was dumped in a small Bavarian town and left to fend for himself. The film is an emotionally supercharged retelling of this famous tale.

As cinematic experiences, Herzog films are ravishing. The mundane plays no part in his fables: Herzog only has eyes for what he calls *ecstatic truth* – moments of visionary reality that defy the rational mind. To make his films, Herzog repeatedly pushed himself to the limits of human endurance. If you're new to Herzog, watch *Aguirre Wrath of God* and you'll be struck by many things, none more so than the realisation that filming this tale of doomed ambition took courage and endurance of barely imaginable proportions.

Yet Herzog's films are not easy. They have plot elisions and moments of logic-defying cinematic sleight of hand. Even when making films with historical antecedents, Herzog invents huge chunks of the story. His may be a cinema of landscape, but it is predominantly a cinema of the imagination. He has said: 'I've always made it very clear that for the sake of a deeper truth, a stratum of very deep truth in movies, you have to be inventive, you have to be imaginative.'

Even with a close reading of Herzog's films you can't hope to understand or grasp every nuance; many of his narrative gestures are so deeply personal and so rooted in childhood experience that only Herzog himself could explain them: this is, as it turns out, precisely what his audio commentaries do. As a lucid and revelatory commentator, he is able to illuminate both the creative process of filmmaking and the labyrinthine business of bringing movies to the screen. The making of films involves a complexity that few art forms can rival, and the conceiving, writing, funding, casting and shooting of even a modest film can often generate its own mythology – a mythology that is sometimes as interesting as the film itself. *Apocalypse Now* is perhaps the most celebrated example of this phenomenon: a film whose gestational process was as interesting as the actual movie.

Much of the material we get from DVD audio commentaries is also available in books and articles. Reading the great film writers – Pauline Kael, Manny Farber, David Thomson – is one of life's great joys. But with this joy comes a small ache: reading about films makes you want to watch them there and then. No matter how good the writing, you want to see the art being described.

But the fusing of words and pictures in DVD audio commentaries creates a potent magic that is rarely achievable in books and articles about cinema. Something special happens when insightful filmmakers talk about their work while we are simultaneously able to view their movies. In a recent Herzog film, the documentary *Grizzly Man*, the director provides a commentary – not as an optional extra, but, as is customary in documentaries, as an integral part of the film. He does this in typically Herzogian style: no cool detachment for him. In fact, he does it in the style of a DVD audio commentary, clearly influenced by the commentaries he has made for his other films: art imitating art, you might say. And technology allowing us to appreciate the deeper truths of art.

Design and royalty
2004

I went to Buckingham Palace the other evening to meet the Queen. I didn't actually 'meet' her in the end, but I saw her standing amid a glittering array of Britain's finest design talent who had graciously accepted an invitation to a reception at her SW1 pad.

My mildly-republican tendencies were tested when I opened an invitation that came in the post to attend a reception to 'celebrate British Design'. I was mystified by the selection process that had thrown up my name. Had a pin been stuck into a list of D&AD members' names? Was Prince Philip an avid reader of my monthly appearance on this page? Who knows? But after about 20 seconds of deliberation I thought what the heck, you don't get invited to meet the Queen every day of the week.

To enter the Palace, guests were required to walk through a courtyard displaying iconic examples of British design: a Routemaster bus, a London taxi, a Mini Cooper S, a red telephone kiosk, the nose of Concord. All worthy specimens, but hardly the modern face of British Design. My heart sank a bit: was this to be a gathering of design's old guard? A small booklet handed to guests as they arrived, listed all the attendees. The list included an imaginative cross-section of figures from fashion, education, graphics, interaction, branding, architecture and product design.

Whoever was responsible for compiling the list did a good job in their generous vision of what constituted British design – but why no Neville Brody, arguably the most influential of all British graphic designers? Names on the list included: Peter Blake, Derek Birdsall, Terrence Conran, Robin Day, Tom Dixon, Mike Dempsey, Mark Farrow, Dan Fern, Norman Foster, Zaha Hadid, Adam Hart Davis (haven't seen much of his work in *Creative Review* lately), Martin Lambie-Nairn, Mary Lewis, Ross Lovegrove, Michael Johnson, Wally Olins, Malcolm Garrett, Quentin Newark, various Pentagram bigwigs, Paul Smith, Peter Saville, Tom Roope, Philip Treacy, Simon Waterfall, Thomas Heatherwick, Christopher Frayling and the editor of this magazine.[1]

Buckingham Palace is less dowdy than we are led to believe. Admittedly there's more flock wallpaper on display than you'll see in a thousand Indian restaurants, and the design revolution that has transformed the homes of millions of Britons hasn't troubled the royal palace yet. But the vastness of the place, and the superabundance of magnificent art hanging on the walls, made walking into Buck House a genuinely awe-inspiring experience. I didn't spot any Tupperware, and the corgis weren't to be seen, but you can see why firebrand Labour politicians and wannabe radicals like me are won over by the sheer grandeur of it all.

The best thing about the evening was watching the other guests. All 400 were crammed into a suite of rooms, and a small posse of Royals led by the Queen, mingled amongst the throng. Witnessing some of British design's finest jockeying for key positions on the Queen's path through the crowd made for great theatre. I saw people strategically positioning themselves in the expectation of catching her eye: some were successful, others got Prince Philip.

The Queen wasn't alone. David Kester, chief executive of the Design Council, appeared to be chaperoning her through the melee, and a small group of public-school-cum-Sandhurst types (although they might have been eminent architects or branding consultants) acted as out-riders, keeping an eye out for any cheeky designers stepping out of line. Beyond the men in regimental ties was a pack of ferocious looking Ladies-in-Waiting who swarmed around Her Maj in a vaguely menacing way.

These women provided the highlight of my evening. Probably never seen outside of Kensington, they looked a bit like Montgomery Burns from *The Simpsons* in drag. They were stick thin, with sharp faces and the most astonishing hairstyles I've ever seen – huge balls of spun steel that looked like more like sculptures than hairstyles. None of the guests, not even the dandyish designers who clearly shared a tailor with Laurence Llewelyn-Bowen, came close to the sheer exoticism of the Ladies-in-Waiting.

I only caught a few glimpses of the Queen. She looked at ease, although you couldn't help thinking that she'd have been happier with an evening celebrating the Ambulance Service, District Nurses or the bloodstock industry. After an hour or so of mingling, she was whisked through some ornate glass doors and the evening was over. The rest of us went home, waking up the next day with mild hangovers caused by the lavish dispensing of drinks (lashings of gin and whiskey). No lie-in for the Queen, however. She had to be up early for the State Opening of Parliament.

1. Lynda Relph-Knight, editor of *Design Week*.

New business and how to get it
2004

New business: arguably the two most important words in a design consultancy's vocabulary. You can use other terminology. You can call it 'business development', 'marketing', or 'sales', but 'new business' has that Ronseal directness that focuses the mind. It means getting new work through your door.

What's the best way to sell design? Is it wise to try and sell it like any other business sector service? Or is design inimical to conventional sales techniques? While we're on the subject, I wonder if it's feasible today for any business sector services to be sold successfully using conventional sales tactics? Consumers seem increasingly resistant to modern selling strategies. Cold calling, most forms of direct mail and the ubiquitous spam are imprecise, intrusive and wasteful. Just ask anyone who has had a call at home at 8.00pm selling double-glazing or financial services, or has had to clear out thickets of unwanted emails from people flogging stuff no one wants. And if the general public doesn't like these tactics, we can be sure they won't be any more popular in the professional sector. In the context of selling design, most sales activities have the effect of saying 'I'm desperate'.

But if you're the new business person in a consultancy, you have to get new work through the door. Even when business is buoyant this is never an easy job. And it's especially difficult today when the buyer is nearly always king, when competition has reached new peaks of intensity, and when new business success is measured, not by the number of jobs won, but by the number of pitch lists you can get on.

If you're responsible for new business in a big, well-upholstered design company you will have the funds to use all the latest sales and marketing strategies. You will be hip to current CRM thinking. You will operate a sophisticated turbo-charged database. Your bed-time reading will be fierce-looking documents with titles like 'Customer Value Maximisation'. You will host seminars, give lectures, publish research, get written about in *The Economist* and maintain an ultra-slick website.

The rest of us have to rely on less sophisticated methods. We might have a brochure and a modest website. We send out email newsletters, and every so often we send out an eye-catching printed mail shot. We enter design competitions in the hope of being able to append the words 'award winning' to our work. We send projects to the design press in the expectation of attracting the camera flash of media attention. And from time to time, we spruce up our portfolio and call existing or potential clients and ask them if we can show them our latest work.

Occasionally, just occasionally, these tactics succeed. But regardless of our best efforts – sophisticated or unsophisticated – most sales activity relating to design is close to worthless. My bet is that a huge proportion of new business opportunities for design are created in one of two ways: the first is via word of mouth, and the second via random encounters in the business and social nexus that most of us live in. In other words, we get most of our work from people who've heard good things about us, and from networking.

Now, I'm not advocating a do-nothing policy here. What I'm saying, however, is that the secret of new business is to get clients to call us. A call from a potential client with a nice project and a bit of cash to spend is the multiple orgasm of new business. But how do we attract those calls? Well, by doing great work which gets people talking, and by shamelessly exploiting the chemistry of human relationships.

I know of consultancies that don't do 'new business': no portfolio, no website, no slick brochure. And yet they have clients queuing up to commission them. They rely purely on their reputation to generate new business. But this policy doesn't work for everyone. For most of us, new business is a never-ending slog and we try anything and everything. A friend of mine thought about opening a design company on his local high street and inviting clients to wander in and commission design just as they might order a new carpet or a holiday in The Maldives. It's a neat idea, but I can't see it catching on.

My own less dramatic recommendation is that you give everyone in your consultancy a second job description. By adding 'new business' to everyone's job description you remind people that no matter what their job is, they also have a business-generating role. Even suppliers and professional advisers can be harnessed into performing an unwitting new business role; treat them right and they become powerful advocates of your company. Then just sit back and wait for the phone to ring. The first call will be from someone selling time-share options, but the next one ...

Safety and comfort
A walk with Paul Davis
2010

London: an early morning train in January. I'm trying to concentrate on my book but the guard is making banal announcements, and I read the same paragraph over and over again. He urges us to be careful on the icy platforms. He is concerned about our safety and comfort.

I'm on my way to see the artist Paul Davis. The train announcer would make a good target for one of Davis' satirical drawings. It's easy to imagine him savaging the guard's unctuous pronouncements and the feigned concern for our safety and comfort.

Davis has asked me to write the introduction to his latest book. I told him I didn't want to write about the usual stuff – art school, his first job, wrangles with clients. He agreed and suggested we go for a walk instead. We decide to stroll around Shoreditch in East London – a once raffish and impoverished district but now a fashionable area of bars, galleries, and design studios. We could be flaneurs for a day, I said. I could be Boswell to his Johnson.

We agree to meet in a café. We are the only customers. We gossip and trade design industry tittle-tattle. Davis moans cheerfully about gutless commissioners who say they like his work and then get other people to rip off his style. He's not bitter – just uncomprehending. He describes a life of furious productivity. He works every day, he says. Drawings pour out of him; he draws as often as other people draw breath. Later, at his studio, he shows me the outcome of all this effort.

We leave the café. The iron-grey sky has been replaced with the brittle yellowy brightness of winter sun. Davis talks about money. His girlfriend. His recent attack by an unknown assailant. I knew Davis had been beaten up, but I didn't know the details. When mutual friends had spoken about it, they had winced sympathetically in a way that discouraged questions. I asked him what had happened. He told me that he had left his flat early one evening. As he walked down the street someone came up behind him and smashed him on the head with an unknown object. He only remembers waking up in an ambulance. The attacker had severed an artery in Davis' head. His face was a mask of blood.

He has no idea why he was attacked. The same thing has happened to other people he knows. He thinks it might have been a gang initiation rite: young bloods earning their stripes by performing acts of random violence. Davis seems an unlikely victim. He's wiry and agile. Not an obvious soft target. But evidently someone thought it was a good idea to bash him on the head. Safety and comfort.

We pound the pavements around Brick Lane. We pass galleries and shops. Everywhere we look we see signs of the bo-ho gentrification that is turning Shoreditch into just another precinct of tourist London. Davis points to the myriad of tiny ovals of flattened chewing gum that cover the roads and pavements. There are thousands of them momentarily illuminated and glowing in the January sun. It's like a shoal of tiny flat fish veering into view. He says that these blobs – and the blobs that appear on his retina – inspired the ovals that populate his newer work.

After Brick Lane we push eastward. We stand in the bandstand at Arnold Circus. Davis smokes a cigarette. The elegant redbrick housing estates are quiet. No one is on the street. No traffic. We wander over to the Rochelle School, a Victorian building with separate entrances for boys and girls. It's no longer a school, but if you listen carefully you can hear the ghostly yelping of hundreds of children from the nearby Boundary estate – one of the first housing estates in the world and a legendary place in East London social history.

The Rochelle School is now a fashionable spot on the map of London, inhabited by a gallery, an artist's agent, a design studio, a publisher and – where the old bike shed once was – a swanky eatery. Davis meets someone he has had professional dealings with. They tap dance around each other – he charming and eager, she wary and distant.

We head back to Davis' studio. We look through his work. I get a reminder of his furious energy and productivity as sheaves of sketches are laid out on every available surface. I notice that the drawings are full of brightly coloured ovals, and I remember the chewing gum [see p.383].

We go to lunch at a nearby restaurant. Afterwards we head off in opposite directions. I keep thinking of Davis' attack. I can't get the thought of it out of my head. I hear footsteps behind me. I look round. It's a gangly youth. In his hand he carries a gun. But it's only a cup of coffee with a plastic lid. Safety and comfort on the streets of London.

Preparing for emergencies
2004

Twenty-five million funky little leaflets were delivered to UK households during August by the British government. The leaflets, and the envelope they were delivered in, featured a vaguely techno-looking graphic device that looks as if it might have been designed for a night club flyer. Picking up the envelope, you half expect it to be a public health warning about the dangers of ecstasy.

In fact, this 22-page, A5 landscape document is the UK government's attempt to advise the nation's citizenry about what to do in case of an 'emergency'. The tenor of the document is friendly – almost casual. The title, *Preparing for emergencies – What you need to know*, appears in VAG Rounded (you can tell when someone's trying to be friendly in print – they use a sans serif font with rounded characters). The government explains its intentions thus: 'This summer we are sending an information booklet ... to every home in the UK. It gives practical common sense advice on what to do in an emergency – for example, a fire, terrorist attack or natural disaster.'

Ah, 'terrorist attacks'. So that's what it's about. But the government is falling over backwards not to alarm us. The document has no pictures: there are no balaclava-helmeted assassins, no gas masks, no cold war mushroom clouds, or any of the imagery traditionally associated with government warnings of immanent disaster. In fact, so keen is the government not to spread panic, we are given a carefully manicured document where graphic design and cautiously modulated prose are used to invoke only the mildest sense of warning. The government has also funded a stylish TV commercial to tell us about the leaflets. The commercial is arty and moodily atmospheric. It makes the point that there are signs everywhere warning us of everyday dangers: fire extinguisher signs and the like. We are calmly requested to look out for the government's brochure, which is really no more alarming than a fire extinguisher sign. The spot makes effective use of Steve Reich-type music to emphasis its simple message.

The brochure itself is agreeably non-threatening. The front cover features six circles with thick black outlines butted up to each other. Each circle contains a symbol (one circle contains the UK emergency telephone number), and each symbol sits on a pleasant, easy-on-the eye colour. The 'techno' graphic device is a step-by-step procedural code (not many people will bother to work it out), but its real purpose, you suspect, is to serve as a sort of visual mnemonic: a 'brand mark' for the government's vigilance in the 'war on terror'.

The page layouts and internal typography deploy techniques commonly used in advertising and retail promotions: lots of text in panels with rounded corners; a mix of type weights and sizes; extensive use of italics; headlines in lower case with key words picked out in colour. The effect is bitty and indicative of a concern that the document won't be read unless everything is put into low-attention-span-friendly, bite-sized chunks.

I said there were no pictures. Not true. There are some tiny black and white portraits of important people: amongst others, we see the Chief Executive of the Emergency Planning Society, Chief Medical Officer, and Head of MI5 (the UK's 'security service'). They all look reassuringly normal. The sort of people you might pass on your way to work. Not a mad-dog general amongst them.

In the event of an attack we are advised to 'Go In, Stay In, Tune In'. This phrase, a clumsier version of Timothy Leary's 1960s mantra of psychedelic subversion ('Turn On, Tune In, Drop Out'), was developed by the National Steering Committee on Warning and Informing the Public. 'It is the key message for people who are not in the immediate location of an attack and therefore not under the direct instruction of the emergency services,' explains the agency.

Designers who advocate radicalism and the avoidance of formulaic design can hardly complain about the 'look' of this small document. It is required to be accessible to a population of nearly sixty million Britons (foreign language editions are available, as is a braille version) and it is required not to exacerbate a climate of general paranoia and widespread concern about the threat of a terrorist attack. It achieves these goals with a light and unpredictable touch.

And yet, because of a willingness to utilise design and communication techniques more suited to advertising, the result is hardly an authoritative piece of communication. If ever a document was crying out for a modernist aesthetic (rational and truthful), it is this slim pamphlet. Of course, modernist design has long since become 'just another style', and if the booklet had been designed in the austere modernist manner it would doubtless have attracted criticism from non-designers who tend to view modernist design as 'boring'.

It raises the question: what is the correct response from the contemporary designer to this sort of task? Clarity and legibility are high priorities; but so too are integrity and plain-speaking. Strange therefore that the UK government, its advisors and its uncredited designers should have turned for inspiration to advertising, rave culture and an American 1960s psychedelic prophet.

The natural digital world
2009

Surely I can't be the only one who sometimes gets confused between the digital realm and the physical world? The other day I was looking for a book amongst the clutter of my studio. I usually know where to find stuff, but on this occasion I was stumped, and for a split second I thought about tapping the title of the missing book into Google. As quickly as the thought occurred to me, I recognised it as loopy.

Yet the fact that I even considered it shows the extent to which life has become unthinkable without the countless online and interactive aids that surround us. For most of us, the digital realm is as natural as the grass that grows in the fields.

And yet, this naturalness, this acceptance of and reliance on digital ways of doing things is transforming how we live and work. I can list dozens of mundane aspects of my life that have changed irreversibly. I haven't bought a CD for months (but I listen to more music and a greater variety of music than ever before); I watch more television on my laptop than on my TV; I still buy *The Guardian* everyday, but probably spend more time on the paper's website than I do with the woodpulp version; I can't imagine how I ever got anywhere in the days before Sat Nav; I have written and posted only one letter this year; I haven't used a call box or payphone since I got my first mobile phone sometime in the 1990s.

Most people would agree that life has been improved by the digital revolution. Yet I wonder if we can be so sure about the psychological impact of this technological eruption? Take the question of memory. It might just be advancing years, but I swear my memory is getting poorer. Could this be because I have come to rely on the great throbbing, always-on brain called the Internet? And does it mean that there will come a time when we will lose long-term memory because there will be no need to remember much since everything will be stored in the limitless vaults of cyberspace? If you think that's far-fetched just remember that our toes were once used for gripping branches. When we learned to walk upright, they changed and ceased to be prehensile. Perhaps our brains are going through a similar transformation?

But it is in the realm of interpersonal relationships that we see the most visible changes. The Archbishop of Westminster, Vincent Nichols, head of the Roman Catholic Church in England and Wales, recently warned against social networking sites. He noted that they built 'transient relationships' that can leave users traumatised and even suicidal when these relationships collapse. His comments came after the inquest into the death of 15-year-old Megan Gillan, a student who took a fatal overdose of painkillers after being bullied on a social networking site. The Archbishop went on to say that the Internet and mobile phones were 'dehumanising' community life and that relationships had been weakened by the decline in face-to-face meetings.

The Archbishop is right to raise concern. But bullying, dehumanisation, and failed relationships have existed in the workplace and the playground for centuries, and seem neither better or worse because of online social networking. All the social networkers I know seem to cope pretty well with the distinction between digital friends and flesh and blood friends.

My concern is slightly different. I'm saddened by the end of privacy. By privacy I don't mean anti-community feeling, or misanthropic tendencies. Instead I'm referring to that perfectly reasonable need to keep aspects of our lives to ourselves. In other words, the need for an inner life. But social networking sites – and many other aspects of digital technology – encourage us to live our entire lives in a blaze of self-revelation. What does this do to our sense of self? If we have no sense of balance between our inner and outer selves, how do we stop ourselves becoming pub bores on a global scale?

One thing's for sure: we'll find out soon. We don't have to wait long for anything in the new digital world.

The myth of originality and the joy of copying 2011

Originality isn't all it's cracked up to be. For a start, it doesn't really exist. The idea that something can be said to be truly original is laughable. There is no immaculate conception. Everything comes from somewhere: everything contains elements of something else. If we were ever to be confronted with an artefact or an idea that was genuinely original, we wouldn't be able to see it or understand it. We wouldn't have any reference points with which to identify it.

If originality is illusory, why then is it so highly prized – especially in the realm of commercial art and design? Nearly all commercial illustration, branding, advertising, etc., is about communication, and if we want to communicate, we have to use recognizable symbols, words and visual tropes. Even when we want to shock, or make statements that are mysterious or enigmatic, we do so by blending visual elements and language in unexpected ways – in other words, we appropriate – but in truth, we are really copying.

To be found 'guilty' of copying in the commercial realm is about the most heinous crime a creative person can commit. Copying and plagiarism are generally regarded as bad, which in turn, forces designers to strive endlessly to be 'original'. This is done with noble intentions. But it is mostly delusional, futile and based on a false understanding of originality and a false understanding of the nature and role of copying.

In his book *In Praise of Copying* (2010),[1] the writer and journalist Marcus Boon delivers a hefty body blow to our cherished notion of copying as evil. He writes: '... suppose copying is what makes us human – what then? More than that, what if copying, rather than being an aberration or a mistake or a crime, is a fundamental condition or requirement for anything, human or not, to exist at all?'

Certainly, the art world doesn't share the commercial world's hang-ups about copying. For centuries, artists have learned their craft by copying the work of the masters who went before. No classical education was complete without the act of studying, absorbing and copying the past – especially antiquity.

Artists were trained in schools of art that made no apology for continuing rigid traditions through the act of copying. In modern times, the unapologetic appropriation of other works of art has been part of the artists' trade since Duchamp slapped a gallery sticker on a mass-made porcelain urinal and called it art.

The shared cultural heritage of the pre-modern era allowed the free exchange of ideas, styles, stories, motifs, symbols and artistic traditions, and also permitted the appropriation of artistic concepts (Shakespeare borrowed plots from other playwrights). But this was jettisoned when capitalism became the western world's dominant economic system, especially the version practised today by the neo-liberal forces that have governed in recent decades. Capitalism meant that the measure of nearly everything became financial rather than cultural, which in turn gave rise to the use of copyright, trademark protection and IP rights to safeguard the financial interests of those who could afford the protection. Yet as Marcus Boon points out, capitalism itself is dependent on the notion of copying and appropriation (as evidence, he cites everything from slavery to the endless replication of consumer goods on the shelves of supermarkets).

But perhaps the most damaging effect of capitalism is that it has created a fractured culture: a dog-eat-dog ethos of snarling competitiveness and enslavement to the never-ending conveyor belt of productivity, progress and profit. It has made everyone we meet into our rivals and adversaries: it has made each of us into psychological isolationists, fearfully watching for invasion from our competitors. It has meant that everything is owned, and not much is shared.

The complexity that surrounds our ideas of originality and copying in the modern world is encapsulated in the laws of copyright. A legal basis for copyright didn't exist until 1710 when the British parliament introduced the Statute of Anne as the world's first copyright law. This related only to printed books, and granted publishers legal protection for 14 years. The Berne Convention of 1886 was the first attempt to secure the rights of the producers of literary and artistic works. The Convention requires its member states to provide protection for every production in the literary, scientific and artistic domain.

This all sounds reasonable. Creative producers should be protected. Plagiarism and theft should be prevented. Yet look at what has happened to the way copyright works today. Think how we'd laugh if we heard of classical painters being sued for 'copying' Greek statues in drawing classes. And yet, thanks to an out-dated and inadequate notion of copyright, this is pretty much what happened to designer/artist Shepherd Fairey, who was successfully sued for basing his famous Obama portrait on a photograph of the US president 'owned' by a picture agency.

This seems to fly in the face of natural justice, but US copyright law states that the making of 'derivative works' – that is works based on or derived from another copyrighted work – constitutes a breach of copyright. The ludicrousness of this is demonstrated by the simple observation that there never was a work of art that in some way wasn't derivative. To further illustrate the bizarre nature of copyright – especially in the digital age – the mere act of providing a link on your website to the website of someone who doesn't want to be linked to, might be cause for litigation. Sampling a single drumbeat from a copyright protected recording can result in prosecution. Unlicensed photocopying of a page from a book is a criminal offense.

In an important contribution to the question of originality and copyright in creative production, the novelist Jonathan Lethem has written: 'few of us question the contemporary construction of copyright. It is taken as a law, both in the sense of a universally recognizable moral absolute, like the law against murder, and as naturally inherent in our world, like the law of gravity. In fact, it is neither. Rather, copyright is an ongoing social negotiation, tenuously forged, endlessly revised, and imperfect in its every incarnation.'[2]

In the pages of *In Praise of Copying*, Marcus Boon further exposes and unravels the paradoxes and conflicts that surround copyright in the digital age. He explains that his book grew out of his observation that: 'Copying is pervasive in contemporary culture, yet at the same time subject to laws, restrictions, and attitudes that suggest that it is wrong, and shouldn't be happening. On the one hand, many of the most visible aspects of contemporary culture – the art of Takashi Murakami or Elizabeth Peyton, electronic music ranging from hip-hop and techno to dubstep and mash-ups, BitTorrent and other digital networks of distribution, software tools like Google Earth or Photoshop, social networking sites like Facebook and Twitter, movies like *Borat* or *Slumdog Millionaire* (all no doubt hopelessly out-of-date by the time you read this) – rely explicitly on something we call 'copying'. Indeed, many of the most vibrant aspects of contemporary culture indicate an obsession with the act of copying and the production of copies, and it seems that we find real insight into what human beings and the universe are like through thinking about how and what we copy. On the other hand, every time we install a new piece of software, listen to music, or watch a movie, we encounter the world of copyright and intellectual property law, and the set of restrictions that have been placed around our access to and use of objects, processes, and ideas produced by the act of copying. Simultaneously, as our ability to make copies expands at both the macro (geophysics and the manipulation of global weather systems) and micro (nanotechnology and the fabrication and replication of matter from the atom up) levels, these same laws are used by corporations to appropriate, copy, and sell increasingly large parts of what was once the "public domain".'

It is clear that we have reached a point where our ideas of originality and copying are being assaulted from all sides. On the one hand we have companies claiming exclusive ownership over things that should be in the public domain (e.g. photos of US presidents taken in public; Deutsche Telekom AG's attempt to register the colour magenta to prevent any other company from using this colour for their communication devices, logos or stationery),[3] and on the other hand we have a generation of digital natives (remixers, DJs, bloggers, file sharers, creative commons activists, Wikileakers, etc.) who have a new concept of the idea of ownership and rights that is at odds with the prevailing capitalist notion of ownership and protected rights.

How then does this relate to working as a creative person in visual communication? To find out, we need to define what originality and copying mean in this context. This is tough, because it almost certainly means letting go of some cherished concepts. But then again, it might lead to a heightened understanding of what and how we function in a world of accelerating change where today's universal law is overtaken by tomorrow's tech wizardry.

Say I produce a smart design execution and sell it to my client. I'm proud of it and I receive an appropriate fee for my work. Happiness reigns. Later, however, I find that someone – another graphic designer – has blatantly copied my idea. The discovery makes me upset. But why? If my objection is that I have been copied, this seems odd since it is nearly always flattering to be copied. But what if my disgruntlement is based on the knowledge that someone has profited financially from my idea? If so, then my displeasure is easier to understand, but it is also irrational, because if I look honestly and critically at my own idea, I will see that it is no more 'original' than that of the person who copied me. And furthermore, what damage has actually been done to me?

Well, I might argue that I have been damaged because my copyist has received a commission – and a fee – that should have come to me. Or, I can say that my reputation might suffer because someone will see the copied work and think that I was the copyist and not the copied. But in reality I can't expect to receive every commission that is going, and the likelihood of my reputation being damaged is slight. Thanks to the new transparency created by blogs, social media and savvy journalists and critics, blatant plagiarism usually gets exposed, or more likely, ignored.

Yet perhaps the most important side effect of being copied is the realisation – if I am honest with myself – that I too am a copyist and that all creative production is essentially mimetic. Owning up to this is hard. I once spoke to a famous designer who railed against his many copyists. When I pointed out that he had produced a celebrated piece of work based on the visual stylings of a famous contemporary artist, he looked at me as if the idea had never occurred to him that, he too, might be guilty of plagiarism.

I also recall a conversation with a musician who spoke murderously about file sharing, yet almost in the same breath, admitted to using undeclared samples from old records. I don't think the designer or musician were guilty of anything other than a philosophical failure to realise that copying is the largest part of the creative process. Like breathing, we can't help but do it – but, as with breathing, we rarely stop to think about it. The realisation that all design is copying – or montage, as Marcus Boon more accurately calls it – takes us to the heart of the matter. The truth is we are incapable of making any graphic statements that aren't a montage of existing elements – typefaces, images, photographs, language, etc. If we do our 'montaging' with wit and style we can hope to make something fresh, novel and unexpected – but we shouldn't kid ourselves that we are making anything that is day-of-creation new.

Pop music, as with folk music before it, is inconceivable without the wholesale borrowing of musical idioms, lyrics and tunes. We see this most clearly in the work of pop giants like David Bowie, Led Zeppelin and Bob Dylan: 'Appropriation,' writes Jonathan Lethem, 'has always played a key role in Dylan's music. The songwriter has grabbed not only from a panoply of vintage Hollywood films but from Shakespeare and F Scott Fitzgerald and Junichi Saga's *Confessions of a Yakuza*. He also nabbed the title of Eric Lott's study of minstrelsy for his 2001 album *Love and Theft*.'

Hip-hop, and other forms of sampling-based music owe their existence to musicians discovering a sophisticated language of montaging pre-recorded sounds to make new musical forms. It is the norm: without sampling, this music doesn't exist. This forces us to ask the question – is it a lesser art form because it uses existing sounds rather than sounds wrung out of musical instruments? For me, the answer is no. It is hard to see how it is any different from the dozens of coded references TS Eliot rolled into his great modernist poetic masterwork – *The Waste Land* (1922). Scholars are still arguing over Eliot's sources – while at the same time, in glass and steel towers in Manhattan, lawyers scour hip-hop records looking for undeclared samples.

Reality Hunger (2010) is a newish book by David Shields which celebrates plagiarism as an essential creative tool. In fact, the whole book is an act of creative literary plagiarism. In a review in *The Guardian*, it was noted that: '*Reality Hunger*'s celebration of plagiarism is contained within its form. Many of the raggedly interwoven collage of thoughts and aphorisms often seem familiar. This is because over half of them are actually other people's thoughts and aphorisms. (This is only admitted in the book's addendum and at the insistence, Shields claims, of the publisher's lawyers.)' Shields brazenly insists on his right to quote freely not only from other writers, but also (his lawyers' insistence apart) to deny attribution to the quotations. Again, this is only what Shakespeare did.

Shields' audacity to produce an entire book out of 'samples' may take the breath away, but it is only what graphic designers, illustrators and image makers, not to mention journalists, bloggers and filmmakers, do every day. Shields' daring is to own up to his act of mass appropriation. As designers and visual communicators, we should be inspired to do the same. Thanks to new technology and new ways of thinking about customs and conventions enshrined in our personal and professional lives, we are obliged to rethink the way we function as creative producers, and recognise that we too are copyists, and recyclers. If we don't, we are guilty of hypocrisy.

In truth, we are trapped. But our first response should be to question the way we function. This is not easy and it will take time to dislodge long-held views on ownership, and to change the way rights are fiercely – often unfairly – protected. It may never happen. Try telling Disney you have included Mickey Mouse in your latest published design and see how accommodating they are. But we can start the process by losing our hang-ups about always trying to be original and insisting that copying is evil.

Just as our biological life is made possible by the ability of our cells to replicate themselves, so too does our creative life depend on our ability to replicate forms, ideas and expressions that already exist. We are all copyists – and for this, we should be glad.

1. A free PDF of this book is available from www.hup.harvard.edu/catalog.php?recid=30094 (December 2012).

2. *The ecstasy of influence: A plagiarism*, www.harpers.org/archive/2007/02/0081387 (December 2012).

3. www.trendhunter.com/trends/t-mobile-magenta-colour-ownership (December 2012).

Sources

New York – still the greatest city in the world. *Design Week*, 3 December 2009. See pp. 282–283.

Apprentice advertisers. *Design Week*, 2 December 2010. See pp. 284–285.

Celluloid, laptops and digital magic. *Motion Blur 2: Multidimensional Moving Imagemakers: v2* by onedotzero. Laurence King Publishing, 2008. See pp. 286–291.

We're all stellar design gurus, now. Design Observer, 9 May 2006. See pp. 292–294.

Charles Dickens and the BBC: the case against dumbing down. Design Observer, 19 December 2005. See pp. 295–297.

Register now to avoid disappointment. Election Aesthetics blog (www.electoaesthetics.blogspot.co.uk), 3 April 2010. See pp. 298–299.

Listomania. Design Observer, 14 November 2006. See pp. 300–302.

The estate we're in. *Design Week*, 2 Febuary 2006. See pp. 303–304.

Branding as fibbing. *Design Week*, 5 February 2009. See pp. 305–306.

The designer as buffoon. Design Observer, 26 April 2005. See pp. 307–309.

Ethics and design. *Design Week*, July 2007. See pp. 310–311.

The joy (and necessity) of collaboration. *Design Week*, 4 November 2010. See pp. 312–313.

Even design gets outsourced abroad. *Design Week*, 1 March 2007. See pp. 314–315.

The 'auto-tuning' of design. *Design Week*, 16 September 2010. See pp. 316–317.

Design internships. *Design Week*, 1 October 2009. See pp. 318–319.

Philosophy, graphic design, and virtue of clarity. Design Observer, 10 May 2011. See pp. 320–322.

Werner Herzog and
the deeper truth.
Design Observer,
16 June 2007.
See pp.323–325.

Design and royalty.
Design Week,
2 December 2004.
See pp.326–328.

New business
and how to get it.
Design Week,
6 May 2004.
See pp.329–331.

Safety and
comfort: a walk
with Paul Davis.
Design Observer,
19 April 2010.
See pp.332–334.

Preparing for
emergencies.
Voice: AIGA
Journal of Design,
7 September 2004.
See pp.335–337.

The natural digital
world. *Design Week*,
Interaction Design
Supplement, 2009.
See pp.338–339.

The myth of
originality and
the joy of copying.
Elephant #6,
Spring 2011.
See pp.340–347.

Image section

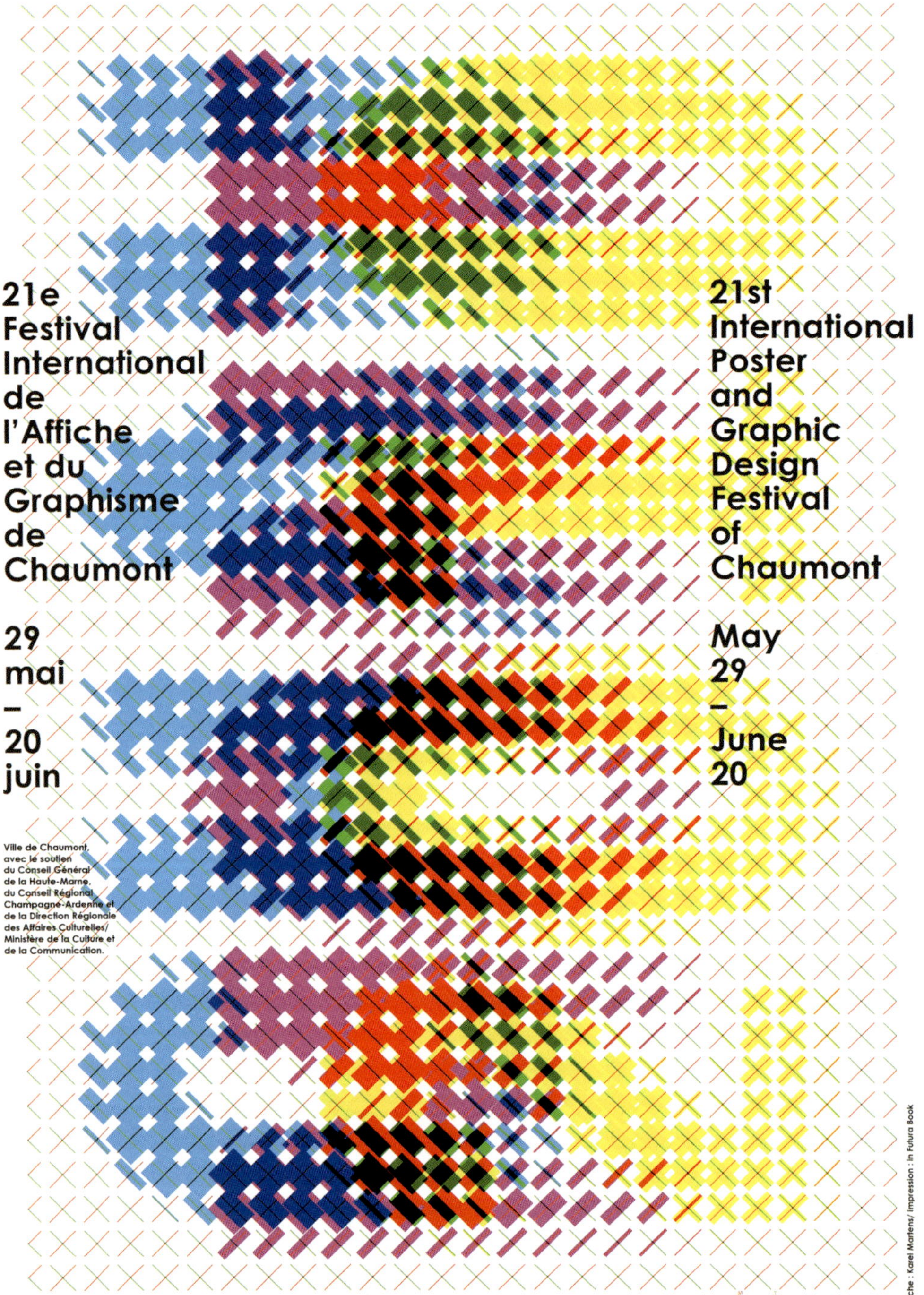
21e
Festival
International
de
l’Affiche
et du
Graphisme
de
Chaumont
29
mai
–
20
juin
Ville de Chaumont,
avec le soutien
du Conseil Général
de la Haute-Marne,
du Conseil Régional
Champagne-Ardenne et
de la Direction Régionale
des Affaires Culturelles/
Ministère de la Culture et
de la Communication.
21st
International
Poster
and
Graphic
Design
Festival
of
Chaumont
May
29
–
June
20
Affiche : Karel Martens/ Impression : In Futura Book

21st International Poster and Graphic Design Festival of Chaumont, 2010. Poster by Dutch graphic designer Karel Martens. See p.24.

Chaumont Festival catalogue, 2010. The catalogue was edited by Etienne Hervy and designed by Frédéric Teschner (with Clémence Michon). The spread shows works by Akatre (left) and Atelier Dirk Behage & Evelyn ter Bekke. See p.24.

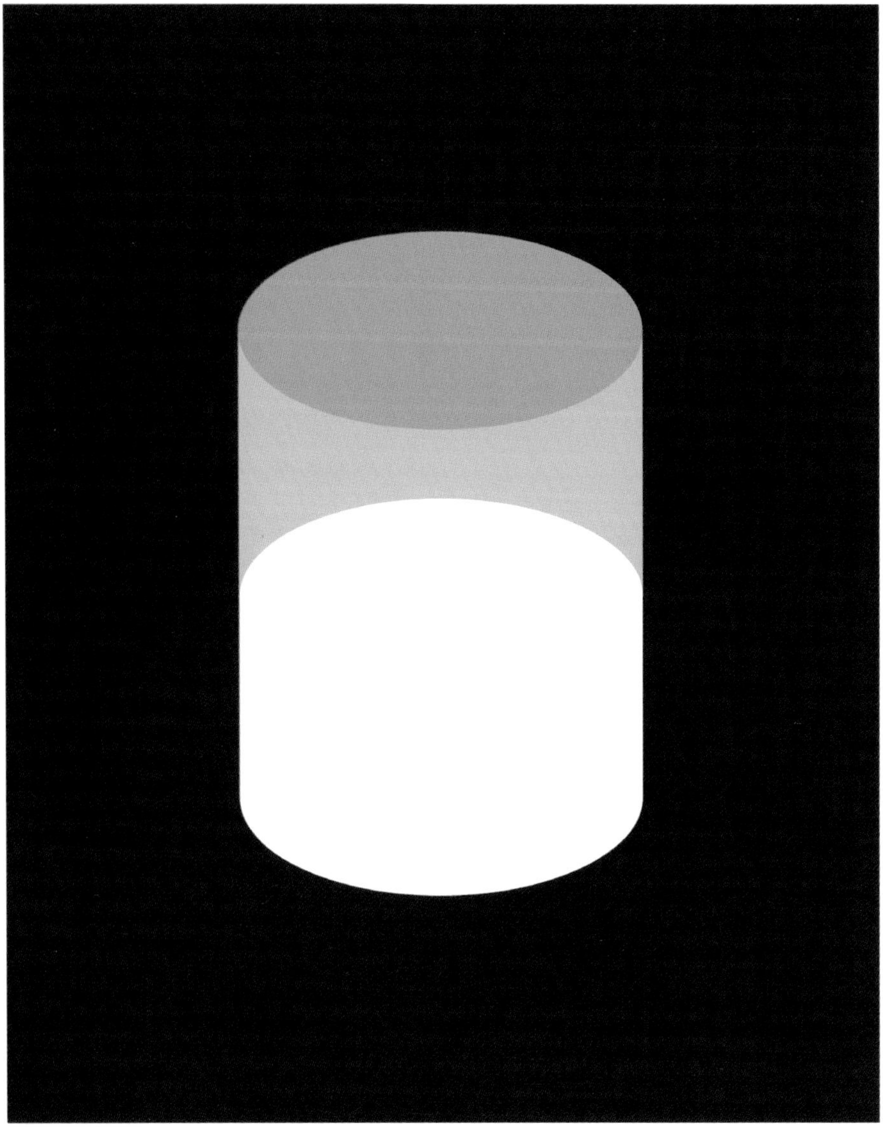

Image section

Alexander Gelman, *Subtraction: Aspects of Essential Design*, Rotovision, 2000. An authentically minimalist front cover. See p.64.

Autechre, *Envane*, Warp Records, 1997. One of the many album covers The Designers Republic designed for Warp Records. Concept and design made in The Designers Republic. © 1997. The copyright in the artwork is owned by Ian Anderson & Sian Thomas licensed to Return Power Shift Control Ltd T/A The Designers Republic. See p.72.

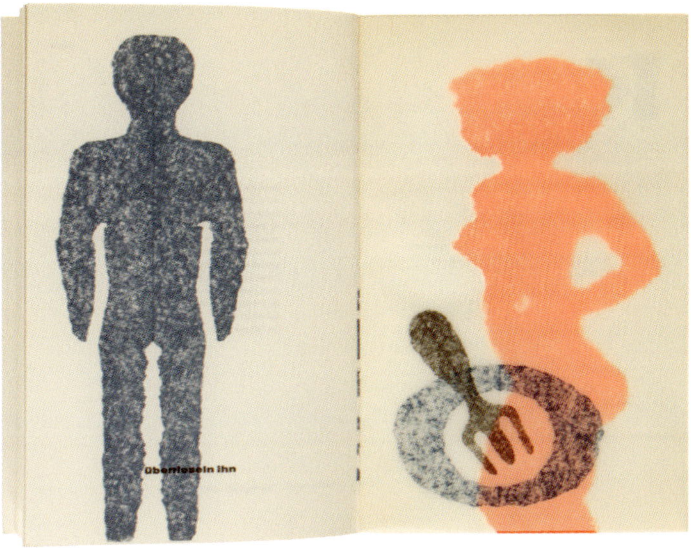

Experimenta Typographica 11, 1956 and *Experimenta Typographica 2*, 1969, both Galerie der Spiegel. Covers and spreads of booklets by Dutch graphic designer Willem Sandberg. He is perhaps better known as the former director (1945–62) of the Stedelijk Museum in Amsterdam. See p.75.

Russian Criminal Tattoo, Encyclopaedia Volume 1, FUEL Publishing, 2009. See p.77.

Ryuichi Sakamoto, */04*, Warner Music Japan, 2004. This album cover designed by Hideki Nakajima illustrates his knack for colourful patterns. Creative directors: Ryuichi Sakamoto and Norika Sora. Art director: Hideki Nakajima. Client: commmons. See p.80.

Pink Floyd, *Ummagumma*, Harvest, 1969. Cover designed by Storm Thorgerson. In an interview with the author he mentions that this image is about 'infinite regression'. See p.88 and p.183.

Pink Floyd, *Atom Heart Mother*, Harvest,1970. Cover designed by Storm Thorgerson. This seemingly simplistic photograph of a cow was offered as a 'serious critique of the record business'. See p.91.

EMI
PINK
FLOYD

du 25 novembre 2004 au 12 janvier 2005 * 13:00 - 17:00 *
* palais de la culture * alger *
quand
les
sciences
parlent
arabe
عندما تكلم العلم بالعربية
ccf Alger
centre culturel français d'Alger
Palais de la Culture
LASTWA

Quand les sciences parlent arabe, A2 offset poster, 2004. A typical example of the typographic work of French designer Toffe, showing his taste for exposing the workings of the computer: 'I use a lot of default settings in my work, I like people to see the nature of the machine I have used.' Client: French Cultural Center of Algiers, Algeria. See p.93.

Album covers by Ghost Box Music, 2004–12. Designer Julian House co-founded record label Ghost Box with Jim Jupp to release their own music and that of like-minded individuals. House also designs the CD covers and promo material. Artwork by Julian House. See p.98.

The Face, 1984. Neville Brody became a graphic design celebrity when he was appointed art director of *The Face* in 1981 (he stayed until 1986). See p.102.

Anti Design Festival, September 2011. Neville Brody created the Anti Design Festival 'out of a need for change. A need for something new, ugly, scary and dangerous'. Anti Design Festival (ADF) © 2011 Neville Brody. See p.105.

Forward-slash ADF is the ongoing idea beyond the world's first Anti Design Festival
Add /ADF to your URL to house experimental, exploratory, risky, failed and non-commercial ideas, then at antidesignfestival.com/ADF we will link everyone to your ideas,
to begin to create the world's biggest online space for creative thought
ANTI DESIGN FESTIVAL 2010
Here to mismanage your expectations
for full programme go to antidesignfestival.com

Image section

Paul Graham, 'Roundabout, Andersonstown, Belfast', 1984. This seemingly subjectless photograph reveals its details only when you look closely. See p.112.

I'll be long gone, 2009. Jonathan Barnbrook can mix a dozen letterforms on a single page and it still looks coherent and exquisitely judged. See p.114.

Rettangoli gialli concentrici senza angoli al suolo, Suglio Lugano, 1998. Felici Varini creates works of art in space. Collection: UBS, Switzerland. Photo: André Morin. See p.117.

Pixies, *Surfer Rosa*, 4AD, 1988. Arguably the most famous Pixies LP cover. Art direction and design by Vaughan Oliver. See p.124.

Bentyl puts a quick stop to SPASM, 1958. One of Herb Lubalin's famous ads from his time as an art director at agency Sudler & Hennessey. See p.127.

Logos for *Mother & Child*, 1965, and *Families*, 1980. Two examples of 'word pictures', the phrase used by Herb Lubalin to describe his typographic concepts. See p.127.

Families

MOTHER & CHILD

PARK
LOOK LEFT
LOOK RIGHT
WALK!
STOP
STREET
CAUTION
Urbanized.
A documentary film by
Gary Hustwit

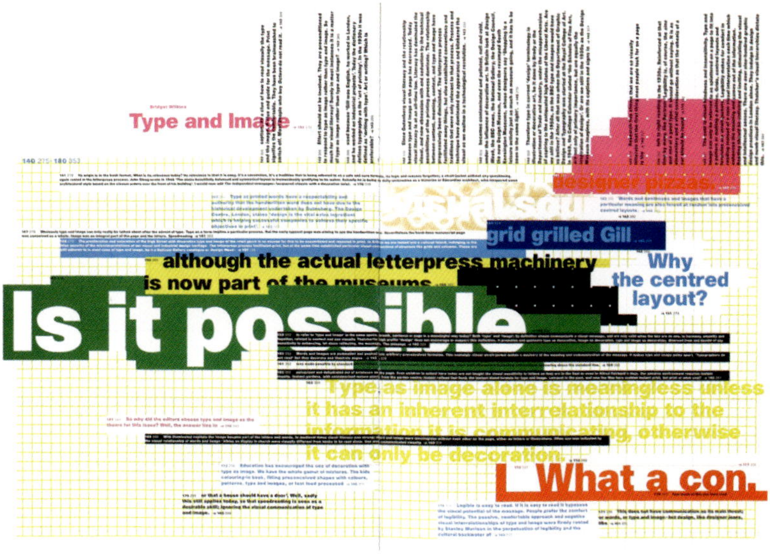

Film poster for *Urbanized*, 2011. Build designed the identity, film posters and DVD packaging for Gary Hustwit's last film in his design trilogy (*Helvetica* and *Objectified* being the other two). Design/direction: Michael C Place. Client: Plexi Films/ Gary Hustwit. See p.133.

Octavo 90.7, 1990. 8vo (1985–2001) was a London-based design group that advocated a rigorous typographic approach to everything they designed. The spread shown here, from their self-published journal *Octavo*, illustrates this point of view. See p.140 and p.143.

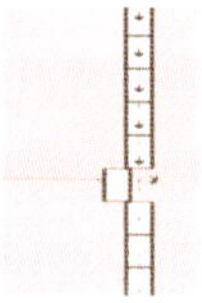

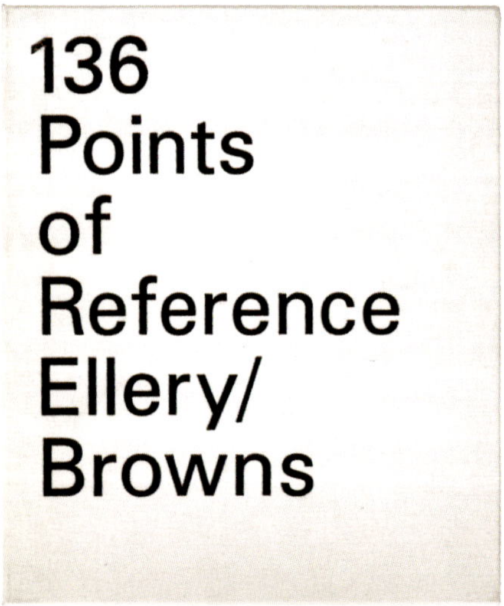

Image section

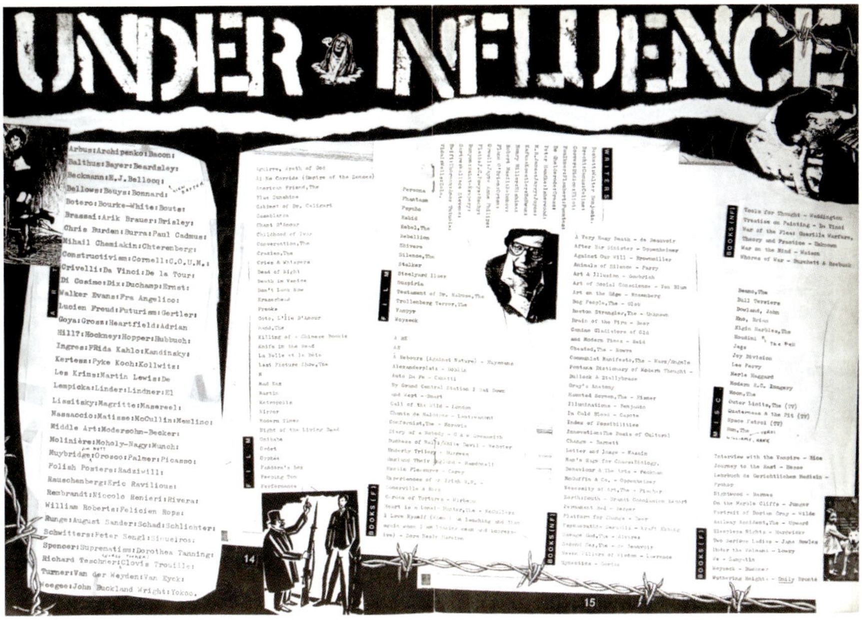

Chaumont Festival catalogue, 2010. This spread from the catalogue shows posters by Ian Wright, Jason Munn and Paul Burgess commissioned by the author for the 'En Tube – Concrete Image' exhibition at Chaumont in 2010. See p.142.

136 Points of Reference by Jonathan Ellery, Browns Editions, 2005. See p.163.

Spread and cover of *Radical Illustrators*, issue 39, 1981. The cover's colour photograph by George Snow was meant as a parody of women's magazines. *Radical Illustrators* kindly loaned by Anne Howeson. See p.150.

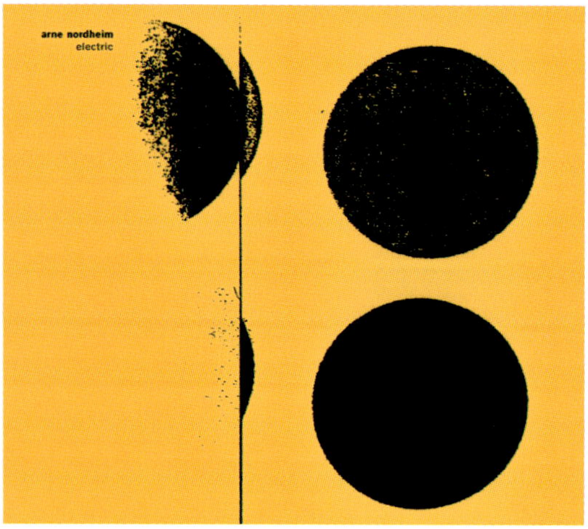

Arne Nordheim, *Electric*, Rune Grammofon, 1998. A typical CD cover by Kim Hiorthøy. See p.168.

Issues 3 and 5 of *Form*, 1966–69. *Form* was edited and designed by Professor Philip Steadman. The magazine was designed in the Swiss modernist style and featured articles on an array of giants of the avant-garde such as Theo van Doesburg, Roland Barthes and Walter Gropius. See p.169.

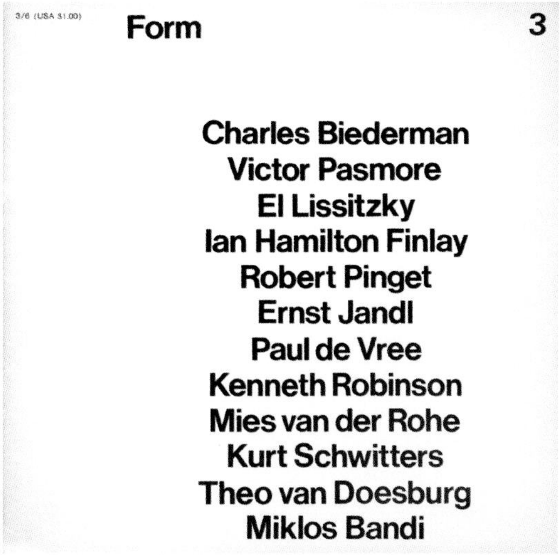
3/6 (USA $1.00)
Form
3
Charles Biederman
Victor Pasmore
El Lissitzky
Ian Hamilton Finlay
Robert Pinget
Ernst Jandl
Paul de Vree
Kenneth Robinson
Mies van der Rohe
Kurt Schwitters
Theo van Doesburg
Miklos Bandi

3/6 (USA $1.00)
Form
5
Walter Gropius and Marcel Breuer: buildings for Black Mountain College, North Carolina, 1939. Dormitory blocks and entrance lobby
De Stijl and Architecture by Hans Jaffe, with writings from 'De Stijl' by J J P Oud and Robert van 't Hoff: Visual Environments and Total Landscape by Bernard Lassus: Meaning and Technique in Phonic Poetry by Raoul Hausmann, with poems: Black Mountain College—A Foreword by John A. Rice, projected buildings by Walter Gropius and Marcel Breuer: A Personal Memoir 1944-45 by George Zabriskie: Great Little Magazines No. 5: Ray

Ralph Towner, *Diary*, ECM, 1974. This CD cover illustrates the enigmatic and austere beauty that typifies the aesthetic of Manfred Eicher and his label ECM. See p.194.

Dave Holland Quartet, *Extensions*, ECM, 1990. CD cover with watercolour lettering by Barbara Wojirsch, the main designer of early ECM sleeves. See p.195.

Still from *Logorama*, 2009. Directed by French filmmakers H5 (François Alaux, Hervé de Crécy & Ludovic Houplain), *Logorama* is a 17-minute film that shows a world where logos festoon every surface. It won an Academy Award for Best Animated Short Film in 2010. Production by Autour de Minuit. See p.202.

OMC
RYOBI
DORFILE
Budget
PERRY
BORDERS
U-HAUL
RODEWAY INN
DAYS INN
BLOCKBUSTER VIDEO
CONVERTERS
bassetti
Best
CHAMPION
吉野家
YOSHINOYA
La Quinta
Best Western
NEW Era
The BuildingBox
CRAFTSMAN
MATCHBOX
EVEREADY
SPIN
NESN
VAT
AVIS
NOMURA
野村證券
SEGA
VNB
WELLS RURAL ELEC. CO.
National Car Rental
Domino's
SHOPPERS DRUG MART
Marlboro
KOHL'S
OREO
Savon drugs
THAMES VALLEY HOUSING
SANTA CRUZ
The Phone Hous
Heinz
7 ELEVEN
RENTAWRECK
EMI
tecno expert
OXXO
nolte

Section 25, *Always Now*, Factory Records, 1981. Typographic cover by Peter Saville. See p.205.

Summer of Love: Art of the Psychedelic Era by Christoph Grunenberg [Ed.], Tate Publishing, 2005. Design by A2/SW/HK. See p.219.

The Breeders, *Pod*, 4AD, 1990. Promotional A2 poster showing Vaughan Oliver himself, dancing naked with flapping eels strapped to his waist. Art direction and design by Vaughan Oliver. Photography by Kevin Westenberg. See p.236.

THE Breeders
POD

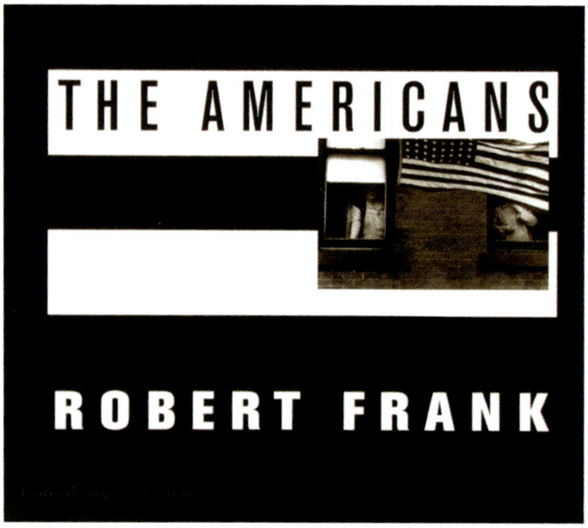

Sleazenation, February 2001. Front cover showing Scott King's now famous Cher Guavara image. King was art director of *Sleazenation* in the 1990s. Art direction and image: Scott King. See p.245.

The Americans by Robert Frank, First Cornerhouse Edition, 1993. During a trip through postwar America in 1958, Frank took photographs of an America that wasn't normally seen. See p.282.

You must be completely reliable and utterly obedient, 2010. Illustration by artist Paul Davis. See p.333.

YOU MUST
YOU MUST
NEVER
BE
TAKE
ANY
COMPLETELY
RELIABLE
IRRATIONAL
&
or
IDIOTIC
UTTERLY OBEDIENT
ORDERS
from
ANYONE
EVER

End matter

End matter

Editorial note

The essays in this book are the outcome of over a decade of writing for magazines, journals, blogs and books. The bulk of the material comes from 2004 onwards, but I have included a few examples from before that date. In nearly all instances, I have used the versions stored on my computer. This means that texts may vary slightly from the published versions.

I have resisted the urge to change any opinions or statements of belief – even where I sometimes now disagree with or would like to modify the views expressed. I have removed a few sentences that are repeated in other essays in this collection, or which relate to the publications or blogs in which they appeared. In a few instances where I have preferred my original title rather than the one inserted by an editor, I have reverted to the original. I have also removed some linguistic clumsiness and a few too many instances of where I have failed to live up to George Orwell's six rules of good writing.[1] However, the majority of essays in this book are unchanged from the day I submitted them for publication.

1. Almost banal in their simplicity, Orwell's rules opened a door that enabled me to progress as a writer. My writing is always poorer when I forget one or more of them:
- Never use a metaphor, simile, or other figure of speech which you are used to seeing in print.
- Never use a long word where a short one will do.
- If it is possible to cut a word out, always cut it out.
- Never use the passive where you can use the active.
- Never use a foreign phrase, a scientific word, or a jargon word if you can think of an everyday English equivalent.
- Break any of these rules sooner than say anything outright barbarous.

Index

Books written by the author

Sampler: Contemporary Music Graphics by Adrian Shaughnessy. Laurence King Publishing, 1999.

Sampler 2: Art, Pop and Contemporary Music Graphics by Adrian Shaughnessy. Laurence King Publishing, 2000.

Display Copy Only: A Book of Intro Work by Adrian Shaughnessy. Laurence King Publishing, 2002.

Radical Album Cover Art: Sampler 3 by Adrian Shaughnessy. Laurence King Publishing, 2003.

How to be a Graphic Designer, Without Losing Your Soul by Adrian Shaughnessy. Laurence King Publishing, 2005.

Look at This: Contemporary Brochures, Catalogues and Documents by Adrian Shaughnessy. Laurence King Publishing, 2006.

Cover Art By: New Music Graphics by Adrian Shaughnessy. Laurence King Publishing, 2007.

Herb Lubalin: American Graphic Designer (1918-81) by Adrian Shaughnessy. Unit Editions, 2012.

Ken Garland: Structure and Substance by Adrian Shaughnessy. Unit Editions, 2012.

Essays – Scratching the Surface by Adrian Shaughnessy. Unit Editions, 2013.

Books edited by the author

Studio culture: The secret life of the graphic design studio by Tony Brook and Adrian Shaughnessy [Eds.]. Unit Editions, 2009.

Supergraphics – Transforming Space: Graphic Design for Walls, Buildings and Spaces by Tony Brook and Adrian Shaughnessy [Eds.]. Unit Editions, 2010.

Wim Crouwel: A Graphic Odyssey – Catalogue by Tony Brook and Adrian Shaughnessy [Eds.]. Unit Editions, 2011.

TD63–73: Total Design and its Pioneering Role in Graphic Design by Ben Bos. Unit Editions, 2011.

Projekt: The Polish journal of visual art and design by Charlotte West and Edgar Bąk. Unit Editions, 2011.

Kwadraat-Bladen: A series of graphic experiments (1955–74) by Tony Brook and Adrian Shaughnessy [Eds.]. Unit Editions, 2012.

Jurriaan Schrofer (1926–90): Restless typographer by Tony Brook and Adrian Shaughnessy [Eds.]. Unit Editions, 2013.

Books the author contributed to

Warp: Labels Unlimited by Rob Young. Black Dog Publishing, 2005.

Paul Davis. Browns/Howard Smith Paper, 2005.

Alexander Gelman. Browns/Howard Smith Paper, 2006.

Paul Graham. Browns/Howard Smith Paper, 2006.

VJ: Audio-visual Art and VJ Culture by Michael Faulkner/D-Fuse. Laurence King Publishing, 2006.

Non-Format (Design & Designer) by Non-Format. Pyramyd, 2006.

Lawrence Weiner. Browns/Howard Smith Paper, 2007.

Storm Thorgerson. Browns/Howard Smith Paper, 2007.

Looking Closer 5: Critical Writings on Graphic Design by Michael Beirut, William Drenttel and Steven Heller. Allworth, 2007.

Erik Kessels. Browns/Howard Smith Paper, 2008.

Felice Varini. Browns/Howard Smith Paper, 2008.

Mute Magazine: Graphic Design by Simon Worthington, Damian Jaques, Pauline Van Mourik Broekman, and Adrian Shaughnessy. 8 Books, 2008.

I Heart Design: Remarkable Graphic Design Selected by Designers, Illustrators, and Critics by Steven Heller [Ed.]. Rockport Publishers, 2011.

FUSE 1-20: From Invention to Antimatter: Twenty Years of FUSE by Neville Brody and Jon Wozencroft [Eds.]. Taschen, 2012.

Writing and Research for Graphic Designers: A Designer's Manual to Strategic Communication and Presentation by Steven Heller [Ed.]. Rockport Publishers, 2013.

Thanks

My heartfelt gratitude to the following people who bravely commissioned me to write for their publications, books, blogs, etc. Without them, this volume wouldn't exist: Lynda Relph-Knight (*Design Week*); Rick Poynor (*Eye* and Design Observer); John L Walters (*Eye*); Storm Thorgerson; Paul A Taylor, Daniel Miller (Mute); Jonathan Ellery (Browns); Caroline Roberts (*Grafik*); Bill Drentell, Michael Bierut, Jessica Helfand (Design Observer); Etienne Hervy, Isabelle Moisy (*Etapes*); Tony Herrington, Anne Hilde Neset, Rob Young (*The Wire*); Partrick Burgoyne, Mark Sinclair (*Creative Review*); Angus Montgomery (*Design Week*); Steve Heller (AIGA); Laurence King (Laurence King Publishing); Shane Walter (onedotzero); AOI; *Blueprint*; Marc Valli (*Graphic* and *Elephant*); Will Hudson, Alex Bec (It's Nice That).

Thanks also to my Unit Editions partners, Tony Brook and Trish Finegan for supporting me in the publication of this book, and to the Spin/Unit team for hard work and enthusiasm. Finally, thanks to my wife Lynda and to our children Ed, Alice and Moll.

Colophon

Essays
Scratching the Surface
Adrian Shaughnessy

Unit 11

Design director:
Tony Brook

Designers:
Elena Carl
Adrian Shaughnessy

Editorial coordinator:
Sarah Schrauwen

Production manager:
Sam Stevenson

Publishing director:
Patricia Finegan

Printer:
C&C Offset Printing Co., Ltd.

Typeface:
Maison Neue Demi
Maison Neue Mono

Unit Editions titles can be ordered direct from the publisher:
www.uniteditions.com

A catalogue for this book is available from the British Library.

ISBN:
978-0-9575114-0-8